Fundamentals of
Private Pensions

Pension Research Council

Fundamentals of
Private Pensions

by
DAN M. McGILL, Ph.D.

Associate Professor of Insurance and
Research Director, Pension Research Council
Wharton School of Finance and Commerce

Published for the
Pension Research Council
Wharton School of Finance and Commerce
University of Pennsylvania
by RICHARD D. IRWIN, Inc., Homewood, Illinois

To
Elaine Kem McGill

Pension Research Council

Purpose of the Council

The Pension Research Council of the Wharton School was created in 1952 for the purpose of sponsoring nonpartisan research in the area of private pensions. It was formed in response to the urgent need for a better understanding of the private pension movement. Private pensions have experienced a phenomenal growth during the last two decades, but their economic, political, and social implications are yet to be explored. They seem destined to play a major role in the quest for old-age economic security, but the nature of that role can be ascertained only on the basis of a more enlightened evaluation of the capabilities and limitations of the private pension mechanism. It was to conduct an impartial study into the facts and basic issues surrounding private pensions, under the auspices of an academic and professional group representing leadership in every phase of the field, that the Council was organized.

Projects undertaken by the Council will be broad in scope and predominantly interpretive rather than technical in nature. In general, attention will be concentrated on areas which are not the object of special investigation by other research groups. Its research studies will be conducted by mature scholars drawn from both the academic and business spheres. Research results will be published from time to time in a series of books and monographs.

Preface

This volume is the initial publication of the Pension Research Council of the Wharton School of Finance and Commerce. It has a twofold purpose: (1) to provide a broad background for the more specialized studies to follow and (2) to serve as a basic text for those persons aspiring to a fuller understanding of the private pension mechanism. It is especially designed to meet the needs of college or university students and trainees in insurance companies, trust companies, and pension consulting firms. It should also prove useful to management personnel, labor union representatives, and others interested in the administration of private pensions.

In keeping with the fundamental objectives of the book, an effort has been made to strike a proper balance between principles and practices. It is in no sense a manual for the pension technician. The emphasis is on why rather than how. Naturally, a great deal of attention has been devoted to how pension plans operate, but the general approach of the book is to analyze—plan provisions, funding media, and funding methods—not to advocate. This is true of even the last chapter which presents a critique of the principal funding media. Attention is focused on the factors which should be considered, not on absolute or final answers.

No consideration has been given to profit-sharing plans and other forms of deferred compensation. While such plans are widely used to provide retirement benefits either alone or in conjunction with a conventional pension plan, their characteristics are so distinctly different from those of pension plans as to warrant their exclusion from this treatise.

As is true of any undertaking of this scope, the author is indebted to many persons and organizations for counsel and assistance. The magnitude of his debt is evidenced by the fact that a minimum of thirty pension specialists, half of them actuaries, read all or a portion of the manuscript before it went to the printer and offered many valuable criticisms and suggestions. The manuscript was reviewed in its entirety by most of the members of the Council and, in many instances, by their pension associates. The author hereby acknowledges his indebtedness to all persons who reviewed the manuscript and expresses his deepest gratitude for their cooperation and his sincerest regrets that space considerations make it impracticable to mention all by name.

Some rendered such valuable assistance that they deserve especial recognition. Mr. John K. Dyer, Jr., Vice-President and Actuary of Towers, Perrin, Forster, and Crosby, Inc., gave generously of his time and counsel and was particularly helpful in connection with actuarial matters. Mr. Preston C. Bassett, Associate Actuary with the same organization, performed extensive actuarial calculations for the author and reviewed large sections of the manuscript. Mr. Ray M. Peterson, Vice-President and Associate Actuary of the Equitable Life Assurance Society of the United States, read the entire manuscript and acted as adviser on group annuity practices. Messrs. Dennis N. Warters, William M. Rae, and Charles L. Trowbridge, Executive Vice-President, Group Secretary, and Associate Group Actuary, respectively, of the Bankers Life Company of Iowa, offered many perceptive criticisms and were especially helpful in the area of group permanent insurance practices. Mr. Laflin C. Jones, C.L.U., Director of Insurance Services and Planning, and his associates at the Northwestern Mutual Life Insurance Company, provided constructive criticism on all phases of the manuscript, with particular emphasis on pension trust or individual contract matters.

Dr. Roger F. Murray, Vice-President of Bankers Trust Company, read the original draft of the manuscript and made numerous suggestions, with special attention to trust company investment operations. Mr. J. W. Myers, Manager, Insurance and Social Security Department, Standard Oil Company of New Jersey, read the entire manuscript and drew upon his rich experience in pension administration to suggest many worthwhile changes. Mr. Robert J. Myers, Chief Actuary of the Social Security Administration, Federal Security Agency, reviewed for factual accuracy the material in Chapter I relating to the economic basis of the old-age problem and governmental pension plans.

The weightiest acknowledgment of all should go to Mr. Ben S. McGiveran, C.L.U., of Seefurth and McGiveran, who not only has contributed generously from his vast storehouse of pension knowledge but was the person who conceived the idea of what is now the

Pension Research Council and assumed primary responsibility for securing the necessary financial support. Special thanks should also go to those individuals and organizations, too numerous to mention, who have participated in a financial way and without whose public-spirited support the project could not have been undertaken.

The private pension field is highly competitive and strong differences of opinion exist with respect to certain practices in the field and particularly with regard to the relative merits of the various funding media. These differences of opinion are reflected within the membership of the Council. It is emphasized, therefore, that the views expressed in this volume are those of the author and are not to be imputed to any other member of the Council or to any other person whose assistance is cited in this preface. Likewise, any factual errors that may still be found in the book are the sole responsibility of the author.

March, 1955
Philadelphia, Pennsylvania

D. M. M.

Contents

LIST OF TABLES

Underlying Forces   1

THE private pension movement is rooted in one of the most significant economic, social, and political developments of the twentieth century—the progressive aging of the population. This development has given rise to a multitude of problems, the most pressing of which, unquestionably, is that of providing a measure of economic security to the aged. Some conception of the magnitude of the problem can be grasped from the following brief account of the gerontological and economic influences at work.

ECONOMIC BASIS OF THE OLD-AGE PROBLEM

POPULATION TRENDS

During the last half-century, the growth in the number and proportion of the aged population has been phenomenal. During that period the general population of the United States has doubled, while the number of persons age 65 and over has quadrupled. In 1900, there were roughly three million persons age 65 and over, whereas fifty years later the number had grown to 12¼ million. The aged population is increasing at the rate of 340,000 per year, which means that at the end of 1954, there were approximately 13.9 million aged persons in the population. It is estimated that by the year 2000, aged persons will number 26 to 28 million.[1] In relative terms, only 4 per cent of the population in 1900 was 65 and over, whereas at the end of 1954, 8.5 per cent of the population fell in that category. Moreover, if present trends continue, from 11 to 13 per cent of the population will be 65 and above by the year 2000.

1. Robert J. Myers and E. A. Rasor, *Illustrative United States Population Projections, 1952*, Actuarial Study No. 33, Federal Security Agency, Washington, 1952.

2 Underlying Forces

This spectacular increase in the absolute and relative number of old persons in the United States reflects the combined influence of a decline in the birth rate, an increase in life expectancy, and the curtailment of immigration. The long-run decrease in the birth rate was reversed during World War II and has remained at a relatively high level since that time, but population experts are reluctant to predict the future course of fertility. The tremendous extension in life expectancy recorded during the last fifty years as a result of advances in medical science, particularly in the control of infectious diseases and the reduction of infant mortality, improvements in public health services, and a rise in general living standards, will certainly not be duplicated during the next half-century, but as medical science devotes more and more study to the diseases of old age, further gains in life expectancy can be anticipated. Immigration, which once contributed large numbers of young people to the United States population, has been a negligible factor for the past twenty-five years and is not expected to assume a more important role in the future.

Employment Opportunities for the Aged

The increase in the proportion of old people has been accompanied by a decline in the employment opportunities of the aged. In 1890, the aged constituted 3.9 per cent of the total population and 4.3 per cent of the total labor force. By 1952, the percentage of the population age 65 and over had more than doubled, but the percentage of the total labor force age 65 and over had barely increased.[2] In 1890, 39.9 per cent of all persons age 65 and over were in the labor force, while in 1952 only 23.4 per cent were in that category. This decline has taken place chiefly among aged males. In 1890, 70 per cent of such males were in the labor force, but by 1952 the percentage had shrunk to 40.9 per cent. The rate of female participation in the labor force declined only slightly during that period, from 8.5 per cent to 8.0 per cent.

Many factors have contributed to the decline in labor force participation by the aged, but one of the most significant, without question, has been the transition from an agrarian and essentially

2. *Retirement Policies and the Railroad Retirement System*, Report of the Joint Committee on Railroad Retirement Legislation, Senate Report No. 6, Part 2, 83rd Congress, 1st Session, 1953, p. 43.

rural economy to an industrial and predominantly urbanized economy. Whereas persons in agricultural employment can continue working, at least on a part-time basis, to advanced ages, industrial employees, because of the physical demands of their jobs or employer personnel policy, must retire at a relatively early age. Other factors which have influenced the trend include the improvement in longevity, extension of social insurance and pension programs, and the institutionalization of age 65 as the normal retirement age.

CAPACITY TO SAVE FOR OLD AGE

The implications of the foregoing are broadened by the lessened capacity of individuals to save for their own old-age maintenance. Several developments within the last quarter-century have magnified the difficulties of accumulating an old-age estate. Frequently overlooked in this connection are the technological changes that have taken place during such period. A greatly improved and expanded industrial plant is pouring forth a vastly increasing quantity of consumer goods, of infinite variety, exerting relentless pressure on all classes of individuals to spend all or the greater portion of their income. High-pressure advertising and liberal extension of installment credit have conspired to tie up the worker's income even before it is earned. As a result, systematic provision for old age has become a secondary consideration in the budget calculations of the majority of families.[3]

A second factor that has complicated the accumulation of an estate is the inexorable rise in personal and corporate income taxes. The stupendous fiscal needs of the Federal government, traceable to war and the threat of war, have led to the imposition of personal tax rates which at the upper income levels approach the point of confiscation and render it difficult for even those persons in the higher income brackets to make adequate provision for their old-age needs. High corporate tax rates have added to the problem.

A third factor has been the corrosive influence of price inflation. This phenomenon requires no documentation but does inspire the comment that inflation impairs the ability of fixed-income persons to save a portion of their income and undermines the purchasing

3. It may be argued that this development reflects a weakened propensity to save for old age rather than a lessened capacity.

power of funds which have already been accumulated by any group of income recipients.

Finally, the economic dependency of many persons now in the aged category was precipitated by the depression of the 1930's which swept away their savings and shrunk their opportunities for economic rehabilitation.

The composite effect of such developments is unmistakably apparent in recent surveys of the personal financial resources of the aged. Information on the net worth of all age groups in the population is made available through the periodic Surveys of Consumer Finances conducted by the Board of Governors of the Federal Reserve System in cooperation with the Survey Research Center of the University of Michigan. The 1953 survey revealed that the median net worth of spending units headed by persons aged 65 and over was $8,400.[4] Inasmuch as 69 per cent of the units headed by persons age 65 and over owned their homes, however, it may be presumed that a substantial portion of the median net worth is represented by the value of the home. Nevertheless, home ownership is not to be discounted, since it reduces the cash needs of aged persons and may produce some income. Retired persons, as contrasted with those age 65 and over, had a median net worth of only $6,000. While these statistics indicate that elderly people as a group are far from destitute—a picture of their economic circumstances painted in some quarters—it is obvious that the resources of the great majority of elderly persons are not adequate to provide even a subsistence income for life.

Surveys by the Social Security Administration of the income, assets, and living arrangements of the beneficiaries of the Old-Age and Survivors Insurance program tend to confirm the findings of the Board of Governors. A survey of such beneficiaries at the end of 1951 disclosed that about two-thirds of the married men owned their homes, 80 per cent of them free from mortgage.[5] About 60 per cent of the beneficiaries had some savings in addition to their home. Only 13 per cent, however, had as much as $5,000 in savings, apart

4. *Federal Reserve Bulletin*, September, 1953, p. 942. A spending unit is defined as all persons living in the same dwelling and belonging to the same family who pool their incomes to meet their major expenses.
5. *Social Security Bulletin*, August, 1952, pp. 3 ff.

from their homes. Approximately 25 per cent of the beneficiaries had no assets whatsoever.

CHANGED CONCEPT OF FILIAL RESPONSIBILITY

In earlier days it was not a matter of particular concern if persons reached old age without adequate means of support. Elderly members of a family resided with and were supported by younger members of the family. In many cases, the elderly persons were able to perform some tasks around the household, or farm, thus lightening the burden on the younger people. With increasing urbanization of society, changes in housing conditions, and many other economic and social developments, the traditional approach to old-age care and support has become outmoded. As a result society is looking increasingly to Government and employers for old-age support.

PUBLIC PENSION PROGRAMS

The limitations of the individual approach to old-age financial security have led to the establishment of various governmental programs of old-age income maintenance. The most comprehensive and significant undertaking of this sort is the Federal Old-Age and Survivors Insurance system. This program has such a profound impact on private pension plans that careful consideration should be given to its structure and underlying philosophy.

FEDERAL OLD-AGE AND SURVIVORS INSURANCE

Coverage.—Federal Old-Age and Survivors Insurance is the national program of old-age insurance created by the Social Security Act of 1935 and, as such, is the foundation of all other programs of old-age income maintenance. Unlike many national programs of old-age insurance, including those of Canada and Great Britain, OASI is not based on the principle of universal coverage. Rather, coverage is conditioned on attachment to the labor market. The broad objective of the program is to cover all gainfully employed persons, including the self-employed. With minor exceptions, coverage for all eligible persons is compulsory and immediate. In other words, OASI is a device by which gainfully employed persons are forced by statute to assume some responsibility for their own old-age maintenance.

As to the technique of coverage, the plan covers by exclusion rather than by inclusion. That is, all gainfully employed persons are covered except those specifically excluded. The original legislation, however, excluded some important groups, the most significant being self-employed persons, domestic servants, agricultural workers, casuals, railroad workers, governmental employees, and employees of educational, religious, and charitable organizations. Based on administrative and constitutional considerations, these exclusions withheld coverage from four out of every ten gainfully employed persons.

The exclusion of such a formidable proportion of employed persons introduced serious inequities into the program and what was even more important tended to frustrate the basic objective of the program. Therefore, in 1950 the coverage was extended to many of the previously excluded groups, bringing an additional ten million persons under the system. At the same time, the concepts of optional coverage (for employees of state and local governments and nonprofit organizations) and qualifying conditions as to regularity of employment (for domestics, farm laborers, and casuals) were introduced. The scope of the program was further broadened in 1954 through compulsory coverage of all self-employed persons who had not been brought under coverage by the 1950 Act, except members of the legal and medical professions, extension of optional coverage to additional groups, and the liberalization of qualification requirements for domestic and farm labor. Today nine out of every ten gainfully employed persons are covered under the system.

Benefits.—

a. Eligibility for Benefits.—The benefits payable under the OASI program are paid as a matter of statutory entitlement and are not conditioned on a showing of need. The quasi-contractual nature of the program not only avoids the administrative complications of a needs test but protects the privacy of the individual and preserves his self-respect. Equally important, it encourages the individual to accumulate savings to supplement the benefits of the OASI program and any other retirement plan of which he might be a member. Retirement benefits are payable upon actual retirement at or after age 65 and the satisfaction of a service requirement. An individual is entitled to retirement benefits only if he has been credited with forty quarters of coverage[6] or, alternatively, coverage equal to half of the calendar quarters that have elapsed since December 31, 1950 (or age 21, if later) up to age 65, subject to a minimum of six quarters. An individual who has met such service requirements is said to be "fully insured." If he has achieved that status through forty quarters of coverage, he is *permanently* as well as fully insured and will retain that status even though he may spend no further time in covered employment.[7] It might be said that the benefits vest after ten years of service (a shorter period for those over age 45 on January 1, 1951), subject to diminution through periods of non-coverage or lower earnings.

Prior to the 1950 amendments to the Social Security Act, a person's insured status was determined by the period since January 1, 1937. The extension of coverage produced by that legislation was accompanied, in the interest of equity, by a "new start" arrangement under which any person, including those previously covered, could become fully insured with six quarters of coverage. This enabled those persons who were within a few years of retirement to qualify for benefits on the basis of service and earnings since 1950. The extension in 1954 was not accompanied by another "new start," since only four years had elapsed since the previous one and, moreover, a new "drop out" provision (explained below) accomplishes roughly the same objective.

As stated above, benefits are conditioned on actual retirement, the test of which has been withdrawal from covered employment. Under the 1939 Act an otherwise eligible claimant was disqualified for benefits for any month in which he earned wages in covered employment of $15 or more. In 1950, the earnings limit was eliminated for persons age 75 and over and raised to $50 for all other persons. In 1952, the limit was increased to $75. Finally, in 1954,

6. A quarter of coverage is any calendar quarter in which an employed person earns at least $50 in covered employment or any quarter in a calendar year in which he earns $4200 in covered employment. A self-employed person is credited with four quarters of coverage in any year in which he earns at least $400.

7. Any individual who reaches age 65 in a fully insured status, or achieves such status subsequently, is also permanently insured, even though he may not have acquired forty quarters of coverage.

an annual limitation of $1200 was substituted for the $75 monthly limitation, and the age below which the limitation is applicable was lowered to 72. The law now provides for suspension of one monthly benefit for each $80, or fraction thereof, of annual earnings in excess of $1200. In no case, however, are benefits withheld for any month in which the beneficiary's remuneration as an employee was $80 or less, and in which he rendered no substantial services in self-employment. On the other hand, all earnings, not just covered earnings, are now taken into account.

Incorporated in the law in the first instance as a device for forcing older workers out of a depressed labor market, the earnings limitation has been retained primarily to hold down the cost of the OASI program. It was estimated prior to the 1954 amendments that the payment of benefits to all fully insured persons at age 65 would increase the cost of the program by 13 per cent.[8] Complete elimination of the earnings limitation today would increase current outlays under the program by $1 billion per year. It is difficult to justify expenditures of such magnitude to persons who have not actually retired, particularly in view of the burdensome level which the cost of the program will eventually reach.

b. Nature of Benefits.—The OASI program provides both retirement and survivorship benefits, all of which are based on the insured's "primary insurance amount," whose derivation is described below. The insured's retirement benefit, a life income, is designated the "old age insurance benefit" and is identical with the primary insurance amount. The wife of a retired worker is entitled to a benefit equal to 50 per cent of the primary insurance amount if she is 65 or over, or, irrespective of her age, if she has under her care a dependent and unmarried child of the insured under age 18. Furthermore, each dependent and unmarried child under 18 is entitled to a benefit equal to one-half of the primary insurance amount. The combined family benefits, however, may not exceed $200 per month, or 80 per cent of the insured's average monthly wage (see below), whichever is smaller.

Prior to the 1939 amendments to the Social Security Act, no survivorship benefits, other than a lump-sum payment, were avail-

8. Federal Security Agency, *Social Security Financing*, Bureau Report No. 17, 1952, p. 51. The average age at which retirement has occurred under the OASI program is 69 years.

able under the OASI program. That legislation not only authorized survivorship benefits but created a special category of insured persons to facilitate the payment of such benefits. Survivorship benefits are now available if the deceased were "currently insured," a status which can be attained with six quarters of coverage, all of which, however, must have been earned within the thirteen quarters preceding the date of death, including the quarter in which death occurs. The same benefits are available if the deceased were "fully insured," a matter of some importance since a person may be "fully insured" without being "currently insured." In addition to a lump-sum benefit equal to three times the primary insurance amount, or $255, whichever is smaller, income benefits are payable to widows age 65 and over, mothers of any age who have dependent children of the deceased under their care, dependent children under 18 and, if there are no other eligible income beneficiaries, dependent parents 65 and over. Dependent widowers age 65 and over are also entitled to benefits if the deceased were both "currently" and "fully insured."

c. Level of Benefits.—All benefits payable under the OASI program are based on the insured's covered earnings, specifically, on his average monthly wage. The average monthly wage is a technical concept and with some administrative refinements, is obtained by dividing the insured's total covered wages, which since 1954 include all wages in covered employment up to a maximum of $4,200 per year, by the number of months that have elapsed since January 1, 1951, or the day preceding the year in which the insured reached age 22, whichever is later. Prior to 1954 all months after the stipulated date were included in the divisor, whether or not the individual had covered earnings in those months. The 1954 amendments, however, provide that up to five years of lowest or no earnings may be dropped out in the calculation of the average monthly wage.[9] In addition, those quarters during which an insured individual is unable to earn income because of a condition of total disability are to be omitted from the denominator in the calculation of the average monthly wage.

The benefit formula is heavily weighted in favor of the lower-income worker. Under the original average wage formula, the

---

9. The law provides a four-year "drop out" for those insured persons with less than twenty quarters of coverage and a five-year "drop out" for those with twenty or more quarters of coverage.

primary benefit was equal to 40 per cent of the first $50 of average monthly wage plus 10 per cent of the excess, up to a maximum monthly wage of $250, multiplied by 1 per cent for each calendar year in which the insured earned at least $200 in covered employment. Successive revisions of the formula have increased the proportion of the average monthly wage reflected in the primary insurance amount until at present the benefit is equal to 55 per cent of the first $110 of average monthly wage and 20 per cent of the excess up to $350 of average monthly wage. The application of this formula produces a maximum primary insurance amount of $108.50, and the law prescribes a minimum of $30. The 1 per cent increment, designed to recognize length of service, was eliminated in 1950 on the theory that the method of calculating the average monthly wage gives adequate recognition to length of service.

Financing.—To the present, the cost of the OASI program, including both benefit and administrative expenditures, has been borne by the covered employees and their employers. The funds have been derived from a payroll tax levied in equal proportions on employers and employees. The original Act was based on the theory that the program should be self-supporting, and a schedule of contributions designed to accomplish that objective was set forth in the Act. The schedule, which called for an initial contribution rate of 1 per cent of covered wages on the part of both the employer and employee, presumed the accumulation of a large reserve, somewhat comparable to the funding of private pension plans. The advisability —and feasibility—of a large reserve was subsequently questioned and, pending a determination of the issue, Congress postponed year after year the scheduled increases in the contribution rate. Finally, in 1950, the rate was permitted to go to 1½ per cent each, or 3 per cent combined, and a new rate schedule was projected, calling for an ultimate combined rate of 6½ per cent of covered earnings by 1970. With the liberalization of the benefit formula in 1954, the contribution schedule was again revised upward, with the rate scheduled to go to 4 per cent each in 1975. The present rate of contribution is 2 per cent each for wage earners and their employers, and 3 per cent for self-employed persons.

The present system of financing is neither a pay-as-you-go nor full-reserve plan. Contributions have been more than adequate to meet benefit and administrative expenditures but less than adequate to accumulate a full reserve. The expenditures of the program in 1954, its eighteenth year of operations, amounted to less than 3 per cent of covered payroll, while in the same year contributions equaled 4 per cent of payroll. The excess contributions have led to the accumulation of a trust fund, or reserve, of more than $20.5 billion. Yet it has been estimated that this fund would not be capable of meeting the obligations of the program to those persons who have already begun to draw old-age benefits, not to mention the accrued liabilities for those persons who are still working. Indeed, official estimates as of the end of 1953, based on the provisions then in effect, placed the present value of the benefits to be paid to those persons already on the OASI benefit rolls at $23 billion and the total accrued liability of the system, including that for all persons who have contributed to the program, at $200 billion.[10] The accrued liability is substantially higher today in view of the liberalization of benefits in the 1954 amendments.

FEDERAL STAFF RETIREMENT PLANS

Entirely distinct from the national old-age insurance program, several staff retirement plans have been established under the aegis of the Federal Government. Designed, with one notable exception, to provide old-age benefits to various categories of Federal employees, these plans bear a close resemblance to private pension plans. Employees enrolled under these plans are not concurrently covered under OASI, although partial integration with OASI has been achieved with respect to the Railroad Retirement System.

Largest of the Federal plans and, in fact, the largest single employer pension plan in existence, is the Civil Service Retirement System, which provides retirement and survivorship benefits to career employees of the Federal Government. Established in 1920, the plan now covers about 1.5 million employees. Participation is compulsory for all eligible employees. During the calendar year 1953, 190,600 persons, on the average, were drawing retirement benefits from the system and another 50,400 were receiving survivorship benefits.[11] Approximately one million Federal employees

10. Social Security Administration, *Long-Range Cost Estimates for Old-Age and Survivors Insurance,* Actuarial Study No. 36, 1953, p. 19.
11. *Social Security Bulletin,* September, 1954, p. 36.

without permanent civil service status are included in the OASI program.

In addition to the Civil Service Retirement System, there are nine other retirement plans covering Federal civilian employees. Some of the more important plans cover members of the foreign service, employees of the Federal Reserve Banks, employees of the Tennessee Valley Authority, and members of the Federal judiciary. Most of these plans provide more liberal benefits than those of the Civil Service Retirement System.

On the periphery of Federal staff plans is the Railroad Retirement System. This program is unique in the American pension field in that it is operated for a group of private employees but is underwritten by the Federal Government. It was established by the Railroad Retirement Act of 1937 in an attempt to restore financial stability to the various individual railroad plans which were threatened with insolvency after years of difficulties. Protection is provided against the five major hazards to economic security—old age, disability, death, unemployment, and sickness—and the benefits are guaranteed by the Federal Government.[12]

State and Local Retirement Systems

A heterogeneous assortment of public pension plans has been established at the state and local level. These plans differ widely in their details, but in most jurisdictions separate plans exist for policemen, firemen, and teachers, all other employees, if covered at all, being lumped together into a general retirement system. Because of the hazardous nature of their work, policemen and firemen were the earliest groups of public employees to obtain retirement benefits, and up to the present, plans for such employees have contained more liberal provisions than those for other public employees. As a rule, police and firemen plans provide for low employee contributions, retirement at an early age after relatively brief service (typically twenty years), liberal survivors' benefits, disability benefits, and retirement benefits based on compensation for the highest grade held. Teacher

12. For a more extended description of Federal staff retirement plans, see Dan M. McGill, "The Goal and Characteristics of Public and Private Pension Plans in the United States," Huebner Foundation Lecture to be published in 1955 by the University of Pennsylvania Press.

retirement systems are less liberal than the policemen and firemen funds, but even so they usually accord more generous treatment than the plans maintained for rank-and-file employees.

Approximately 1700 in number, state and local plans are characterized by low benefits, long service requirements, nontransferability of credits, and inadequate financing.

Noncontributory Pension Programs

Noncontributory pension programs represent another broad source of old-age benefits and deserve brief mention. The best known of these programs is Old Age Assistance, which came into existence with the enactment of the Social Security Act and was broadly designed to complement the old-age insurance scheme which is now termed OASI. It was intended that Old Age Assistance should provide benefits to those indigent old persons who could not qualify for insurance benefits, or who could qualify but for one reason or another would not receive adequate benefits. This objective was to be accomplished through a system of Federal grants-in-aid to states which already had or would establish old-age assistance programs which could meet certain standards prescribed in the law. Conceived as a transitional device, the program has shown no tendency to diminish in importance and continues to rival OASI in number of beneficiaries and dollar value of benefit expenditures. The Federal Government is currently bearing about 53 per cent of benefit expenditures and one-half of the costs of administration.

Other noncontributory pension benefits are provided by the Veterans Administration and the regular military establishments.

THE PRIVATE PENSION MOVEMENT

Rationale

Industrial pensions appeared on the American scene during the last quarter of the nineteenth century, but only within the last two decades have they assumed any significance in the old-age financial picture. In the beginning, private pension benefits were universally regarded as gratuities from a grateful employer in recognition of long and faithful service. The payments were usually discretionary, the employer assuming no legal obligation to provide benefits. In fact, most plans stated in specific terms that no employee rights were being created thereunder and reserved to the employer the right to deny benefits to any employee and to reduce or terminate benefits which had already commenced. A few plans promised to continue benefit payments to retired employees but made no commitment to active employees.

As the years went by, certain groups, anxious to encourage and strengthen the pension movement, sought to place on the employer a moral obligation to provide pensions to superannuated employees. As early as 1912, one student of the old-age problem wrote: "From the standpoint of the whole system of social economy, no employer has a right to engage men in any occupation that exhausts the individual's industrial life in ten, twenty, or forty years; and then leave the remnant floating on society at large as a derelict at sea."[13] This point of view was frequently expressed during the next few decades, being the subject of widespread debate in the early 1920's. It was adopted by the United Mine Workers and used by that organization in its 1946 campaign to establish a welfare fund. The union's position has been expressed by its President as follows:

> The United Mine Workers of America has assumed the position over the years that the cost of caring for the human equity in the coal industry is inherently as valid as the cost of the replacement of mining machinery, or the cost of paying taxes, or the cost of paying interest indebtedness, or any other factor incident to the production of a ton of coal for consumers' bins . . . [The agreement establishing the Welfare Fund] recognized in principle the fact that the industry owed an obligation to those employees, and the coal miners could no longer be used up, crippled beyond repair and turned out to live or die subject to the charity of the community or the minimum contributions of the state.[14]

The concept received its most influential endorsement in the report of the fact-finding board in the 1949 steel industry labor dispute. The board wrote, in part, as follows:

> As hereinafter amplified, we think that all industry, in the absence of adequate Government programs, owes an obligation to workers to provide for maintenance of the human body in the form of medical and similar

13. Lee Welling Squier, *Old Age Dependency in the United States* (New York: Macmillan Company, 1912), p. 272.
14. United Mine Workers of America Welfare and Retirement Fund, *Pensions for Coal Miners* (undated), p. 4.

benefits and full depreciation in the form of old-age retirement—in the same way as it does now for plant and machinery.[15]

And again:

. . . the steel companies have, with some exceptions, overlooked the fact that the machines and plant on which the industry has prospered, and on which it must depend in the future, are not all made of metal or brick and mortar. They are also made of flesh and blood. And the human machines, like the inanimate machines, have a definite rate of depreciation.[16]

Despite its respectable following, this concept, now known as the Human Depreciation Concept, clearly rests on some logical imperfections. In the first place, aging is not a result of employment but of physiological processes. Even if it could be established that certain occupations tend to accelerate the aging process, the employer logically should be responsible for only the increase in the rate of aging. Secondly, the responsibility for providing retirement benefits is placed entirely on the last employer. Only the terminal employer is accused of casting away the worn out human machine, leaving it "floating on society at large as a derelict at sea." The same disapprobation does not attach to an employer who discharges an employee in his middle years without providing paid-up pension benefits. Finally, and this is the crux of the matter, the cost of replacing a human machine is not comparable to that of replacing a physical machine. A human machine can be replaced with only the cost of training a replacement, whereas the purchase price of a new unit must be accumulated to replace a worn out physical machine.[17]

The Human Depreciation Concept has been supplanted—or supplemented—in some quarters, by the theory that pensions are nothing more than deferred wages. The latter concept holds that an employee group has the prerogative of choosing between an immediate wage increase and a pension plan, and, having chosen the latter, is entitled to regard the benefits as deferred wages. Like the

15. Steel Industry Board, *Report to the President of the United States on the Labor Dispute in the Basic Steel Industry*, September 10, 1949, p. 55.
16. *Ibid.*, p. 64.
17. Of course, if social pressure forces an employer to provide old-age support for his employees, he will have to accumulate a capital sum for each employee or provide for such maintenance out of current earnings. In such event, the replacement of a superannuated employee would be comparable to the replacement of a worn out machine.

Human Depreciation Concept, this point of view found early expression:

> Theoretically, the simplest way of dealing with labor would be the
> payment of a money wage, requiring the employee to provide for the
> hazards of employment and his old age. While here and there an employee
> does this, by and large the mass of employees do not.
> In order to get a full understanding of old-age and service pensions,
> they should be considered as a part of the real wages of a workman.
> There is a tendency to speak of these pensions as being *paid* by the
> company, or, in cases where the employee contributes a portion, as being
> *paid* partly by the employer and partly by the employee. In a certain
> sense, of course, this may be correct, but it leads to confusion. A pension
> system considered as part of the real wages of an employee is really paid
> by the employee, not perhaps in money, but in the foregoing of an
> increase in wages which he might obtain except for the establishment of
> a pension system.[18]

Pursued to its logical conclusion, this concept has some far-reach-
ing implications. Certainly it would call for full, immediate vesting
of all benefits in the employees. It would also require that the minimum employer contribution to the plan be equal to the proposed
wage increase. (As a matter of fact, the concept usually carries the
implication that the employer should assume the full cost of the
plan.) Finally, it might be argued, as Dearing does,[19] that all contributions should be paid into an irrevocable trust fund administered by the employees, entirely free of either employer or union
control.

The unions which quite naturally are the most articulate advocates
of this concept have not insisted on its rigorous application to specific bargaining situations. In fact, many inconsistencies are found
between theory and practice. Perhaps the most basic inconsistency
is the almost universal absence of any vesting provisions in negotiated pension plans. Furthermore, there is rather general insistence
on union participation in the administration of the plan, jointly with
the employer, as opposed to unfettered administration by the employee group. Nevertheless, the concept assumes a certain realism
when the cost of the pension plan is translated into cents per hour

18. Albert deRoods, "Pensions as Wages," *The American Economic Review,*
Vol. 3 (June, 1913), p. 287.
19. Charles L. Dearing, *Industrial Pensions* (Washington: The Brookings
Institution, 1954), pp. 254-55.

and the employer averts a wage increase by agreeing to a pension plan.

It is doubtful that the private pension movement can be explained in terms of any one social or economic philosophy. Its rationale lies in broad and conflicting forces that do not lend themselves to definitive characterization. One might conclude that the only tenable explanation of the development is business expediency. Yet this expression is so pervasive that it furnishes only the vaguest of clues as to the specific forces that motivate employers to adopt pension plans. It might be helpful, therefore, to examine some of the significant factors and developments that have made it seem expedient to an employer to establish a pension plan.

FORCES INFLUENCING THE GROWTH OF PRIVATE PENSION PLANS

Productivity of the Employee Group.—Unquestionably, one of the most compelling employer motives in adopting a pension plan is the desire to increase the productivity of his employees. This motive is usually mixed with others, including a sincere desire to provide financial security to retired or superannuated employees. Nevertheless, unless the employer believes that the cost of the pension plan can be substantially offset by savings in other phases of company operations, including production costs, he may not be overly receptive to the idea of pensions.

On balance there is little doubt that the efficiency of the labor force is enhanced through the establishment of a pension plan. American industrial development has reached the stage where most concerns of any size now face or will soon face the problem of dealing with large numbers of employees near or beyond normal retirement age. This problem may be handled in one of three ways. The first possible approach is for the employer to discharge his employees without retirement benefits as they become superannuated. With Federal OASI benefits available in increasingly generous proportions, such action would not be as callous as it might otherwise be. Nevertheless, in the present state of social consciousness, most employers shun such an approach, not only for humanitarian reasons but because of the risk of public censure. A second possibility is for the employer to retain his superannuated employees on the payroll at full or reduced pay but in a capacity commensurate with their diminished ability and vitality. This policy is usually disruptive of employee morale and may prove to be uneconomical in other respects. The third approach, and in the great majority of cases the only one offering a satisfactory solution, is for the employer to establish a formal pension plan. This permits the employer to remove over-age employees from the payroll in an orderly fashion, without fear of adverse employee and public reaction, and to replace them with younger, presumably more efficient, workers. The inevitable result is a more productive work force.

The installation of a pension plan is thought to boost production in other ways. It is argued, for example, that the morale of the employee group will be elevated through the elimination of the workers' anxiety over their old-age security, not to mention the favorable attitude engendered by such tangible evidence of the employer's concern for the welfare of his employees. While a pension plan is definitely a positive morale factor, one may wonder whether its influence among the rank and file employees, particularly those distant from retirement, is not overshadowed by more immediate considerations, such as wages, hospitalization benefits, and working conditions.

It is also argued that the establishment of a pension plan will reduce turnover and hence the cost of training replacements. This argument is difficult to evaluate, since it is impossible to isolate the influence of a pension plan from the other factors that have a bearing on turnover. It is of some pertinency to point out that the highest rate of turnover occurs among employees who because of their youth or short service may not be eligible for membership in the plan, or even if active participants, may be only slightly influenced in their choice of employment by the promise of a retirement benefit many years in the future. Moreover, it should be remembered that any reductions in turnover will be reflected in higher pension costs, since a higher percentage of employees will qualify for severance or retirement benefits.

A pension plan is a particularly effective instrument of personnel policy with respect to supervisory employees. Supervisory personnel represent a more stable and permanent group of employees, to whom the promise of a pension appears less illusory than to the hourly workers. They tend, therefore, to be more responsive to the stimulus of a pension plan and to carry out their responsibilities more effectively. Furthermore, since the responsibilities of the supervisory personnel are, by definition, on a higher level than those of the ordinary employee, it is especially important that a means exist whereby the executives and other supervisors can be readily retired when they have passed the peak of effectiveness. Related to this is the importance of keeping open the channels of promotion. In a large organization, one retirement can precipitate a chain of promotions—all to the betterment of employee morale and efficiency. Finally, a pension plan unquestionably enables an employer to attract and hold better qualified executives than would otherwise be possible. This is particularly true of those firms which normally draw their executives from external rather than internal sources.

Tax Inducements.—Related to the foregoing in the sense that both are cost-reducing factors are the tax inducements offered by the Federal Government. The Revenue Act of 1942 is frequently—and erroneously—cited as the genesis of the favorable tax treatment of private pension plans, but the real beginning of such policy is found in much earlier legislation. As a matter of fact, before the enactment of any legislation directed specifically at private pensions, reasonable payments made by an employer, as pensions to retired employees or as contributions to a trust to fund current pension credits, were deductible from the employer's gross income for tax purposes. Such payments were deductible only as an ordinary and necessary business expense and then only if, together with other payments, they represented reasonable compensation. However, payments to a trust to fund liabilities for past service credits or to place the trust on a sound financial basis were not deductible. Moreover, the income of the trust was currently taxable to the employer, employees, or the trust, depending on the provisions of the trust instrument.

The latter condition was removed by the Revenue Act of 1921, which exempted from current taxation the income of a trust created by an employer as part of a stock bonus or profit-sharing plan for the exclusive benefit of some or all of his employees. The income of pension trusts was not exempted by statute from current taxation until the enactment of the Revenue Act of 1926, but by administrative ruling pension trusts were accorded the same status as stock bonus and profit-sharing trusts after 1921. In all cases, the income was to be taxable to the employees when actually distributed or made available.

Inasmuch as the Revenue Act of 1921 did not authorize deductions for past service contributions or contributions to establish the financial soundness of a plan, many employers adopted the practice of carrying balance sheet reserves against their pension obligations. Credits to these reserves were not deductible in arriving at net taxable income. The increase in the number and size of such reserves led to the enactment of a provision in the Revenue Act of 1928 which permitted an employer to take deductions for reasonable amounts paid in to a qualified trust in excess of the amounts required to fund current liabilities. In effect, this meant that an employer could transfer his balance sheet reserve to a trust or make other payments to a trust for the purpose of funding past service liabilities. However, deductions for any contributions in excess of the amount required to fund current service credits had to be apportioned in equal parts over a period of ten years. While this was a reasonable requirement when the past service liability was liquidated in one year, it was burdensome and unduly complicated when only a portion of the past service liability was funded each year, with each portion having to be spread over a ten-year period. It is interesting to note that this limitation on past service contributions did not apply to plans funded through group annuities, such discrimination existing until 1942 when all plans were made subject to the limitations of Section 23(p) of the Revenue Act of that year.

Unfortunately, as the law stood after 1928, pension plans lent themselves to tax-avoidance schemes. This was made possible through two broad loopholes in the law. In the first place, a pension trust could qualify for favorable tax treatment if it were created for the exclusive benefit of "some or all of the employees." Thus, the owners and officers of close corporations could establish a plan for the benefit of themselves and perhaps a few key employees, gaining an immediate tax deduction for the corporation without an immediate tax to themselves as participants. In the second place, the law did not require that the trust be irrevocable. An employer could make substantial contributions to a trust during years of high earnings, taking deductions against his income tax, and then recapture the earnings in poor years by revoking the trust. This practice not only deprived the Government of tax revenue but perhaps more important was detrimental to the interests of the participating employees.

Abuses under the law led to the inclusion of the so-called Non-Diversion Rule in the Revenue Act of 1938. This rule stated that it must be impossible at any time prior to the satisfaction of all liabilities under the trust for any part of the trust funds to be diverted to purposes other than the exclusive benefit of the employees. In brief, the trust had to be irrevocable. No attempt was made in that legislation, however, to broaden the participation in qualified plans, so that it remained possible to establish qualified plans for a few favored employees.

The impetus given to the adoption of pension plans by the sharp increase in corporate income taxes in 1940, and other influences, forced the Congress to tighten up the requirements for qualification. This was accomplished in the Revenue Act of 1942. The provisions of this Act, as subsequently amended, were re-enacted in the Internal Revenue Code of 1954 and, along with implementing regulations, constitute the law under which pension plans operate today.

At the present time, in order for an employer to deduct his contributions to a pension plan, whether for current or past service, the plan must meet the general requirements of Section 401(a) of the Internal Revenue Code of 1954 [Section 165(a) of the 1942 Code]. As implemented by Sec. 29.165 of Regulations 111, these requirements are:

(a) There must be a trust, contract, or other legally binding arrangement. The plan must be in writing and must be communicated to the employees. Furthermore, it must be a permanent and continuing program.

(b) The plan must be for the exclusive benefit of the employees or their beneficiaries, and it must be impossible prior to the satisfaction of all liabilities under the plan for any part of the corpus or income to be diverted to any other use. In fact, the trust agreement or other applicable document must contain a specific statement to the effect that no funds can be diverted.

(c) The plan must benefit employees in general and not just a limited number of favored employees. To meet this requirement the plan must cover either a prescribed percentage of employees or a classification of employees found by the Commissioner of Internal Revenue not to be discriminatory in favor of officers, shareholders, supervisors, or highly compensated employees.[20]

(d) The plan must not discriminate in favor of officers, shareholders, or highly compensated employees with respect to contributions or benefits. Variations in contributions or benefits are permissible so long as the plan in its over-all operations does not discriminate in favor of that class of employees with respect to which discrimination is prohibited. It is of special significance that contributions or benefits based on remuneration excluded from the OASI wage base may differ from contributions or benefits within such base so long as the resulting differences in benefits are approximately offset percentage-wise by the benefits available under the Federal OASI program. If such an equivalence obtains, the plan is said to be integrated with OASI.[21]

✓ (e) The plan must provide definitely determinable benefits. This requirement is designed to distinguish a pension plan from a profit-sharing plan. A plan to provide retirement benefits to employees or their beneficiaries will be deemed a pension plan if either the benefits payable to the employee or the contributions required of the employer can be determined actuarially. Benefits are not definitely determinable if funds arising from forfeitures on termination of service, or for other reasons, may be used to provide increased benefits for the remaining participants rather than being used to reduce employer contributions. There is an implication that the plan should be actuarially sound but as will be apparent from later discussions Treasury approval of a plan carries with it no certification that contributions under the plan will be adequate to provide the accrued benefits.

Contributions to a plan which qualifies under Section 401(a) are deductible under Section 404 of the Code [Formerly Section 23(p)]. In order to be deductible under Section 404, however, the contributions must fall within a class of expense deductible under Section 162 (relating to trade or business expenses) or Section 212 (relating to

20. See pp. 31-34 for a fuller explanation of the coverage requirement.
21. See pp. 42-48 for a more detailed explanation of the integration requirement.

expenses for the production of income). That is to say, contributions may be deducted under Section 404 only to the extent that they are ordinary and necessary expenses incurred in carrying on a trade or business or in the production of income and are in the nature of compensation for personal services actually rendered. In no case is a deduction allowable for a contribution on behalf of an employee in excess of an amount which, together with other deductions allowed as compensation for such employee's services, constitutes a reasonable allowance for compensation.

After employer contributions have qualified as ordinary and necessary expenses, they must conform to the detailed limitations contained in Section 404(1)(A) through (D). These limitations are dealt with at length at a later point[22] and will not be discussed here.

In addition to the encouragement offered private pension plans through deductibility of employer contributions, the income of a qualified trust is exempted from Federal income taxation until disbursed in the form of benefits. Furthermore, employer contributions to a qualified plan are not taxable to the participating employees until actually received.[23]

The deductibility of employer contributions has given rise to a general impression that the Government bears a share of the burden of providing pension benefits, a factor which has acted as a strong stimulus to the establishment of pension plans. This view was particularly prevalent during World War II when an excess profits tax was being levied in addition to the normal corporate income tax, the combined levy being 85.5 per cent at the top income bracket. The thesis that a corporation subject to the maximum levy could finance a plan with fifteen-cent dollars was universally accepted. As recently as 1953, before the postwar excess profits tax expired, many companies could logically conclude that their pension plan was costing them only eighteen cents per dollar of outlay.

This conclusion is based on the assumption that employer contributions come out of the top bracket of income and in the absence of a pension plan would go to the Government in the form of tax pay-

---

22. See pp. 133-36.

23. The taxability of employee benefits is a separate and involved subject which because of space limitations cannot be discussed here. It is not particularly relevant to the subject of employer motivation, except with respect to plans for management employees, where the primary incentive may be the deferred taxation of employer contributions.

ments. Such an assumption is undoubtedly valid in the short run, particularly during a period when prices and wage rates are virtually frozen, as they were during World War II. Other things being equal, any type of expenditure not incurred in earlier years or one that is increased over former years, reduces the net taxable income of the taxpayer by the amount of the expenditure and, in effect, is passed on to the Government in the proportion that the tax reduction bears to the increase in expenditures.

Other things do not remain equal indefinitely, however, and an expenditure that was marginal in one period may have become a permanent feature of the cost structure in the next period. In the long run, pension outlays may lose their marginal status and come to be regarded as a normal cost of labor, similar to wages and other benefits that go to employees. In such event an attempt will almost certainly be made to pass such costs on to consumers in the form of higher prices. Whether this can be done will depend on a number of variables, including the elasticity of demand for the company's product, competition from other firms, and the nature of the industry.

To a considerable degree, the question of whether the pension contributions of a particular employer will be treated as a special outlay to be charged against profits or as an element of ordinary labor cost to be passed on to consumers will be determined by the extent to which pension plans are adopted and pension outlays are incurred by other firms in the industry or competing industries. So long as pension plans are established by only those firms with a better-than-average earnings record, employer contributions will undoubtedly have the effect of reducing profits and, hence, the tax liability of the firms. If, however, virtually all firms in an industry, including the marginal firms, should adopt plans, a situation might be created in which all employers could shift their pension costs to consumers.

Pressure From Organized Labor.—A third broad factor influencing the adoption of pension plans has been the attitude of organized labor. Until recently, organized labor was, in the main, either indifferent to the pension movement or openly antagonistic to it. Many of the older and well-established craft unions viewed

employer-sponsored pensions as a paternalistic device to wean the
allegiance of the workers away from the unions to the employer.
They also harbored a fear that pensions would be used to hold down
wages. Over the years, however, these attitudes have changed to
such an extent that in 1949, when another round of wage increases
seemed difficult to justify, a large segment of organized labor de-
manded pensions in lieu of wages. The way was paved for such a
switch when a Federal Court ruled that pensions are a bargainable
issue.

This case arose out of a union grievance filed with the National
Labor Relations Board in 1946, alleging that the unilateral action of
the Inland Steel Company in enforcing a policy of compulsory retirement at age 65 constituted a breach of the provision of the general
labor contract relating to separation from service. The grievance
stemmed from the refusal of the company to negotiate the matter
with the union on the grounds that compulsory retirement was an
essential part of the company's pension plan and that pension plans
did not fall within the scope of collective bargaining. The union did
not contend that the provisions of a pension plan were of themselves
subject to collective bargaining, but argued that the company could
not take unilateral action with respect to any provision of a pension
agreement that was also a part of the general labor contract and
hence conceded to be within the scope of mandatory collective
bargaining.

In 1948 the National Labor Relations Board ruled in effect that
the Labor Management Relations Act of 1947 imposes a duty on
employers to bargain with representatives of their employees on
the subject of pensions. This decision was based on the dual
premise that the term "wages" as defined in the statute includes
any emolument of value such as pension or insurance benefits and
that the detailed provisions of pension plans come within the pur-
view of "conditions of employment" and therefore constitute an
appropriate subject for collective bargaining.[24]

Upon appeal by the Company, the Seventh Circuit Court of
Appeals approved the view of the National Labor Relations Board
that the terms of a pension plan are subject to mandatory collective

24. *Inland Steel Company* v. *United Steelworkers of America* (CIO), 77
NLRB 4 (1948).

bargaining on the ground that they constitute "conditions of employment" but expressed some reservation with respect to the wage analogy:

> We are convinced that the language employed by Congress, considered in connection with the purpose of the Act, so clearly includes a retirement and pension plan as to leave little, if any, reason for construction. While, as the Company has demonstrated, a reasonable argument can be made that the benefits flowing from such a plan are not "wages," we think the better and more logical argument is on the other side, and certainly there is, in our opinion, no sound basis for an argument that such a plan is not clearly included in the phrase, "other conditions of employment."[25]

The Inland Steel Decision established a legal framework within which no employer can install, alter, or terminate a pension plan for organized workers without the assent of the labor bargaining unit. This obligation rests on the employer whether or not the plan was installed prior to certification of the bargaining unit and whether or not the plan be compulsory or voluntary, contributory or noncontributory.

The CIO took advantage of the new legal status of pensions to launch a concerted drive for pensions and other welfare benefits. The purpose of the drive was twofold: (1) to secure pension benefits directly from employers, and (2) to induce employers to join labor in seeking liberalization of the Federal OASI program. The CIO argued that the Federal program did not provide adequate benefits, a condition which they ascribed to the organized opposition of employers and insurance companies. By pressing for pension benefits to be financed entirely by management, union leaders felt that employers would be more receptive to proposals for liberalization of the Federal program which is jointly financed by management and labor. In line with this policy, the CIO agreed to deduction of OASI benefits from the benefits to be provided by the employer pension plan. The strategy was carried out through a unified collective bargaining program, the local unions being required to observe the standards prescribed by the governing bodies.

The CIO program does not reflect the views of all segments of organized labor. The AFofL, for example, has urged more reliance on the Federal program, advocating employer plans for only those

---

25. *Inland Steel Company* v. *National Labor Relations Board*, 170 F. 2d 247, 251 (1949). Certiorari denied by the Supreme Court, 336 U.S. 960 (1949).

workers whose wages provide a margin above the current necessities of life. It cautions against an ill-considered or poorly-designed plan, pointing out that "such a plan may impair other vital trade union aims and functions, while offering relatively little in return."[26] Furthermore, the AFofL has made no attempt to impose a patterned pension program on its local unions. The locals have been given full discretion as to whether or not they will bargain with employers for pension coverage and, if so, as to what type of plan to seek. As a result, wide differences are found among the unions affiliated with the AFofL as to pension philosophy and practice.

Social Pressure.—A final factor that has encouraged the spread of pension plans is the social and political atmosphere that has prevailed during the last quarter-century. During that period the American people have become security-conscious. The economic upheaval of the early 1930's swept away the life savings of millions and engendered a feeling of insecurity that shook the very foundations of the country. Prominent among the proposals for economic reform were those that envisioned social action in the area of old-age income maintenance. The Federal OASI program was the outgrowth of these proposals.

Since the Federal program was deliberately designed to provide only a "floor of protection," the way was left clear for supplemental benefits to be provided through private measures. In view of the general inability—or unwillingness, as some would have it—of the individual to accumulate through his own efforts the additional resources required, society has come to expect the employer to bear a share of the burden. The employer may successfully shift his share of the costs to the consumer, but a great deal of social pressure is exerted on the employer to provide the mechanism through which additional funds can be accumulated. If the employer chooses not to install a formal pension plan, he may find that social pressure forces him to take care of his superannuated employees in some other manner. In anticipation of such a development, employers are turning in increasing numbers to formal pension programs as the most economical and satisfactory method of meeting the problem.

26. American Federation of Labor, *Pension Plans Under Collective Bargaining*, A Reference Guide for Trade Unions (1952), p. v.

28 Underlying Forces

PRESENT SCOPE

Complete and up-to-date information on the number and coverage of private pension plans is not available. As of the end of 1953, there were 15,730 plans underwritten by life insurance companies, covering 3,940,000 employees.[27] Individual contract pension trusts accounted for 10,470, or approximately two-thirds, of the plans but only 610,000, or about 15 per cent, of the persons covered. Group annuity contracts, comprising only one-fourth of the plans, accounted for more than 75 per cent of the coverage.

The number of self-administered trusteed plans is not known. Estimates run as high as 5,000 plans. These plans cover an estimated 8,000,000 employees. This would mean that insured and self-administered plans combined cover 12,000,000 persons, or about 20 per cent of the current working population.

The following chapter indicates the range of provisions that may be found in these plans. Later chapters describe the legal arrangements, called funding media, under which the benefits of the plans may be provided; the actuarial techniques, called funding methods, that govern the rate at which the necessary funds are accumulated; and, finally, the factors which should be considered by the employer in selecting a funding medium.

27. Institute of Life Insurance, *Fact Book*, 1954, p. 31.

Basic Features
of a Pension Plan

2

IT is axiomatic in pension planning that the benefit pattern and
other substantive provisions of a pension plan should be determined before consideration of the method of financing and the legal
form of the plan. Certain basic provisions are common to all types
of pension plans and can be discussed independently of the financial
and legal characteristics of the plan. It is the purpose of this chapter
to outline the essential features of any pension plan, indicating in a
general manner the various arrangements and combinations that are
available. The chapter is not intended as a manual or guide for pension technicians but rather as background for subsequent discussions
of the more complex and controversial issues encountered in pension
planning. Despite the many facets of a pension plan, the essential
features can be summarized under the three general headings of
coverage, benefit structure, and source of financing.

COVERAGE

From the standpoint of broad coverage, a pension plan may be
of the multi-employer or single-employer type. The multi-employer
type of plan is a product of collective bargaining and has emerged
principally in industries characterized by skilled craftsmen, numerous small employers, and a high rate of business failure. It may be
industry-wide in scope or it may cover only the members of the
negotiating union located in a particular geographical area. Some
examples of industry-wide plans are those of the United Mine Workers; the United Brotherhood of Carpenters and Joiners of America,
AFL; the International Brotherhood of Electrical Workers, AFL;
the International Typographical Union, AFL; and the Amalgamated
Clothing Workers of America, CIO. Among the multi-employer

29

plans that operate in a restricted geographical area are those covering (1) the Detroit tool and die workers, United Automobile Workers, CIO; (2) the brewery workers of the New York City area, the International Union of United Brewery . . . Workers, CIO; (3) the longshoremen in the New York City area, International Longshoremen's Association, AFL; and (4) the employees of a number of small employers in the Toledo, Ohio area, the bargaining unit being the United Automobile Workers, CIO. By the nature of things, however, the great majority of pension plans cover only the employees of a single employer.[1]

If a pension plan is to qualify under Section 401(a) of the Internal Revenue Code of 1954, it must not discriminate in favor of officers, stockholders, supervisory personnel, or highly paid employees. Discrimination may occur in three broad areas—coverage, benefits, or contributions—but as a safeguard against discrimination as to coverage, the Internal Revenue Code requires that a plan cover an arbitrary percentage of employees or, in lieu thereof, satisfy the Commissioner of Internal Revenue that it is, in fact, not discriminatory in favor of the specified categories of individuals. In order to qualify under the so-called Arbitrary Rule, a plan must cover 70 per cent or more of all employees, exclusive of short service, seasonal, and part-time employees, or 70 per cent or more of all employees, similarly defined, must be eligible for coverage under the plan, of whom at least 80 per cent must actually participate.[2] Thus, so long as 70 per cent of the employees are eligible for coverage, a plan may qualify if only 56 per cent of the employees participate (70% x 80%). Moreover, in satisfaction of this requirement, an employer may treat as a unit any number of pension plans he may have in effect.

A plan may fail to meet the foregoing requirement and still qualify by satisfying the Commissioner that no discrimination will occur. Section 401(a)(3)(B), referred to as the Discretionary Rule, permits the Commissioner to approve any classification of employees which he finds not to be discriminatory in favor of officers, stock-

---

1. As of June 30, 1953, 22,168 profit-sharing and pension plans had been approved by the Treasury Department, of which only 99 were industry-wide plans. Prentice-Hall *Pension and Profit-Sharing Report No. 56,* September 4, 1953. For statistical purposes, an industry-wide plan is defined as a negotiated plan of all subscribing employers located in areas under the jurisdiction of more than one District Director of Internal Revenue.

2. Section 401(a)(3)(A), Internal Revenue Code of 1954.

holders, supervisory personnel, or highly compensated employees. In practice, most plans are approved under this discretionary provision. The Commissioner has approved plans covering as few as 10 per cent of the employees.

Very few pension plans cover all employees of a particular employer. The employee group may be stratified in various ways without jeopardizing Treasury approval of the resulting plan or plans. The most common bases for exclusion from participation in a particular plan are as follows:

Type of Employment.—The basis for exclusion under this category is normally the part-time or seasonal nature of the work performed by the excluded employees. Section 401(a)(3)(A) of the Code, it may be noted, permits exclusion of those persons who do not work more than twenty hours per week or whose customary employment is not for more than five months in any calendar year in computing the percentage of coverage under a plan. Under this category, however, a plan may cover the employees of only one department of a plant or the employees of only one or a few plants of several operated by the employer. Likewise, a negotiated plan may cover only one bargaining unit at the plant, excluding other bargaining units and unorganized groups.

Type of Pay.—A distinction is sometimes made between salaried and hourly employees. If such a distinction is made, it is usually to exclude hourly employees. The employer may feel that he cannot afford to provide retirement benefits to all his employees and prefers to provide adequate benefits to a limited group (the salaried employees) rather than inadequate benefits to the entire group. Occasionally, a plan is limited to salaried employees in the beginning, with the objective of extending it to hourly employees as soon as the financial circumstances of the employer permit. Finally, if the hourly employees are organized, the union representatives may request wage increases and other benefits in lieu of pensions.

On the other hand, plans are frequently established which exclude salaried workers, particularly at the outset.

Amount of Pay.—The rationale for a distinction on this basis is the treatment of earnings under the Federal OASI program. As was pointed out earlier, the benefit formula under this program is designed to favor the low income worker. For example, under the present law the primary OASI benefit replaces 35.4 per cent of the total wages of a covered employee earning $2,400 per year, while it replaces only 21.7 per cent of the total compensation of an individual earning $6,000 per year. A person earning $18,000 has only 7.2 per cent of his salary replaced through his primary OASI benefit.

In an effort to achieve an equilibrium between earnings and retirement income, many employers throughout the years have established plans covering only those employees with earnings above the limit of OASI coverage, currently $4,200, with a benefit formula designed to replace the same percentage of earnings above the limit as is replaced below the limit by the OASI program. Such plans are approved by the Treasury if they meet the integration requirements discussed below and are otherwise acceptable. In many cases, a company has one plan covering all employees and another plan, intended to equalize benefits, covering only employees earning more than the income limitation under OASI. As might be expected, revisions in the OASI wage base and benefit formula have precipitated amendments to many plans integrated with earlier formulas.

Length of Service.—Most plans require that an employee complete a minimum period of service before achieving membership in the plan. Early plans tended to require five years of service as a qualification period, but the trend in recent years has been to shorten the period. An analysis of 217 "conventional" plans established or amended during the period 1950-52 revealed that 49 had no service requirement and 87 others had a requirement of one year or less.[3] Only 31 plans required as much as five years of service. In about 40 per cent of the cases, the service requirement was combined with an age requirement, the most frequent combination being one year of service and age thirty.

The purpose of a service requirement is almost purely administrative. There is a high rate of turnover among recently hired

3. Bankers Trust Company, *A Study of Industrial Retirement Plans,* 1953 Edition, New York, p. 8. A "conventional" plan is defined in the study as one whose benefits vary with both years of service and rate of compensation. It is to be contrasted with the negotiated or "pattern" plan whose benefit is a flat amount, sometimes varying with years of service but seldom with rate of compensation. Plans negotiated in the steel and rubber industries are an exception to the above definition, since their benefits almost always vary with the rate of compensation.

employees, particularly those at the younger ages, and it is an un-necessary administrative expense to bring such persons into the pension plan, with the attendant records, only to have them with-draw a short time later. The matter of employer contributions is normally not involved, since such short-term employees would rarely have any vested interests and the contributions on their behalf would thus be recovered by the employer in any event. The requirement does reduce the number of years of credited service and, hence, the pension benefit of the employee who remains with the employer until retirement, or to the point of vesting.

A service requirement may occasionally be found in a different connection or at the other end of the scale. If the plan requires a minimum period of service for entitlement to benefits, as opposed to membership in the plan, an employee who cannot accumulate the requisite period of service before the normal retirement age may be excluded from membership in the plan. In that event, he may be denied retirement benefits altogether or he may receive benefits outside the plan. In the Bankers Trust Company study referred to above, it was found that 18 per cent of the conventional plans re-quired a minimum period of credited service, ranging from ten to twenty years, before entitlement to benefits.[4]

Age.—An employee may be excluded from membership in a pen-sion plan because he is either too young or too old. Many plans require that the employee must have attained the age of 25, 30, or 35 before he may become a member of the plan, while at the other extreme, persons who are employed after, or have not elected to become members of the plan before, age 50, 55, or 60 are excluded from membership.

A minimum age limitation has much the same purpose as a service requirement—to exclude high turnover employees—and, as was indi-cated previously, is frequently combined with a service requirement. When the plan is contributory, a minimum age requirement has the additional function of excluding those employees who because of their youth have scant interest in pensions and would object to making contributions for that purpose.

The maximum age limitation has a purely financial basis—the desire to hold down the cost of pensions. Dollar for dollar, the cost

4. *Ibid.,* p. 9.

of providing a pension increases with the age of the employee. For example, a widely used rate basis requires a single premium of $45.60 for a life income of $1.00 per month at age 65 purchased at age 30, with no refund, while the same benefit purchased at age 50 is $82.32.[5] At the same time, an employer normally feels little responsibility for the retirement needs of a person who was in his service only five or ten years before retirement. Companies which do not include a maximum age provision in their pension specifications may achieve the same objective through a hiring limitation. Such a device may be effective for this purpose, but its widespread adoption creates serious economic and social problems for the economy as a whole.

BENEFIT STRUCTURE

The benefit provisions of a pension plan constitute the very heart of the plan. They define the type of benefits that will be paid, the size of the benefits that will be paid, the circumstances under which they will become payable, and the manner in which they will be paid. Together, they represent the disbursement aspect of the plan. There is obviously a close logical relationship between the benefit pattern of a plan and the methods of financing such benefits. In this section, however, benefits will be discussed independently of financing techniques.

RETIREMENT BENEFITS

Size of Benefits.—The underlying purpose of a pension plan is to enable the employer to remove his superannuated employees from the payroll in a manner that is morally and socially acceptable. Basic to this objective is the continuation of an income which, supplemented by OASI benefits, will be large enough to sustain the retired worker and his dependents on a decent standard of living. Otherwise, the employer will not feel justified in forcing the aged worker off the payroll, and the pension plan will fail of its purpose.

Ideally, perhaps, the goal of a pension plan, in conjunction with the Federal program, should be the continuation, in full, of the

5. Rates based on 1937 Standard Annuity Table, 2½ per cent interest, and loading of 8 per cent of gross premium.

worker's wages or salary at the time of his retirement. As a practical matter, however, it has not been found possible, or perhaps even desirable, to provide retirement benefits on such a scale, and the objective has been, rather, to provide benefits that bear a "reasonable" relationship to the wages which were earned by the employee during his working years. The concept of reasonableness is obviously subjective, but pension technicians have generally regarded as adequate a plan which will replace, inclusive of OASI benefits, one-third to one-half of the employee's average earnings during the five or ten years preceding retirement.

A. Benefit Formulas.—Pension plans may be classified with respect to benefit formulas into two categories: money purchase and definite benefit.

(1) Money Purchase Plan.—The money purchase plan is one in which the contribution of the employer—and employee, if the plan is contributory—is fixed in the formula and the benefit is treated as the variable factor. The annual contribution to the plan on behalf of a particular employee is normally expressed as a percentage of the employee's earnings, the percentage typically being uniform for all employees. The percentage is normally not less than 10 nor more than 15 per cent. Most money purchase plans are contributory, with the employer matching the employee's contribution or sometimes contributing a multiple of the employee's rate. A typical plan might provide for a 5 per cent contribution on the part of both the employer and employee, with an upper limit of perhaps $5,000, $7,500, or even $10,000 on the earnings to which the percentage will be applied.

The benefits which can be purchased in any given year for a particular employee depend upon the attained age of the employee and will decrease with increasing age. For an employee, age 30, earning $3,000 per year, a total contribution of 10 per cent or $300 would purchase a life income of $78.95 per year beginning at age 65, with no guaranteed payments.[6] The same contribution would purchase an annual benefit of only $76.73 at age 31 and at age 40, assuming no change in earnings, the $300 contribution or premium would

6. All rates in this paragraph are based on the 1937 Standard Annuity Table, 2½ per cent interest, and loading of 8 per cent of gross premium.

purchase an annual benefit of only $59.76. Normally, of course, increases in earnings can be expected to offset to some extent the effect of the age increase.

The money purchase plan is attractive to the firm or organization which is forced to budget its funds very carefully and must know in advance what its outlay for pensions will be. Under this plan, an organization can determine its pension commitment by multiplying its projected payroll, adjusted for maximum limitations, by the appropriate percentage. It is used extensively in public retirement plans and plans of non-profit institutions, such as universities, hospitals, and charitable organizations. The technique is used in connection with industrial plans of the definite benefit type which permit voluntary contributions by the employees to provide benefits supplemental to the basic plan.

As the basic formula, however, the money purchase plan has certain undesirable features particularly from the standpoint of the employees. Through the operation of compound interest, relatively greater weight is given to compensation of the early years of service, when wages are low, than to earnings of the later years, the resulting benefit being particularly deficient during an inflationary period. The scale of contributions, adequate for younger employees, tends to produce inadequate benefits for older entrants. Furthermore, the plan does not lend itself to simple calculation or expression of benefits. For these and perhaps other reasons, the money purchase plan has not been widely adopted by industrial firms, and many plans which were originally set up on that basis have subsequently been converted to the definite benefit basis.

(2) Definite Benefit Plan.—The definite benefit type of plan is one in which the benefits are determined in advance by a formula and the contributions are treated as the variable factor. There are many variations of the plan. In its study of 346 group annuity plans established during 1946-50, the Federal Security Agency found 166 different formulas of the definite benefit type.[7] The Bankers Trust Company in its most recent study,[8] found 24 variations among the benefit formulas of 97 pattern plans, which by definition should

7. Weltha Van Eenam and Martha E. Penman, *Analysis of 346 Group Annuities Underwritten in 1946-50,* Actuarial Study No. 32 (Washington: Federal Security Agency, Social Security Administration), October, 1952, p. 20.
8. *Op. cit.,* p. 14.

have common characteristics, and virtually 217 different formulas among the 217 conventional plans. It might be said that the only uniformity among the benefit formulas of the latter plans was their nonuniformity. Nevertheless, the various plans of the definite benefit type can be broadly classified into four categories:

(a) <u>Benefits related to both earnings and services.</u>—The type of formula in which the benefit payable at retirement age is based on both earnings and length of service is by far the most popular. This type of formula has the merit of providing a benefit that is related to the employee's previous standard of living but is limited, in a rough measure, to the employer's moral responsibility to the employee. It appears to be elemental justice that an employee with a long period of service should receive a larger benefit at retirement than the employee with a limited or short period of service. The view that an employee's relative earnings status should be extended into retirement has not been as widely embraced.

For the purpose of the benefit formula, both "earnings" and "service" must be carefully defined. The pension agreement must spell out clearly the items of compensation which will be treated as part of the earnings base. Such items as overtime pay, holiday pay, sick pay, bonuses, and commissions must be specifically excluded or included. More important from the standpoint of the benefit formula, however, is the question of the period whose earnings will be used. Specifically, the question is whether the benefits shall be based on the earnings of the employee during his entire period of credited service or whether they shall be based on a selected period, such as the final five or ten years of employment.

The great majority of plans that relate benefits to earnings base the benefits on earnings for the total period of employment or the "career average," as the concept is called. The benefit formula of such a plan provides that each employee is to be credited with an annual benefit at retirement equal to a specified percentage of average annual compensation multiplied by the number of years of credited service. The percentage used in the formulas ranges from ½ to 2½ per cent, with 1 per cent predominating. The percentage may vary with the level of earnings, as many as four earnings classifications sometimes being employed. It is quite common to apply one percentage to the earnings subject to OASI and another, perhaps higher, percentage to earnings in excess of the OASI base. There is normally a distinction between past and future service, with a lower percentage being applicable to the former.[9] As a matter of administration, wage or earnings brackets are frequently established, with the formula percentage or percentages being applied to the midpoint of the bracket.

An increasing number of plans use a formula based on average earnings for the last five or ten years preceding retirement.[10] Under normal circumstances, this type of formula will produce an earnings base higher than that of the career average, since most employees reach the peak of their earnings in the years immediately preceding retirement. This bias in favor of the employee is offset in many such formulas by crediting a lower percentage of earnings toward retirement benefits.

A more significant characteristic of this type of formula, however, is the fact that it is more responsive to changes in price level and other economic developments. In periods of inflationary pressures, wages have a tendency to rise with the price level, and an employee whose earnings base for retirement purposes embraces such a period obviously receives larger benefits. The final average type of formula thus appears to be a partial hedge against the effect of inflation, and employers are currently being urged by employees and labor unions to adopt such plans. Naturally, the plan would operate in the opposite direction in a period of depressed business activity, assuming no amendments to the benefit formula. From a long range point of view, however, this formula should produce higher benefits than those of the career average formula, since the secular trend of prices and wages in the United States has been upward.

The benefit formula normally gives credit only for "continuous service," which is usually defined as the period extending from the last date of hiring to date of retirement. The pension agreement, therefore, must stipulate the types of personnel actions that will be interpreted as breaks in continuous service.

9. See pp. 39-40 for a discussion of past and future service.
10. As a matter of fact, the early important plans in this country, such as those of the petroleum industry, the Bell System, Bethlehem Steel, and International Harvester, were of the "final average" type. The depression of the 1930's caused a shift to the career average type, a trend which continued into World War II. The inflation since 1945 has reversed the trend back to the original type of program.

Another concept involved in the service aspect of the benefit formula is the distinction between future and past service. Future service means all service of a continuous nature performed after the date of establishment of the pension plan, while past service is all continuous service performed for the company in question prior to that date.[11] Virtually all plans give credit for future service, although there may be a limitation on the number of years that will be recognized for benefit purposes. Future service alone, however, will not provide adequate benefits to employees who have been with the company for years but have only a few more years before retirement. For this reason, the great majority of pension plans afford some recognition to past service. A relatively small percentage of plans, however, grant full credit for past service.[12] Various forms of limitations are used, the most common being the exclusion of (a) all service performed before a specified age, such as thirty; (b) the first few years of service, such as five; and (c) all service over a maximum number of years, such as 10, 15, or 25, or before a specified date. Exclusions (a) and (b) are frequently combined to exclude, for example, all service performed before age 30 and during the first five years of employment. The first two types of exclusion, or the combination, have the general purpose of placing the past service of old employees on the same basis as the future service of new employees. The primary purpose of the type (c) exclusion is to limit the cost of past service benefits, an accrued liability which is invariably borne by the employer.

The recognized portion of past service is generally given credit for a specified percentage of earnings for each year of service, although some plans grant a stated dollar amount for each year of credited service. For administrative reasons, past service benefits are usually based on the employee's compensation as of the effective date of the plan or for a short period preceding establishment of the

11. Service with a company which was absorbed by or merged with the firm installing the pension plan may or may not be recognized. If the previous firm had had a plan in effect, it is likely that the acquiring firm will assume the pension obligations of the other firm or at least integrate its employees into the new plan.

12. The Federal Security Agency found only 31 plans out of 346 group annuities, or 9 per cent, which granted full credit for past service. Twelve per cent of the plans granted no recognition of past service. Van Eenam and Penman, *op. cit.*, p. 25.

plan. If the plan is of the final average type, the same compensation base is likely to be used for both past and future service, and the same percentage is normally credited toward retirement. In connection with the career average type of formula, however, a lower percentage, typically 3/4 per cent, is applied to past service earnings than to future service earnings on the grounds that the rate of compensation for most employees will be higher as of the date of the plan than the average up to that point.

(b) Benefits related to earnings but not to service.—Some plans utilize a benefit formula which provides a benefit at retirement equal to a specified percentage of compensation, without regard to years of service. The compensation base is normally the earnings or salary at retirement, but the average for a period before retirement or even the career average may be used. A wide range of percentages is found. The distinctive feature of the plan is that the percentage is flat and does not vary with years of service. Service is not ignored, however, since entitlement to benefits is based on a minimum period of service, such as twenty years. Past service may be credited against this requirement. The philosophy of this plan is that an employee who remains with the employer for twenty years, or whatever period is specified, is entitled to the same consideration as one who has served a longer period. However, the longer service employee will tend to have a higher earnings base than one who barely qualifies.

(c) Benefits related to service but not to earnings.—This type of formula has been rather popular in negotiated plans. The pattern appears to be $21 per year at age 65 for each year of credited service up to a maximum of thirty years. This would provide a benefit of $630 per year. Many of these plans, however, have a minimum benefit of $100 per month, including Social Security benefits, payable on normal retirement after 25 years of service. Some of the plans provide benefits ranging up to $30 per year of credited service, exclusive of Social Security benefits. In these plans, past service is credited with the same benefits as future service.

(d) Benefits related to neither earnings nor service.—This type of formula emerged from the contract negotiations in the steel and automobile industries in 1949 and has been incorporated in many negotiated plans since that time. It provides a flat benefit, including the primary Social Security benefit, to the employee who retires with 25 or 30 years of credited service. The basic formula of this type provides $100 per month after 25 years of service but a few plans pay $125. No benefit is paid unless the employee has accumulated a minimum period of credited service, typically 10 or 15 years, the latter being more common. Creditable service is carefully defined, and partial credit, measured by the number of hours worked, is granted for years during which the worker was employed only part-time. An employee who has accumulated the minimum period of service but falls short of the basic requirements receives a benefit adjusted to his years of service. To this extent, then, the benefit is affected by service.[13] But below the minimum and above the basic requirement, no recognition is given to service.

A variation of this formula treats the flat benefit as a minimum and provides larger benefits, based on compensation, on earnings in excess of a specified amount, such as $3,500 or $4,000.

B. Minimum Benefit Provisions.—There has been a trend in recent years to incorporate minimum benefit limitations in pension plans. The flat benefit of the negotiated pattern plans is, of course, the equivalent of a minimum pension. The provisions used almost defy classification, but they may be broadly classified as to whether the dollar minimum includes or excludes the primary OASI benefit. The tendency is to include OASI benefits in the minimum. The provision found most frequently promises a minimum benefit of $1,200 per year, including OASI, after 25 years of service, with reduced benefits available for shorter periods of service. A plan is occasionally found which guarantees an annual benefit of $1,500, including OASI. The minimum benefits in plans which exclude OASI range from $200 per year to $800 per year. It might be pointed out, with reference to the discussion of past service, that plans which do not provide past service benefits usually guarantee a minimum benefit at retirement.

C. Maximum Benefit Provisions.—The flat benefit of the pattern plan operates as both an upper and lower limit to benefits. Many

---

13. The employee who has accumulated the minimum period of service but falls short of the basic requirements, frequently receives a zero benefit because of the OASI deduction.

conventional plans, as well, impose an upper limit to the benefits which they will pay. This maximum may take the form of a dollar limit or as a limitation on the compensation which will be recognized for benefit purposes. The dollar limitations are usually very generous, some ranging as high as $40,000. The most common limitation, perhaps, is $10,000 per year, although a few plans impose a limit as low as $3,000 per year.

The limitations expressed in terms of compensation tend to be less generous when converted into benefits. The median salary figure in the Federal Security Administration study of 346 group annuity plans was $10,000, the maximum being $30,000.[14] This tendency has been confirmed by other surveys.

The trend, significantly, is to liberalize maximum limitations or to remove them altogether.

D. Integration with Federal OASI Program.—With few exceptions, private pension plans are superimposed on the Federal program of old-age benefits. Motivated by the desire to avoid pyramiding of benefits or to provide equitable treatment to all wage or salary classifications, most employers seek to integrate the coverage and benefits of their plan with the Federal program. This integration must be accomplished in consonance with Treasury directives on the subject, which are designed to prevent discrimination in favor of the more highly paid employees.[15]

Three general approaches may be used in integrating a private pension plan with the Federal OASI program:

(1) Deduction of OASI Benefits.—The simplest method of integrating is to deduct at retirement the benefits that are payable under the Federal program from those that would otherwise be payable under the private plan. This is referred to in Treasury regulations as the "offset plan." This is the approach used in many negotiated pattern plans and in a sizable percentage of conventional plans. It is not feasible for plans underwritten by individual insurance or annuity contracts or deferred group annuities, but it is adaptable to uninsured plans and group annuity contracts which

14. Van Eenam and Penman, *op. cit.*, p. 31.
15. The guiding principles on integration are set forth in Sec. 401(a)(5), IRC; Sec. 29.165-3, Regulations 111; Mimeograph 5539, July 8, 1943; Mimeograph 6641, May 3, 1951; and Revenue Ruling 13, January 5, 1953. The basic directive on integration is Mimeograph 6641.

do not allocate funds to individual employees until retirement. Nor is it feasible for contributory plans, particularly money purchase plans. Many plans, however, which do not subtract the primary OASI benefit from the basic benefit of the plan include it as a part of any minimum benefit that might be guaranteed.

In recognition of the supplementary and survivors benefits payable under the Federal OASI program, Treasury regulations permit the deduction of 130 per cent of the primary OASI benefit from the retirement benefit of a noncontributory plan that provides no death benefits before or after retirement.[16] Smaller deductions are allowed for plans which do provide death benefits before or after retirement. As a practical matter, the maximum deduction is seldom applied and most plans using the offset method deduct at most 100 per cent of the primary OASI benefit.

The offset approach has been criticized by many pension experts.[17] In the first place, it is argued, to deduct anything from benefits is poor psychology. It would be better to offer lower benefits under the private plan and treat OASI benefits as *additions* to the plan.[18] In effect, of course, the offset method is applied in that manner under some plans, particularly those which provide a flat benefit. Secondly, the employee may object to the deduction of the full OASI benefit on the grounds that he has purchased half of the benefit with his own contributions. This argument is recognized in some plans by a provision that only half of the primary OASI benefit shall be deducted. Finally, under this arrangement, any increase in OASI benefits would not benefit the employee; it would only decrease the cost of the private plan. An argument from the employer's point of view is that if Congress should ever lower the level of OASI benefits, not entirely inconceivable, the benefits under the private plan would be automatically increased and probably at

16. Paragraph 6, Revenue Ruling 13, January 5, 1953. If the employee's primary insurance benefit is computed under the formula in the Social Security Act amendments of 1950 rather than under the amendments effected by Public Law 590, 82nd Congress, 2nd Session, July 18, 1952, the permissible percentage is 140 per cent.

17. For example, see J. W. Myers, "Governmental and Voluntary Programs for Security," *Harvard Business Review*, Volume XXVIII, No. 2, March, 1950, p. 36.

18. Or, as suggested in some quarters, OASI should be viewed as the base to which the benefits from the private plan are *added* to produce an adequate over-all pension.

a time when the employer could least afford the increase in cost.

(2) Exclusion of Portion of Earnings.[19]—A second method of integration is to exclude from a pension plan that portion of earnings on which duplication might otherwise occur. Since the 1950 amendments to the Social Security Act, this has meant the exclusion of the first $3,600 of earnings; prior to that time only the first $3,000 had to be excluded. This approach, which is referred to as an "excess plan," is feasible only when the employer does not wish to supplement the retirement benefits of OASI for those employees earning less than $3,600. Furthermore, the plan must not provide for employees earning over $3,600 benefits proportionately greater than those available under OASI for employees earning less than $3,600. For the purpose of this comparison, the total benefits available under each program must be considered.

The Treasury has promulgated various rules to indicate whether a private plan is integrated with the Social Security program. Underlying all such rules is an evaluation of the benefits available under the OASI program.

For the purposes of integration it is assumed that all covered employees who retire in the future will be entitled to the maximum primary benefit payable under the OASI program. Under the Social Security Act, as amended in 1950, the maximum primary benefit was $80, 50 per cent of the first $100 of average monthly wage plus 15 per cent of the next $200 of average monthly wage. The 1952 amendments to the Act raised the maximum to $85 by crediting 55 per cent of the first $100 of average monthly wage, but the basic directive on integration, Mimeograph 6641, is still based on the 1950 amendments. Therefore, the primary old-age benefit under OASI is assumed to be $80, or 26⅔ per cent of the employee's average monthly wage. It is further assumed that the total benefits available under the OASI program, including the wife's old-age benefits and all survivorship benefits, are, on the average, equal to 150 per cent of the employee's primary insurance benefit. Thus, the total OASI benefits may be considered as equivalent to a straight life annuity beginning at age 65 of $120 a month, or 40 per cent of the assumed average monthly wage.

19. This section is based on the Social Security Act as it existed prior to the 1954 amendments, since the Treasury has not as yet issued integration rules based on the new formula.

This figure, however, takes no account of the fact that the OASI program is contributory and the employee has purchased a portion of his benefits. If it is assumed that the benefits under the Federal program will be completely financed through employer and employee contributions, in the long run the employees, in the aggregate, should bear approximately one-half of the cost of the program. Employees retiring within the next several years, however, will have contributed much less than one-half of the cost of their OASI benefits. In fact, for integration purposes, the Treasury assumes that at present employee contributions under OASI will pay for benefits equivalent to a straight life annuity of only 2½ per cent of average monthly wage, or one-sixteenth of the total OASI benefits payable, on the average, to an employee whose average monthly wage is $300. Accordingly, a $3,600 excess plan is considered to be integrated, subject to the conditions noted below, if the normal annual retirement benefit of no employee can exceed 37½ per cent of his average annual compensation in excess of $3,600.

This percentage, however, is based on the following conditions:[20]

(a) There are no benefits payable in case of death before retirement;

(b) The normal form of retirement benefit is a straight life annuity and optional forms of annuity, if available, provide benefits which are the actuarial equivalent of those payable under the normal form;

(c) No employee can become eligible for normal retirement benefits before completion of 15 years of service with the employer;

(d) Normal retirement age is not lower than age 65 for men and age 60 for women and any early retirement or severance benefits are actuarially adjusted to reflect the lower age and shorter period of service;

(e) The employees do not contribute.

A $3,600 excess plan which conforms to the conditions set forth above, except that it provides benefits in the event of death before retirement not exceeding the higher of the reserve or the total prior contributions on a typical individual level annual premium funding method, is integrated if the normal annual retirement benefit for

20. Paragraph 5, Mimeograph 6641, May 3, 1951.

any employee cannot exceed 33⅓ per cent of his average annual compensation in excess of $3,600.

If the normal form of annuity is one other than a straight life or pure annuity, the maximum retirement benefit, as a percentage of average compensation in excess of $3,600, cannot exceed the rate obtained by multiplying 37½ or 33⅓ per cent, as the case may be, by the appropriate percentage shown below.

Annuity for 10 years certain and life thereafter.........90%
Annuity for 15 years certain and life thereafter.........80%
Annuity for 20 years certain and life thereafter.........70%
Life Annuity with instalment refund...................80%
Life Annuity with cash refund........................75%

For example, a $3,600 excess plan which conforms to all the required conditions, except that the normal form of retirement benefit is a life annuity with payments guaranteed for ten years and benefits equal to the reserve are payable in case of the employee's death before retirement, is integrated if the normal annual retirement benefit for any employee is 30 per cent (33⅓% multiplied by 90%) of his average annual compensation in excess of $3,600.

If a plan provides normal retirement benefits for service of less than fifteen years, the benefits cannot exceed 1/15 of those that would otherwise be permissible, multiplied by the number of years of actual service. In other words, a $3,600 excess plan that satisfies all the required conditions except (c) is integrated if it provides a normal annual retirement benefit of 37½ per cent of average annual compensation in excess of $3,600 less 2½ per cent of such average annual compensation for each year that the employee's total service at normal retirement falls short of fifteen years.

With respect to the condition stated in (d) above, the permissible percentage of average annual compensation that can be provided in the retirement benefit must be reduced by 10 per cent for each year that the normal retirement age is lower than age 65. Early retirement benefits must not exceed the actuarial equivalent of the contributions or reserve standing to the credit of the employee at the time of his withdrawal or early retirement.

Finally, if the plan is contributory, with the exception of the money purchase type, an employee's annual retirement benefit may be increased by 10 per cent of his aggregate contributions exclusive of those devoted to the current cost of insurance or death benefits in excess of the reserve or cash value. Such an increase is permitted regardless of the form of retirement benefit or provision for death benefits. Furthermore, no reduction in the level of permitted benefits is required by a provision that the employee's contributions, with interest, shall be returned in the event of his death before or after retirement. Separate rules have been promulgated for money purchase plans.

The increase in the maximum primary insurance benefit that was authorized by the 1952 amendments to the Social Security Act should have raised to a slight extent the percentage of average annual compensation that could be replaced through the benefit formula of excess plans. The Treasury authorities decided, however, that an increase in the basic integration limits was not warranted in view of the fact that the present 2½ per cent adjustment for employee contributions to the OASI programs appears to be inadequate. Nevertheless, changes were made in the limits for excess plans which cover earnings between $1,200 and $3,600 and in the rules pertaining to offset plans. In the latter case, the permissible percentage of offset was lowered in recognition of the heavier weighting assigned to employee contributions.

(3) Adjustment of the Benefit Formula.—This is the approach that is used when the employer wishes to supplement OASI benefits for all his employees yet at the same time desires to remove the bias in favor of lower paid employees that exists in the OASI benefit formula. This is referred to in official literature as a "Stepped-up Benefits Plan" and is defined as "A plan in which no employee and no portion of compensation is excluded by reason of a minimum compensation requirement and in which all the provisions apply uniformly to all covered employees regardless of the rate of compensation, except that a higher rate of benefit or of employer contributions (and possibly of employee contributions) is applicable to compensation above a specified level . . . than to compensation below such level . . ."[21] An example of such a plan is one which provides retirement benefits equal to ½ per cent of the first $3,600 of

21. Paragraph 16, Mimeograph 6641, May 3, 1951.

annual compensation and 1½ per cent of the excess for each year of credited past service and ½ per cent and 2 per cent, respectively, for each year of future service.

For integration purposes this type of plan is treated as two separate plans—one providing the lower rate of benefit or employer contribution on all compensation, and the second providing the balance of the higher rates on the compensation in excess of the specified level. The first or underlying plan does not involve integration requirements, since it provides uniform rates and types of benefits on all compensation, while the second plan may be treated as an excess plan which would be subject to all the rules outlined in the preceding section. The example cited would satisfy the integration requirements.

Time of Payment.—A second broad aspect of retirement benefits relates to the conditions under which the benefits become payable. Under the great majority of plans, an employee who is a member of the plan is entitled to receive full retirement benefits upon the attainment of a specified age, referred to as the normal retirement age. This is a contractual right and can be exercised without the consent of the employer. In some plans, however, the age requirement is supplemented by a minimum service requirement. Perhaps one-third of the plans that have been established since 1943 either require a minimum period of service or entry into the plan before a specified age, which has the same effect. Under negotiated pattern plans, the service requirement is normally 25 or 30 years, with no benefits for service of less than 10 or 15 years, while among conventional plans 15 years is the most common requirement. A service requirement is rarely used in insured plans of the group annuity type.

A. Normal Retirement Age.—The normal retirement age is the earliest age at which eligible employees are permitted to retire with full benefits. It may or may not be the automatic retirement age. If the employees do not have the option of continuing their employment beyond the age designated as the normal retirement age, then the normal retirement age is, in effect, the automatic retirement age. If, however, the employees are permitted to defer their retirement to a later date, with or without the employer's consent, it is customary to specify an age at which retirement will automatically become effective. This is known as the automatic retirement age. In some plans, particularly the pattern plans, an employee may remain in service beyond the automatic retirement age with the consent of the employer.

From the standpoint of an individual employer, the normal retirement age should be the age beyond which the services of his employees would be uneconomical. This point, of course, is not easy to determine. In theory, multiple retirement ages should be adopted in many cases, since a retirement that would be suitable for one class of employees might be completely inappropriate for another group. In the airlines industry, for example, flight personnel should undoubtedly have a lower retirement age than non-flight employees. Jobs which require physical strength and endurance may call for a lower retirement age than those which emphasize mental ability. Within particular job classifications, moreover, there are differences in individual employees which, ideally, should be recognized. Nevertheless, the practice, subject to certain exceptions, is to have a normal retirement age that is applicable to all employees, with provisions in a majority of plans for adjustments to particular situations through optional retirement arrangements, which are discussed below.

Age 65 is almost universally designated as the normal retirement age for male employees. This is undoubtedly a reflection of the Social Security program. A small percentage of plans specify an age lower than 65 for female employees, age 60 being the most common variant. An exception to the normal retirement age is generally made for employees who are beyond a specified age at the time the pension plan is established. The lower limit for such exception is usually 55 or 60, and such employees are permitted to work five or ten years beyond the normal retirement age or age 70, whichever occurs first. The purpose of such staggered retirement is primarily to spread the cost of the benefits, composed principally of past service credits, over a longer period than would otherwise be available. This is particularly important in insured plans, since the insurance company usually insists that the benefits payable to a retired employee must have been purchased in full before actual retirement. Another reason for staggered retirement at the inception of the plan is to permit high-age low-service employees to accumulate larger pensions.

B. Early Retirement.—It is customary to provide that an employee may retire earlier than the normal retirement age. The plans are about equally divided as to whether employer consent is required. About half of the plans permit early retirement on the sole basis of age, usually 55, while the other half require a period of service, typically ten years, in addition to the attainment of a specified age. Only rarely does a plan permit early retirement on the basis of service alone, in which case 25 or 30 years are usually required. Plans which require employer consent tend to rely on the age requirement alone, while those which permit early retirement at the option of the employee are inclined to impose both an age and service requirement.

Some plans permit early retirement only in the event of total and permanent disability. In such plans, age and service requirements are also imposed. Some of the plans provide a special disability benefit, while others pay only the actuarial equivalent of the regular accrued benefit.

The benefit which is paid to an employee who takes advantage of the early retirement privilege is the actuarial equivalent of the benefit that would have been paid at the normal retirement age. The actuarial equivalent, however, is smaller than the normal benefit. All benefits are calculated in the first instance on the assumption that no benefit payments will be made until the normal retirement age and that all contributions will earn interest until that date. If an employee retires early, the contributions on his behalf will have accumulated to a smaller sum, through loss of interest, than was originally assumed, and each dollar of accumulations will purchase a smaller benefit, since the payments begin earlier than was anticipated and, therefore, extend over a longer period of time. If the benefit formula is based on years of service, the anticipated benefit will be further reduced by the loss of the additional contributions, plus interest, that would have been credited to the account of the employee. Finally, if the plan is insured, the calculation of actuarial equivalency recognizes the fact that a high percentage of early retirements stem from poor health, and in providing benefits in such cases, the insurance company is disbursing benefits to some employees who would not have survived to normal retirement age. The result is a further reduction in the early retirement benefit.

The percentage of normal retirement income which is available for early retirement at ages 55-64 is shown in Table 1. The percentages are applied to the annuity credits earned to the date of early retirement and not to the benefits that would have been payable at age 65 had the employee continued working to that age. A distinction is made between male and female employees because of the difference in their life expectancy. Females have a longer life expectancy at 65 than males, which means that the early retirement of a female employee has a smaller effect, percentage-wise, on benefits than the early retirement of a male employee. Since retirement

TABLE 1

PROPORTION OF NORMAL RETIREMENT INCOME AVAILABLE
IN EVENT OF EARLY RETIREMENT AT VARIOUS AGES*

Age at Early Retirement	Normal Retirement Age 65	
	Male Employees	Female Employees
64	90.6%	92.1%
63	82.5	85.0
62	75.3	78.7
61	68.9	73.0
60	63.3	67.9
59	58.3	63.2
58	53.8	59.0
57	49.8	55.2
56	46.2	51.7
55	42.9	48.6

* These percentages apply to the benefits earned to the date of early retirement and not to the benefits that would have been payable had the employee continued working to age 65.

ten years prior to the normal retirement age produces a benefit of less than half the normal benefit, most plans do not permit retirement earlier than ten years prior to the normal retirement age.

When a separate disability benefit has not been provided, employers occasionally supplement the early retirement benefit for an employee who retires because of poor health. The supplement may take the form of an informal benefit provided on a year-to-year basis until OASI benefits begin or a temporary life annuity of an amount equal to the benefit that will be available at normal retirement age. The temporary annuity is really a benefit paid in lieu of rather than in addition to the early retirement benefit. Apart from the foregoing, many plans permit an employee who retires early to level out his income including OASI benefits, by converting a portion of his normal retirement benefit into a temporary annuity payable to age 65.[22]

C. Deferred Retirement.—Under relatively few plans is retirement at the normal retirement age compulsory in the sense that no provision is available under which an employee could continue in employment. A sizable percentage of plans, perhaps a fourth, contain an automatic retirement age, as well as a normal retirement age, and under those plans an employee is permitted to remain in service up to the automatic retirement age, usually without the employer's consent. Continuation beyond the automatic retirement age, if permitted at all, is only with employer consent. Those plans which do not specify both a normal and automatic retirement age usually make express provision for continuation of an employee's service beyond the normal retirement age with the employer's consent.[23] It should be understood, of course, that the employee is entitled to retire at the normal retirement age and can be retained in service only with his consent. As a matter of practice, it is usually at the employee's request that he does so.

Practice is divided as to whether the employee who defers his retirement will, nevertheless, begin to receive his retirement benefits at the normal retirement age. The companies which provide for immediate payment of retirement benefits feel that the employee has earned the benefits and should receive them in addition to his regular wages or salary. Occasionally, a plan will provide for deduction of all or a portion of the retirement benefits from the employee's earnings.

Those companies which postpone the payment of benefits until actual retirement argue that the employee is not forced to continue in service but does so only because his full salary is more attractive than his retirement benefits. The majority of the plans which postpone the retirement benefits pay the employee, upon actual retirement, only the amount of income which would have been paid at the

22. This is known as the Social Security adjustment option, which is discussed briefly on pp. 55-56.

23. Retirement later than the normal retirement age is expressly provided for in 274, or 79 per cent, of the 346 group annuity plans analyzed by the Federal Security Agency. Van Eenam and Penman, *op. cit.*, p. 17. No mention of deferred retirements is made in the other 21 per cent of the plans, so it is likely that continuation of employment would be authorized under some of those plans by administrative decision.

normal retirement age. The payments which would have been made from the normal retirement age to the date of actual retirement inure to the credit of the employer. Some plans, however, pay a larger benefit at actual retirement than would have been paid at the normal retirement date. In technical terms, the actuarial equivalent of the normal benefit is paid at actual retirement. Such plans recognize the right of the employee to retire and receive his full benefits at his normal retirement age, yet they postpone the benefits until a time when they will be more vital to him. The actuarial equivalent of a given benefit increases substantially with each year of postponement beyond the normal retirement age.

Only in exceptional cases does an employee earn additional retirement credits by continuing to work beyond the normal retirement age.

Manner of Payment.—Implicit in any pension plan is the payment of a retirement benefit that continues throughout the remaining lifetime of the superannuated employee. The plan may provide various collateral benefits, but underlying the whole scheme must be the promise of a life income to the employee upon his retirement. If this promise is underwritten by a life insurance company, the life income will be provided in the form of an annuity of some type. If the plan is self-administered and handled through a trust company, the benefits may be provided through an annuity purchased from an insurance company, probably at the time of the employee's retirement, or they may be paid by the trust company directly.

Several forms of annuities are available for the disbursement of pension benefits. Classified broadly, annuities may be of the single life or joint life variety, and within that classification they may be either of the pure or refund type. As indicated by its title, a single life annuity is one which is based on only one life. The pure form of single life annuity, usually referred to as a "straight life annuity," provides periodic, usually monthly, income payments that continue as long as the annuitant lives and terminates upon his death. The annuity is considered fully liquidated upon the death of the annuitant, and no guarantee is given that any particular number of monthly payments will be made. Because of the absence of any refund feature, this type of single life annuity provides the largest monthly income per dollar of premium or outlay.

The refund type of single life annuity includes any annuity which guarantees to return in one manner or another a portion or all of the purchase price of the annuity. The annuity may promise that a certain number of monthly payments will be made whether the annuitant lives or dies, with payments to continue, of course, if the annuitant lives beyond the guaranteed period. In insurance circles, this type of annuity is referred to as a "life annuity certain and continuous," and the annuitant may elect 60, 120, 180 or 240 guaranteed instalments.[24] The cost of the annuity increases with the number of guaranteed instalments, since life contingencies are not involved during the guaranteed period. One type of refund annuity promises that, if the annuitant dies before receiving monthly payments equal to the purchase price of the annuity, the payments shall be continued to a contingent beneficiary or beneficiaries until the full cost has been recovered. This type of annuity is known as an "instalment refund annuity." If the contract promises, upon the death of the annuitant, to pay to the annuitant's estate or a contingent beneficiary in a lump sum the difference, if any, between the purchase price of the annuity and the sum of the monthly payments, it is designated a "cash refund annuity." The only difference between the "cash refund annuity" and the "instalment refund annuity" is that under the former the unliquidated purchase price is refunded in a lump sum at the time of the annuitant's death, whereas in the latter case the monthly instalments are continued until the purchase price has been recovered. These two types of annuities are the most costly of the single life variety, with the "cash refund annuity" being somewhat more costly than the "instalment refund annuity" because of the loss of interest.

A joint life annuity is based on two or more lives. It provides an income of a specified amount as long as the annuitants designated in the contract live, the income ceasing, however, upon the death of the first annuitant. Theoretically, this annuity could contain a refund feature, but it is not customary to incorporate such a feature. The joint life annuity has only a limited applicability and has been all but supplanted by the "joint and last survivor annuity" which provides a periodic payment of a specified amount as long as either of two or more persons shall live. For most combinations of ages, this is

---

24. Such a range of options is rarely provided under a pension plan.

the most expensive of all annuity forms. This type of contract is ideally suited to provide old-age income to a husband and wife. The contract is available in a form in which the income is reduced upon the death of the first annuitant to either one-half or two-thirds of the original amount, on the theory that the survivor does not require as large an income as do the two annuitants.

The benefits under a pension plan, and their cost, are calculated on the assumption that a particular form of income settlement will be used. The normal form of settlement specified in most noncontributory plans is the straight life annuity, although it is not unusual to guarantee a certain number of instalments. Contributory plans usually adopt a "modified" cash refund annuity. This form promises that should the employee die before receiving retirement benefits equal to the accumulated value of his contributions, with or without interest, the difference between his benefits and his contributions will be refunded in a lump sum to his estate or a designated beneficiary. Some contributory plans prescribe a life annuity with payments guaranteed for five or ten years, either form of which will, in the typical case, assure the return of the employee's accumulated contributions.

Despite the fact that a specific type of annuity is prescribed in the pension plan, the employee is usually given the option, at retirement, of electing a different type of settlement. In the case of group annuities, at least, such election must be accompanied by evidence of good health, unless made a prescribed time, usually five years, prior to retirement. Some plans provide a wide choice of options, while others are fairly restrictive. One form that is almost always available is the joint and survivorship annuity, in the thought that the employee may wish to extend the protection of his annuity to his wife. Since a regular joint and survivorship annuity sharply reduces the size of the retirement benefit, most plans also permit the type of joint and survivorship annuity that provides a smaller benefit to the survivor. Since under this option the surviving employee would receive only 40 per cent or less of the original benefit that was intended for him, many plans, including all group annuities, modify the option by stipulating that the income is reduced only when the employee dies first. If the wife or other dependent should die first, the employee continues to receive the full benefit.

An option that is available only in the case of early retirement is the so-called "Social Security Adjustment Option." The purpose of the option is to provide a level benefit throughout the period of retirement, notwithstanding the fact that OASI retirement benefits are not available until age 65. This objective is accomplished by converting such portion of the normal retirement benefit into a temporary annuity as is needed to provide an income to age 65 equal to the benefits, composed of the reduced normal benefit and the primary OASI benefit, that will be payable after age 65. The amount of the normal retirement benefit that must be converted can be easily determined from available tables.

A provision designed for the protection of the employee's dependents is found in some plans whose normal annuity form provides for 60 or 120 guaranteed instalments. This provision stipulates that if an employee should die between the ages of 55 and 65, or the period during which early retirement is permitted, but before he has actually retired, the beneficiary will receive benefits for five or ten years, as the case may be, in the same amount that would have been paid to the employee had he retired on the date of his death. This provision is a manifestation of the increasing interest in widows' benefits under pension plans. Another provision occasionally encountered presumes the election of a joint and survivorship annuity where the employee continues to work beyond the normal retirement age and dies before retirement.

The benefits under self-administered plans are distributed in essentially the same manner as those of insured plans, since, if an annuity is not actually purchased from an insurance company, the benefits prescribed under the plan provisions will be calculated in accordance with the same actuarial principles.

The monthly benefits which are payable at various retirement ages under some of the commonly used annuity forms are shown in Table 2. In each case, the benefits are those which would be paid for each $1,000 of accumulations available at the age indicated.

TERMINATION BENEFITS

While a pension plan is set up for the primary purpose of providing retirement benefits, it must be recognized that a relatively small percentage of the persons who enter the service of a particular employer remain with that employer until retirement. It is necessary,

TABLE 2

MONTHLY BENEFITS PER $1,000 OF ACCUMULATIONS PROVIDED AT
VARIOUS RETIREMENT AGES UNDER COMMONLY USED
ANNUITY FORMS—MALE EMPLOYEES*

Age at Retirement	Life Annuity			Full Cash Refund Annuity	Joint and Survivorship Annuity†
	No Period Certain	5-Year Certain	10-Year Certain		
55	$4.91	$4.86	$4.71	$4.02	$3.53
60	5.66	5.56	5.28	4.38	3.90
65	6.63	6.44	5.94	4.79	4.37
66	6.87	6.65	6.08	4.88	4.48
67	7.11	6.86	6.22	4.97	4.59
68	7.37	7.08	6.36	5.06	4.72
69	7.65	7.32	6.50	5.16	4.85
70	7.95	7.56	6.65	5.26	5.00

* Rate basis: 1937 Standard Annuity Table, 2½ per cent interest, and loading of 8 per cent of gross premium.

† Contingent or joint annuitant assumed to be five years younger than the employee in each case. Full income to continue to survivor.

therefore, for the pension agreement to outline the rights of those employees who qualify for membership in the plan but sever their connection with the company, for one reason or another, before reaching retirement. These rights can be discussed under the three principal headings of withdrawal from employment, death, and disability. A fourth section deals with the rights of employees in the event that the pension plan itself is terminated.

Withdrawal From Employment.—It is a basic rule of pension planning that an employee must be permitted under all circumstances to recover the contributions, with or without interest, which he has made toward his own retirement. The trend today is to credit the employee's contributions with a moderate rate of interest, although many of the older plans return the accumulated contributions without interest. Under insured plans, the employee usually has the option of taking cash or a paid-up annuity that will be payable at the normal retirement age. If he elects to leave his contributions with the insurance company, he retains the right, nevertheless, to withdraw their cash value at any time before the annuity payments begin. If the plan is of the individual contract or group permanent type,[25] the employee is not only permitted to retain the benefits which his contributions have purchased up to the time of his withdrawal, but he may supplement the benefits by continuing premium payments on the contract.

In self-administered plans, the employee usually can take his contributions only in the form of cash, since annuities are normally not purchased for the employee until he reaches the retirement age and perhaps not then.

The rights of the withdrawing employee in the contributions of the employer depend upon the vesting provisions, if any, in the pension agreement. The term "vesting" refers to the right or interest which an employee acquires in the contributions made on his behalf by the employer. Vesting never refers to the right of the employee to the return of his own contributions, since that right is unquestioned. It refers only to the right of the employee to retain the benefits which have accrued from the employer's contributions.

The vesting provisions of pension plans can be classified according to at least four different bases: the *time*, the *amount*, the *form*, and the *type* of vesting. From the standpoint of *time*, the employer's contributions may vest immediately or the vesting may be deferred until certain age and service requirements have been met. As to *amount*, the employer's contributions may vest in full or only in part. Most plans vest in full upon satisfaction of the basic requirements, but some plans utilize an arrangement known as graded vesting in accordance with which only a portion of the contributions vest upon satisfaction of specified minimum requirements. The percentage of vesting increases on a sliding scale as additional requirements are met until 100 per cent vesting is eventually attained. An example of this arrangement is a plan which provides for 40 per cent vesting after ten years of service, with full vesting after 25 years of service or, alternatively, 15 years of service and the attainment of age 55. With reference to *form*, the employee may be permitted to take the employer's contributions in a variety of ways, including a lump sum, or he may be restricted to a deferred paid-up annuity without a cash value.

Finally, a distinction may be made as to whether the vesting is *absolute* or *conditional*. In theory at least, absolute vesting would

25. See pp. 69-75 and 75-84, respectively, for a description of these two types of contracts.

place full title to the employer's contributions in the employee whenever the basic requirements are met, and his rights could be exercised under any circumstances that might terminate his employment. Specifically, the employee, or his estate, would be entitled to receive the employer's contributions in one form or the other whether the termination resulted from withdrawal (severance), death or disability. Conditional vesting, on the other hand, permits the employee to exercise his rights only under certain circumstances, usually only in the case of withdrawal. In fact, this type of conditional vesting provision is so widely used that in common usage "vesting" refers to entitlement to employer contributions only in the event of withdrawal. Yet the term has a broader application, and careful usage requires that the circumstances under which the vesting is to occur be clearly indicated.

Another example of conditional vesting is a provision found in many plans, including the vast majority of group annuity plans, that upon withdrawal, the employer's contributions vest in the employee only if the latter elects to take his own contributions in the form of deferred annuities, rather than in a lump sum. In such plans the employer's contributions vest only in the form of deferred pension credits.

The great majority of pension plans provide for some type of vesting in the event of withdrawal.[26] A significant exception is the negotiated pattern plans in which no vesting is provided other than that which is available under the early retirement provisions of the plans.[27] Vesting rights are virtually always conditioned on service or a combination of service and age, with full, immediate vesting being extremely rare. Seldom will age alone confer vesting privileges.[28] The most common requirements from a service stand-

26. Over 75 per cent of the conventional plans analyzed by the Bankers Trust Company in its 1950-52 survey contained some form of withdrawal vesting. *Op. cit.*, p. 12. Ninety-four per cent of the 346 group annuity plans studied by the Federal Security Agency provided for withdrawal vesting under some conditions. Van Eenam and Penman, *op. cit.*, p. 42.

27. Employer contributions vest absolutely and in full upon retirement, so an early retirement provision may be regarded as a method of accelerating the vesting process.

28. Only nine plans out of the 346 group annuities analyzed by the Federal Security Agency provided for vesting on the basis of age alone, although 46 per cent of the plans which provided for vesting contained an age requirement in combination with a service requirment.

point are 5, 10, 15 or 20 years, with the latter being the most widely used. If an age requirement is imposed, age 45, 50, 55 or 60 is usually used. A summary of the vesting provisions found in the two most recent surveys of conventional plans by the Bankers Trust Company is presented in Table 3. For graded vesting provisions, minimum service and age requirements are shown.

TABLE 3

WITHDRAWAL VESTING PROVISIONS IN RECENTLY ESTABLISHED OR AMENDED PENSION PLANS

Type of Vesting Provision	1948-50 Plans*	1950-52 Plans†
	%	%
No vesting	19	24
Vesting upon Completion of Period of Service:		
10 years or less	14	13
15 years	7	6
20 years or more	10	10
Total	31	29
Vesting upon Attainment of Age:		
50	1	1
55	2	1
60	2	2
Total	5	4
Vesting upon Completion of 10 to 20 Years of Service and Attainment of Age:		
45 or less	7	9
50	9	10
55	17	12
60	5	7
Total	38	38
Immediate Vesting Without Age or Service Requirement	3	2
Vesting only on Layoff	3	2
Information Incomplete	1	1
Total	100	100

* Includes 100 new plans and 117 amended plans.

† Includes 97 new plans and 138 amended plans.

Source: Bankers Trust Company, *A Study of Industrial Retirement Plans,* 1953 Edition (New York), p. 12.

Death Before Retirement.—In a contributory plan there will almost invariably be a death benefit equal to the accumulated value, with or without interest, of the contributions of the deceased employee. This benefit is paid in a lump sum to the deceased's estate or designated beneficiary. In some states this disposition of the employee's contributions is required by law. Any other death benefits that might be available would depend upon the type of plan selected, the various possibilities being outlined in the discussion of noncontributory plans.

There may or may not be death benefits under noncontributory plans. The right of an employee to his employer's contributions does not normally vest in his estate in the event of his death before retirement, so there is no assurance that a death benefit will be paid. Death benefits may, of course, be provided in other forms. A self-administered plan may provide a specific death benefit, unrelated to the contributions made by the employer toward the employee's retirement, sometimes expressed as a flat amount and sometimes equal to one year's salary of the deceased. Among insured plans, the individual retirement income policy and group permanent policies automatically include a death benefit with the retirement benefit. The amount of the death benefit in the retirement income policy is normally $1,000 for each $10 unit of monthly income at retirement, or the cash value, whichever is larger, while the group permanent plan, when it does not utilize the retirement income policy, affords $1,000 of insurance for each $10 unit of monthly income.

Plans using the group annuity contract normally provide no death benefits as a part of the pension plan, other than return of the employee's contributions, if any. Under the bulk of group annuity plans, the contributions of the employer are applied to the purchase of pure or nonrefund deferred annuities in accordance with which mortality is discounted in advance and no refund is available upon death of an employee.[29] Nevertheless, many companies which have a pension plan of the group annuity type provide death benefits through a separate group life insurance program.

Benefits paid by reason of death after retirement depend upon the

29. This procedure, it might be added, maximizes the retirement benefit per dollar of employer contribution.

type of annuity under which retirement benefits are paid. As was indicated earlier, the normal form of settlement under noncontributory plans does not provide any death benefit, while contributory plans, in keeping with the fiduciary treatment accorded employee funds in every aspect of pension administration, return the unliquidated portion of the employee's contribution through the operation of the modified cash refund option. Under either type of program, annuity forms are usually available under which death benefits of varying magnitude can be obtained—all at the expense of the retirement benefit, or at extra cost.

Disability Benefits.—Virtually all pension plans contain provisions which protect the interests of employees who are temporarily unable to work because of illness or injury. The real problem, however, is created by the employee who is permanently unable to work because of injury or disease.

The majority of pension plans make no provisions for permanent and total disability other than the relief afforded by the early retirement privilege. As was indicated earlier, this provision permits an employee who has met certain age and service requirements to retire with a reduced benefit earlier than the normal retirement age. Experience has shown that most early retirements are based on physical disabilities and, moreover, a large percentage of employees who become permanently and totally disabled can satisfy the eligibility conditions for early retirement. To afford greater relief, some plans permit a disabled employee to retire at a younger age and with fewer years of service than would otherwise be possible. Such an employee would receive only the actuarial equivalent of his accrued pension credits, which in most cases would constitute a very modest benefit. In recognition of this, a few plans vest the employer's contributions upon the occurrence of permanent and total disability and permit the employee to withdraw them in a lump sum. Other employers, while making no attempt to increase the amount of disability income, purchase an additional annuity at retirement of such amount as to bring the total retirement income up to that which the employee would have received at the normal retirement age, based, however, on the credits earned up to the date of the disability retirement. Since, with few exceptions, the disability benefits under these plans are the actuarial equivalent of the pension credits accrued at the inception of disability, they constitute only an alternative rather than supplemental benefit.

Many large plans, particularly those resulting from collective bargaining, provide a separate and distinct benefit for permanent and total disability. The benefit is definitely stated in advance and may be a percentage of the normal retirement benefit, a percentage of current compensation, or a flat amount. Several recently negotiated plans provide a disability benefit of $50 per month up to age 65, at which time the disabled employee becomes entitled to a normal retirement benefit based on his credits as of the date of disablement. In self-administered plans, the benefits are usually paid from the same fund used to finance retirement benefits, although an occasional employer charges them to current payroll. Disability benefits under insured plans may be provided as an integral part of the plan or, if the insurance company is unwilling to underwrite the disability hazard, through a self-administered disability fund apart from the retirement plan itself.

Termination of the Plan.—The conditions under which a pension plan can be terminated without retroactive tax penalty have been carefully circumscribed by the Treasury in order to prevent discrimination in favor of stockholders, officers, and highly paid employees of the company. Without adequate safeguards, a company with a small core of permanent officers and employees, for example, might establish a pension plan with illiberal vesting provisions which, after being credited with tax-deductible contributions for all employees for a number of years, could be terminated, with distribution of the total accumulations among the favored few participants who could meet the stringent vesting requirement. This scheme is particularly attractive during years of high profits and large tax liabilities.

In order to forestall such practices, the Treasury has ruled that a plan can be terminated only for reasons of "business necessity."[30] If a plan is abandoned for any cause other than business necessity within a few years after it has taken effect, such action will be construed by the Treasury as evidence that the plan, from its inception, was not a bona fide program for the exclusive benefit of employees in general. Some of the motivating forces for termination

30. Section 29.165-1 of Regulations 111.

which have been recognized by the Treasury as reasons of business necessity include bankruptcy, insolvency, change of ownership, change in management, and financial inability to continue contributions toward the pension program. If the Treasury finds that a plan, from its inception, was not a bona fide permanent program for the exclusive benefit of employees in general, employer contributions toward the plan will be disallowed as Federal income tax deductions for all open taxable years.

Upon termination, all funds credited to the pension plan vest in the employees, active and retired.[31] This is in accordance with the so-called Non-Diversion Rule[32] which forbids the employer to divert any portion of the principal or income of the pension plan to purposes other than for the exclusive benefit of his employees or their beneficiaries. The only exception to this rule is that which permits the employer to recover any balance remaining after all liabilities of the plan have been satisfied, provided that the surplus arose out of an "erroneous actuarial computation."[33] Plans under which units of benefits are purchased for employees on a current basis usually vest title to such paid-up benefits, including those purchased with employer money, in the employees. This is the practice in connection with deferred group annuity plans, for example. A different procedure may be prescribed by plans which pool the contributions and make no allocations to individual employees on a current basis. Even in those plans, any funds contributed by the employees will be returned to them upon termination, either in a lump sum or in the form of deferred pension credits; employer contributions, however, may be distributed in any manner which does not violate the provisions of Mimeograph 5717, which imposes restrictions on the amounts which may be paid to the 25

31. An exception to this rule exists whenever a plan is terminated in order to reactivate it with another funding agency, i.e., with another trust or insurance company. In such cases, the basic provisions of the plan continue to apply, and all accrued credits are transferred to the new funding agency.

32. Section 401(a)(2), IRC; Section 29.165-2 of Regulations 111.

33. A balance due to an "erroneous actuarial computation" is the surplus arising because actual requirements did not equal the projected requirements based on reasonable assumptions as to mortality, interest, turnover, salary scales, and other pertinent factors. It is to be contrasted to a surplus which arises out of a downward adjustment in the benefit formula, which does not inure to the benefit of the employer.

highest paid employees. If there are sufficient funds to purchase annuities for all accrued credits, the money would, of course, be applied in that manner. If funds are not sufficient to meet all accrued liabilities, a system of successive preferential classes of employees or classes of benefits may be followed. For example, the highest priority may be assigned to benefits for retired employees, the benefits for employees who have met the requirements for retirement but have not actually retired, then benefits to employees who have met the vesting requirements, and so on until the funds have been fully exhausted. On the other hand, the funds might first be used to liquidate future service credits, with any excess being applied on a pro rata basis to past service benefits. Any excess remaining after the satisfaction of all liabilities, if not due to an actuarial error, would be applied to provide additional benefits on some equitable basis.

SOURCE OF FINANCING

From the standpoint of financing, a pension plan may be contributory or noncontributory. Under a contributory plan the employee provides the funds for a portion of his benefits, with the employer assuming the cost of the remaining portion. Under a noncontributory plan the employer bears the total cost of the program, the employee making no contribution.

THE CASE FOR AND AGAINST EMPLOYEE CONTRIBUTION

Traditionally, the cost of providing retirement benefits has been borne jointly by the employer and employees and even today contributory plans predominate in number. Joint financing has the obvious and, in some cases, controlling advantage of making possible larger benefits to the employees. In many cases, the employer's financial position is such that he cannot assume the entire cost of pensions, and unless the employee group is willing to contribute toward the program, no plan will be installed. In other cases, employees contribute in order to enlarge the benefits. Finally, some plans are made contributory on the assumption that the members have a fuller appreciation of the plan if they bear a part of its cost.

The case for noncontributory plans rests largely on the deferred wage concept, which was discussed earlier. If retirement benefits can be regarded as the equivalent of wages, then, logically, the employer should assume the total cost of the program. If that view is rejected, the argument for unilateral financing loses much of its strength.

Entirely apart from the philosophical or moral aspects of the question, there are strong practical considerations in favor of employer financing. Arguments frequently cited in favor of noncontributory plans are relative freedom from employee interference, administrative convenience, and flexibility in funding. A more compelling argument revolves around the fact that the contributions which an employer makes toward a qualified pension plan are deductible as an ordinary business expense for income tax purposes and, in the short run at least, a substantial portion of the cost is shifted to the Federal government. On the other hand, the contributions which an employee makes toward his own retirement are not deductible and, as a consequence, are made from residual or net income. Dollar for dollar, therefore, employee contributions are more burdensome than employer contributions.

CURRENT PRACTICE IN FINANCING

As might be expected, the tendency in negotiated plans has been to place the entire burden of financing on the employer. None of the 97 pattern plans analyzed by the Bankers Trust Company in its 1950-52 survey requires nor accepts contributions from employees.[34] Under a few programs, however, employees covered by a pattern plan are permitted to elect voluntarily to make contributions to and participate in a conventional contributory plan which the company has established.

The majority of conventional plans require employee participation in financing, although a trend in the opposite direction seems to be developing among newly established and amended plans. In its surveys, the Federal Security Agency found, for example, that 94 per cent of the group annuity plans established during the period of 1938-42 were on the contributory basis, whereas during the 1942-46 period the percentage dropped to 58.[35] With the termina-

34. Bankers Trust Company, *op. cit.*, p. 13.
35. Van Eenam and Penman, *op. cit.*, p. 5.

tion of World War II, contributory plans gained in popularity, the peak being reached in 1948 when 85 per cent of the group annuity plans were on the contributory basis. The trend was reversed again, however, and by 1950, only 59 per cent of the newly established plans were of the contributory type.

The general pattern revealed in the Bankers Trust Company studies of conventional plans is similar to that disclosed in the Federal Security Agency studies, but within the category of contributory plans a trend away from employee contributions on the first $3,000 or $3,600 of annual compensation is manifested. Only 35 per cent of the conventional plans established during 1950-52 required no employee contributions, but another 25 per cent excluded contributions on annual earnings of less than $3,000.[36] The bulk of the plans in the latter category excluded contributions on annual earnings of less than $3,600. Only 37 per cent of the plans require employee contributions on all earnings.

AMOUNT OF EMPLOYEE'S CONTRIBUTION

In a contributory plan, the amount of an employee's contribution should bear a reasonable relationship to his ability to pay. This is important from a practical as well as an ethical standpoint, since if the contribution rate is set too high, a sufficient number of employees may not elect coverage under the plan. Under group contributory plans, at least 75 per cent of the eligible employees must elect coverage before the plan will be installed and under any plan the objectives of the program can be defeated by inadequate participation.

In the definite benefit type of plan, an employee's contribution rate is usually set at a multiple of his retirement benefit. The most common practice has been to establish employee contributions at two to three times the rate at which future service benefits accrue. If future service benefits accrue at the rate of 1 per cent of each year's compensation, for example, the employee contribution rate would usually be set at 2 to 3 per cent of each year's compensation. The amount of retirement benefits which such contributions will purchase varies with the attained age of the employee, and other factors, but the employer contributes such additional sums as are

36. Bankers Trust Company, *op. cit.*, p. 13.

needed to provide the future service benefits guaranteed under the plan. In addition, the employer almost invariably bears the entire cost of past service benefits.

In connection with money purchase plans, the employee's rate of contribution bears a fixed ratio to the contribution rate of the employer, although both are normally expressed as a percentage of the employee's compensation. As a minimum, employers are expected to match the employee's rate, with each, for example, contributing 5 per cent of the employee's compensation. In some plans, however, the employer contributes at a rate of two or three times that of the employee. The appeal of this approach is that the employer knows in advance what his rate of contribution will be, as contrasted with the definite benefit type under which his contributions are supplemental in nature and, hence, indeterminate.

Under both definite benefit and money purchase plans, the employee's rate of contribution on earnings subject to OASI coverage may be lower than that on earnings in excess of that limit. The rate of contribution on the first $3,600 of earnings tends to fall within a range of 1 to 4 per cent, while the rate on earnings in excess of $3,600 falls within a range of 2½ to 7 per cent.

Types of
Formal Pension Plans

3

THE preceding chapter outlined the features which are common to all types of pension plans, with particular emphasis on the benefit structure. This chapter will describe the basic characteristics of the legal arrangements under which the benefits of a pension plan may be provided. These forms can be broadly classified as (1) insured and (2) self-administered. Some pension plans are partially insured and partially self-administered, the over-all program being designated as a combination plan. Only the substantive features of the plans will be described in this chapter.

INSURED PLANS

INDIVIDUAL CONTRACT PLAN

The benefits promised under a pension plan may be provided in the form of an individual annuity or insurance contract issued on the life of each employee eligible to participate in the plan. This method is generally referred to as an individual contract pension trust or even as a pension trust, since it operates through a trustee, either an individual or corporation, who holds title to and possession of the individual contracts issued under the plan. The trust arrangement is used in order to qualify the plan under Treasury regulations and for administrative reasons. The provisions of the pension plan are usually incorporated in the trust agreement, the trustee being charged with the responsibility of administering the plan.

The trustee makes application for the insurance or annuity contracts on the lives of the eligible employees and upon issue holds the policies subject to the terms of the pension trust agreement. If insurance is involved, evidence of insurability satisfactory to the insurance company will be required. In some companies, a medical examination will be required for each new employee as he enters the plan and for each employee who receives an increase in his benefits under the plan. Companies which write nonmedical insurance may issue the policies on the basis of the individual's statement of past medical history and present condition of health. The plan may be contributory or noncontributory, but in either case the employer turns over to the trustee sufficient sums of money to pay the premiums on the insurance or annuity contracts, and the trustee transmits the money to the insurance company. Upon certification by the trustee, benefits are normally paid directly to the employees by the insurance company, but under a few plans the latter makes payment to the trustee for transmittal to the employees.

Nature of the Contracts.—Several types of contracts may be used under the individual contract plan, the choice depending upon the benefit provisions of the pension plan. The contracts used most extensively, however, are the retirement annuity and the retirement income policy, the latter sometimes being referred to as a retirement endowment or endowment annuity policy.

The retirement annuity contract embodies the two concepts of accumulation and liquidation. Prior to retirement, the contract is nothing more than a method of accumulating a principal sum by the use of the investment facilities of an insurance company; the annuity or liquidation feature does not go into operation until the employee retires. This dual nature of the contract can best be explained by an illustration.

In accordance with the rate basis of several leading companies, $1,623 would have to be on hand at age 65 for each $10 unit of monthly life income to be paid to a male employee, with payments guaranteed for ten years.[1] If a particular employee should be entitled to a retirement benefit of $100 a month at 65, with 120 guaranteed instalments, any insurance company using the rates cited would have to have $16,230 on hand when the employee reached 65. Theoretically, it would be immaterial to the insurance company whether the $16,230 was paid to it in a lump sum at the time of the employee's retirement or was accumulated over a period of years by periodic

1. The maturity value of a retirement annuity providing a life income of $10 per month to a male age 65, with payments guaranteed for 10 years, ranges from $1,582 to $1,706 among the leading life insurance companies.

payments. If, however, a retirement annuity should be purchased for the employee at age 45, an annual deposit of $709.70 with the insurance company would accumulate to the required sum of $16,230 at 65.[2] At that time, the employee would begin to liquidate the principal sum at the rate of $100 per month if he elects the normal annuity, or at a slower rate if he chooses an annuity with a larger death benefit.

The deposits, or level premiums, as they are called, are credited with a guaranteed rate of interest, and should the employee die at any time before 65, a death benefit equal to the premiums paid on the contract or the cash value, whichever is larger, is available.[3] Whether such sum would be paid to the deceased's beneficiaries or credited against future employer contributions would depend upon the vesting provisions of the pension plan. If the plan were contributory, the employee's estate would be entitled, as a minimum, to the benefits purchased with his contributions. The cash value would also provide any withdrawal benefits that the plan might authorize. It can be seen, then, that during the period of accumulation the employer has a number of pure investment accounts, represented by the individual retirement annuities on the lives of the active employees. After retirement, the benefits are distributed on the basis of the same annuity forms that are available under any other pension plan.

Retirement annuities are generally issued only in units of $10 monthly income at retirement, although a few companies will provide additional units on a $5 basis. This means that the benefit formula of the pension plan must be set up in such manner as to produce retirement benefits only in units of $5 or $10, as the case may be. Wage increases can be recognized only if, alone or in conjunction with prior increases, they are of such magnitude as to entitle the employee to an additional unit of $5 or $10 of monthly retirement income. Adjustment of retirement credits because of decreases in compensation is subject to the same limitation.

The contract is issued originally in that multiple of $10 monthly

2. The annual deposit of $709.70 includes a charge for expenses and varies among the companies whose policies have the same maturity value.

3. The cash value under a retirement annuity is the equivalent of the premiums paid, plus interest, less a charge for expenses. After a few years, the cash value will exceed the accumulated value of premiums paid, without interest.

income which is equivalent to the benefit that would be payable to the employee if he should continue to work at his current salary until normal retirement age. If a subsequent increase in compensation should entitle the employee to one or more additional units of retirement income, an additional policy in the appropriate amount is purchased for the employee. Each such increase is assumed to remain in effect until normal retirement age. Over a period of years, the trustee may purchase half a dozen or more policies for a single employee, each one, after the original, representing an additional increment to the employee's retirement income. A wage decrease is likewise assumed to be permanent and, if large enough, will cause the cancellation of one or more units of retirement income, the cash values being applied to the purchase of paid-up insurance and appropriate adjustments being made in future premium payments.

The retirement income policy is identical with the retirement annuity contract except that the former incorporates an insurance feature.[4] Whereas the retirement annuity, in the event of the employee's death before retirement, only returns the premiums paid or the cash value, whichever is larger, the retirement income policy pays $1,000 for each $10 unit of monthly income or the cash value, whichever is larger.[5] The excess of the death benefit over the cash value represents the insurance element. The amount of insurance protection decreases as the cash value increases and eventually declines to zero when the cash value equals the face of the policy. The type of insurance involved is decreasing term since it is both temporary and reducing in nature. The effective amount of insurance protection afforded by a retirement income policy of one large life insurance company, issued to a male employee at age 45, is shown in Table 4. If the policy had been issued at a younger age the cash value would have accumulated more slowly and the effective amount of insurance would have been somewhat larger and extended over a longer period. In policies which provide $1,500 of

4. Technically, the retirement annuity contract contains a minor insurance element in that, during the first few years after issue, the accumulated value of paid-in premiums exceeds the cash value of the policy.

5. Some retirement income policies provide $1,250 or even $1,500 of insurance for each $10 unit of monthly income.

TABLE 4

DEATH BENEFITS PER $10 OF MONTHLY INCOME AVAILABLE UNDER
RETIREMENT ANNUITY AND RETIREMENT INCOME CONTRACTS
ISSUED TO MALE EMPLOYEE AGE 45*

Duration or Years After Issue	Retirement Annuity Contract†	Retirement Income Contract		
		Death Benefit	Cash Value	Insurance Element
1	$ 70.97	$ 1,000.00	$ 33.00	$ 967.00
2	141.94	1,000.00	97.49	902.51
3	212.91	1,000.00	163.54	836.44
4	283.88	1,000.00	231.26	768.74
5	354.85	1,000.00	300.75	699.25
6	425.82	1,000.00	372.15	627.85
7	496.79	1,000.00	445.61	554.39
8	567.76	1,000.00	521.31	478.69
9	638.73	1,000.00	599.45	401.55
10	709.70	1,000.00	680.28	319.72
11	784.01	1,000.00	761.09	238.91
12	868.35	1,000.00	845.20	154.80
13	954.80	1,000.00	933.02	66.98
14	1,043.40	1,024.44	1,024.44	—
15	1,134.24	1,118.14	1,118.14	—
16	1,227.34	1,214.19	1,214.19	—
17	1,322.77	1,312.64	1,312.64	—
18	1,420.58	1,413.55	1,413.55	—
19	1,520.84	1,516.98	1,516.98	—
20	1,623.00	1,623.00	1,623.00	—

* Gross annual level premium for retirement annuity contract, $70.97; for retirement income policy, $79.30.

† During first ten years death benefits equal to gross premiums paid, without interest; thereafter death benefits equal to cash value.

insurance for each $10 of monthly income, an insurance element will be present until shortly before retirement. For comparative purposes, the death benefit that would be available under a retirement annuity contract issued at age 45 is included in Table 4.

If the insurance company writes disability income insurance, upon evidence of insurability and the payment of an additional premium it will attach a disability income rider to the insurance or annuity contracts issued under the pension trust agreement. The endorsement would be the standard rider which in most cases would provide a monthly income of $5 or $10 per $1,000 face amount of insurance in the event that permanent and total disability commences before age 55 or 60. Total disability is presumed to be permanent after it has continued for a period of six months. Premiums are waived and the income payments are continued as long as the disability exists but not beyond the maturity date.

Premium Rates and Dividends.—The retirement annuity and retirement income contracts issued under the provisions of a pension plan are usually the standard contracts available to any member of the public. The policy provisions and actuarial assumptions are the same as those contained in contracts issued to individual policyholders, although restrictions on the exercise of certain rights in the contract are likely to be written into the pension trust agreement. As in all individual contracts, the premium rates and annuity benefits applicable to any particular contract are guaranteed for the lifetime of that contract. The insurance company, however, makes no guarantee as to the rates which will apply to contracts issued in the future to new participants or to old employees who qualify for additional retirement benefits. Such contracts are subject to the rate basis currently being applied by the insurance company. Thus, all contracts issued pursuant to a pension trust agreement will not necessarily contain the same actuarial assumptions.

Contracts written by mutual life insurance companies, and those written by some stock companies, are credited with dividends, if earned. Any such dividends are credited against the employer's contributions for the following year, even in the case of contributory money purchase plans. This disposition of dividends is dictated, in effect, by a Treasury ruling that a qualified pension plan must provide "definitely determinable benefits" to the employees after retirement.[6] The view is held that the use of dividends to provide paid-up units of retirement benefits would violate the requirement that the benefits under the plan be "definitely determinable." Contributory plans, predominantly of the money purchase type, covering the employees of nonprofit organizations sometimes provide that dividends attributable to employee contributions will be applied to the purchase of additional benefits, but such a provision is feasible

6. Section 29.165-1, Regulations 111.

only because of the tax-exempt status of the corporation and the special tax treatment accorded the employees of such organizations.[7]

Dividends are earned on the same basis as that applicable to all other contracts of the same type written by the insurance company. That is, dividends are derived from company-wide experience rather than the segregated experience of the one pension plan.

Group Plans

The individual contract plan is normally confined to a group of employees which is not large enough to qualify for coverage on a group basis. In fact, many insurance companies will not write an individual contract plan on a group of more than 100 or 200 employees, although a company that does not write group insurance may impose no limit on the number of lives that may be included.[8] In terms of total employee coverage, however, group pension plans overshadow individual contract plans.

Plans with widely varying characteristics are combined in the general category of group pensions. At one extreme are found plans which differ only slightly from the individual contract plan, while at the other extreme plans will be found which closely resemble self-administered trusteed plans. The plans will be discussed in the order in which they depart from the pattern of conventional insurance principles.

Group Permanent Plans.—The group permanent type of pension plan is essentially the individual contract plan modified to conform to the principles of group underwriting and administration. The insurance company takes the place of the trustee, and the master contract between the employer and the insurance company supplants the trust agreement. All the provisions of the pension plan

---

7. An employee of an organization exempt from taxation under Section 501(c)(3) of the Internal Revenue Code of 1954 is not required to include in his income the contributions made by the employer toward the purchase of his retirement benefits, even though the plan fails to satisfy the requirements of Section 401(a) of the Code and the rights of the employee are nonforfeitable. The contributions of the employer become taxable to the employee, however, when the benefits are actually received. See Section 29.22(b)(2)-5, Regulations 111 and PS No. 17, August 24, 1944.

8. Some individual contract plans cover up to 8,000 or 10,000 employees, but plans of such size are definitely the exception and can be serviced only by the largest pension firms.

are incorporated in the master contract, and each eligible employee receives, as evidence of his participation in the program, a certificate which contains a summary of the important provisions of the plan. Individual contracts are not issued. The employer remits all premiums to the insurance company, and the latter pays all benefits of the plan directly to the employees. Premiums may be payable monthly or annually and, if the plan is contributory, the employer reimburses himself by means of payroll deductions.

The plan must meet the legal requirements for group insurance, the most basic of which is that there must be at least 25 employees in the group. This is a matter of state regulation, and some states still require as many as 50 employees. Irrespective of the legal minimum, many insurance companies will not issue a group contract on fewer than 50 to 100 lives. If the plan is noncontributory, all eligible employees must be covered; if contributory, at least 75 per cent of the eligible employees must be enrolled. This latter requirement is for the purpose of avoiding adverse selection.

The insurance is written without evidence of insurability up to the limits specified in the plan. The only requirement is that the employee be at work on the day that the insurance becomes effective. The amount of insurance which the insurance company will issue on the automatic, "no-evidence"[9] basis to any one employee is determined by the same underwriting limits that apply to the writing of group life insurance on the term basis. The individual limit is a function of the total volume of insurance on the group and the amount on the lives of the 50 employees with the largest coverage. For example, if there is $1,000,000 of insurance on the group, and each of 50 employees is covered for at least $5,000, then any member of the group might obtain up to $15,000 without giving evidence of insurability. If an employee is entitled to more insurance by the benefit formula than the master contract permits on a "no-evidence" basis, he can obtain the additional amounts by meeting the medical requirements of the insurance company. If he should prove uninsurable at standard rates, many companies will write the insurance on a substandard basis, at least one company being willing to write up to 1000 per cent extra mortality. Otherwise, the additional retire-

9. "No-evidence" is to be distinguished from "nonmedical," in connection with which a health statement is always required and a medical examination may be prescribed at the option of the company.

ment benefits will be provided in the form of a retirement annuity, which contains no insurance feature and, hence, requires no medical examination. The latter procedure is used in the case of an employee whose retirement credits entitle him to more insurance than the insurance company is willing to write on one individual, even on a medical basis.

A. Basic Features of the Plan.—The group permanent plan is appropriate only for those pension plans which provide a death benefit as well as income at retirement. Theoretically, the plan can be underwritten by any type of life insurance or annuity contract which develops a cash value, but, as a matter of practice, the retirement income contract is generally used. The popularity of the retirement income contract is undoubtedly traceable in great measure to the fact that the group permanent arrangement grew out of the individual contract pension trust, which has utilized the retirement income policy almost exclusively. Another factor, which, however, may reflect the same influence, is that virtually all pension plans which include an insurance feature set the amount of insurance at $1,000 for each $10 of retirement benefits.[10] As it happens, the retirement income contract is the only policy that can produce a $10 retirement benefit out of a face amount of $1,000 of insurance. No policy, however, can produce death and retirement benefits in the exact proportion of $1,000 to $10, respectively. The retirement income policy in its later years provides an effective death benefit

10. An interesting exception is the widely publicized Module plan introduced in 1953 by The Mutual Life Insurance Company of New York. This plan provides a death benefit before retirement equal to the commuted value of the guaranteed instalments after retirement, payments under the annuity being guaranteed for either five or ten years, usually five. If a life annuity with five years certain and continuous payments is prescribed, the death benefit is $560 per $10 of monthly life income; if 120 monthly payments are guaranteed, the death benefit before retirement is $1,120 per $10 of monthly retirement income. In addition to the normal death benefit, which is included in all Module plans, the employer may elect to provide, on behalf of married male employees only, a supplemental death benefit, called the widow's pension but payable to any beneficiary including the employee's estate, equal to one-half of the retirement benefit that would have been payable to the employee had he lived to age 65, but not in excess of $100 per month. This benefit, patterned after the familiar family income rider, is payable from the date of the employee's death until the date he would have attained age 65 but may be commuted at any time. The basic death benefit is payable in a lump sum but the beneficiary may elect at the time of the employee's death to take the proceeds as income.

greatly in excess of $1,000 per $10 unit of retirement income. If an employee should die shortly before retirement, his estate or designated beneficiary would receive $1,582 to $1,706, depending upon the company, for each $10 of retirement benefits.

Some employers wish to avoid the additional cost involved in providing a death benefit in excess of the face of the policy and, therefore, prefer a benefit formula that promises a level death benefit of $1,000 for each unit of retirement income.[11] That type of plan can be financed by an ordinary life, life paid-up at 65, endowment at 65, or any other type of level premium contract. Under none of these contracts, however, will the cash value at 65 be sufficient to provide a monthly income of $10 for each unit of insurance. This means that the cash value will have to be supplemented at retirement by funds accumulated in some other manner.

The additional sums may be supplied out of the current revenue of the employer, or they may be accumulated in an auxiliary or "side" fund. It is customary to accumulate the required cash by means of a fund administered on the deposit administration plan by the same life insurance company that underwrites the group permanent policies.[12] In fact, the agreement governing the administration of such a fund is usually made a part of the master contract by means of a rider. Occasionally the additional money is accumulated through a trust arrangement, which converts the program into what is known as a combination plan, the details of which are discussed later in this chapter.[13]

B. Benefit Structure.—

(1) Retirement Benefits.—The group permanent plan can be adapted to any type of benefit formula, but it is most widely used with a formula which bases the benefit on compensation, either as a flat percentage of earnings or as a unit of benefit for each year of service. Under either arrangement, the benefits are purchased on a level premium basis in units of $5 or $10 monthly income on the assumption that earnings will continue at the same rate until retire-

11. The cost of that portion of the death benefit in excess of the face amount of the retirement income contract is nominal, amounting to between 2 and 3 per cent of the gross premium.

12. See pp. 101-09 for a description of the deposit administration type of group annuity contract.

13. See pp. 121-25.

ment. As under the individual contract plan, salary changes are recognized only if they are large enough to add or take away a unit of $10 monthly income. Furthermore, such changes are taken into consideration only on the contract anniversary. This procedure is followed in order that all premiums will fall due at the same time and all coverages for a particular employee will mature at the same time. Most companies will provide short duration coverage for salary increases within the ten-year period preceding the normal retirement date.

The benefits are normally payable under a life income option with payments guaranteed for five or ten years. Other annuity forms are available, however, and the employee is usually given the right to elect the optional forms up to the date of retirement. The adverse selection which is made possible by this privilege is usually hedged by the use of special rates for the optional settlements, frequently arrived at by a one-year setback in the employee's age.

(2) Withdrawal Benefits.—Severance benefits are based on the policy cash values, including in some instances any sums that may have been accumulated in an auxiliary fund, except that with respect to the latter the sums are released only if the employee be in good health at the time of his withdrawal.[14] Unless employer contributions have vested, the withdrawing employee is entitled to only that portion of the cash values that is attributable to his contributions.

The withdrawal benefit is equal to the cash value under the policy, which, contrary to the procedure prescribed for individual policies under the standard nonforfeiture legislation, is based on the full level reserve, less a surrender charge. Designed to reimburse the company for first year expenses in excess of the loading, this charge will usually not exceed $5 or $10 per $1,000 during the first policy year and will decrease each year thereafter, terminating completely from five to ten years after issue. In some companies, the employee receives the full level reserve, the employer absorbing the charge for expenses in the credit which he is allowed against future contributions.

The employee may elect paid-up benefits for whatever amounts can be purchased at net premium rates with his cash value and any other values vested in him. In such event, the employee may obtain, without evidence of insurability, any plan of insurance other than

14. See pp. 97-98 for an explanation of the good health requirement.

term in an amount equal to the difference between the amount of insurance terminating on his life and the amount of paid-up insurance to which he is entitled. The conversion is usually on an attained age basis, although some companies have offered the conversion privilege on the original age basis. The latter procedure may result in the issuance of several policies to one terminating employee, since a separate policy would have had to be issued for every increase in benefits.

(3) Death Benefits.—As has been indicated, death benefits prior to retirement are always provided under group permanent contracts. The minimum benefit is $1,000 for each $10 unit of retirement income, while, if the retirement income contract is used, the benefit may be much larger than that. The death benefit may be taken under the same settlement options as those available under individual poli- cies, except that the interest option is not usually available. The options may be selected by either the insured or the beneficiary.

The normal annuity form under group permanent contracts is a life income with instalments guaranteed for either five or ten years. The employee, however, may elect an annuity which will provide a larger death benefit than the normal annuity form. In such case, the insurance company, to protect itself against adverse selection, levies a selection charge, usually in the form of a one-year setback of the employee's age. This procedure automatically produces a charge of about 3 per cent of the maturity value.

(4) Disability Benefits.—Two types of disability benefits may be available under group permanent plans: waiver of premium and income payments. The benefits are available only for permanent and total disability.

The waiver of premium benefit is identical with that available under individual contracts. Most contracts provide that premiums will be waived after the employee has been totally disabled for a period of six months prior to his sixtieth birthday. Many employers prefer to continue premiums on disabled employees and, in effect, administer their own disability provision.

The income benefits are likewise conditioned on the existence of total disability for a period of six months prior to age sixty. The monthly payments, the number and size of which depend upon the amount of insurance in force on the life of the employee, are deductible from the face of the policy or policies. This is based on the theory that the occurrence of total disability matures the insurance. If the disabled employee should die before the disability payments have exhausted the insurance, the unliquidated balance is paid to his estate or designated beneficiary, either in a lump sum or as a continuation of the income.

If the employee recovers from his disability prior to his normal retirement date and resumes his service with the employer, his insurance coverage is revived but is limited in amount to the commuted value of the remaining unpaid instalments. Recovery from disability after the employee's normal retirement age is ignored. The liquidation of the insurance coverage through the payment of disability benefits does not affect the retirement benefits that would otherwise be payable to the employee, although, of course, the disablement may prevent the employee from qualifying for any retirement benefits.

C. Premiums and Rates.—

(1) Rate Factors.—With respect to mortality prior to retirement, or the insurance coverage, most companies use the Commissioners' Standard Ordinary Table, although some still use the American Men(5) Table. For mortality after retirement virtually all companies are using the 1937 Standard Annuity Table, in some cases with the ages set back one year. A few companies are using annuity tables which have been developed within recent years.[15] The interest rate assumed is generally 2½ per cent, although some companies are using lower assumptions. The loading is usually around 12 or 13 per cent of the gross premium, which is lower than that of individual contracts and higher than that of deferred group annuity contracts. The benefits which are purchased from the auxiliary fund, when a contract other than the retirement income policy is used, are generally purchased at regular group annuity rates, except that the

15. For instance, the Module plan referred to in footnote 10 calculates the maturity value of the annuity on the basis of the 1949 Annuity Table without projection (see Appendix D) and 2½ per cent interest with no loading. The insurance benefits, however, including the pure endowment used to accumulate the maturity value of the annuity benefits, are calculated on the basis of the C.S.O. Table and 2½ per cent interest, with a loading which approximately reproduces the "U" rates promulgated for group life insurance by the Insurance Department of the State of New York.

rates sometimes carry a lower loading than the customary 5 to 8 per cent in recognition of lower acquisition costs and other expenses.

(2) Rate Guarantees.—As under the individual contract plan, each unit of retirement benefit is purchased by a level annual premium payable to the normal retirement age from the date on which the employee qualified for the benefit. This means that the premium and annuity rates are guaranteed for the lifetime of each unit. Furthermore, the master contract usually specifies that no rate changes will be applicable to policies issued under the pension plan for a period of three to five years, depending upon company practice. Thereafter, any new rates that might be promulgated by the company would be applicable to any additional units of benefits purchased for new or old employees.

The same rate guarantees will normally apply to the benefits which are to be provided by an auxiliary fund. In other words, sums set aside to purchase specific units of benefits will carry a rate guarantee with them to the date of conversion. Additional units will be subject to the rates which are in effect at the time they are set up, but all sums set aside to purchase the benefits at retirement enjoy a guaranteed conversion value. When such a guarantee is not given by the insurance company, the employer must make up any deficiencies that might arise.

D. Employer Credits.—The group permanent contract ordinarily provides certain credits to the employer, which, in order to meet the requirements of the Internal Revenue Code, cannot be paid in cash but must be applied against future premiums under the contract.

(1) Withdrawal Credits.—The total withdrawal credit under a group permanent contract is equal to the reserve less a deduction that may amount to $5 or $10 per $1,000 of insurance during the first policy year and reduces to zero by the end of ten years at the longest. The employer's credit is equal to the total withdrawal credit less the amount credited to the employee. If the employee takes advantage of the conversion privilege, the employer credit is allowed immediately only if the employer furnishes satisfactory evidence that the employee is in good health. In the event that evidence

of good health is not furnished, the employer withdrawal credit is allowed only if the converted policy remains in force for five years or if it terminates other than by death within the five-year period. In the latter event, the withdrawal credit is granted in the form of a pure endowment payable at the end of five years.

(2) Deferred Retirement Credits.—The normal method of handling delayed retirement under group permanent plans is to continue the normal salary of the employee and credit the employer with the benefits that would have been paid to the employee if he had retired

(3) Dividends or Premium Rate Adjustments.—Group permanent policies are normally credited with dividends, if underwritten by a mutual company, or with experience credits, if a stock company is on the risk. As a rule, the dividends are calculated in precisely the same manner as those of deferred group annuities, which procedure is described in a later section. Each plan is treated as a unit for dividend determination, with the degree of credibility increasing with the size of the case.

E. Suspensions.—Some group permanent contracts contain a "stop and go" provision under which the employer may temporarily discontinue the permanent insurance and later reinstate it. Upon suspension of the plan, the full termination value of each employee's insurance and retirement annuity, if any, is applied to purchase paid-up insurance and a paid-up retirement annuity. The cash values under such policies can be withdrawn only on termination of employment. Each employee is protected during the period of suspension by yearly renewable term insurance in an amount equal to the difference between the original amount of permanent insurance and the amount of reduced paid-up insurance. New entrants to the plan during the period of suspension receive term insurance in accordance with the benefit formula.

Premium payments on the permanent insurance can be resumed on notice to the insurance company. The reversion to permanent insurance is made on the basis of attained age rather than original age, thus relieving the employer of the necessity of repaying in one sum the premiums which were suspended. Retirement benefits are not affected since the attained age insurance plus the paid-up insurance will provide the benefits promised under the formula. The right to suspend premium payments on the permanent insurance may not be exercised more often than once every five years and not more than three years may elapse during a period of suspension.

F. Discontinuance.—On discontinuance of a plan, all benefits which have been purchased become fully vested in the employees regardless of the vesting formula applicable before discontinuance. A termination charge is levied to cover unamortized expenses, the balance being applied to purchase paid-up insurance and paid-up annuities. Any policy which has been in force for at least five years may be converted to any type of permanent insurance and continued by the employee. These paid-up benefits are purchased at net single premium rates. The employees retain the same right to optional retirement as they would have had if the pension plan had remained in effect.

The sums in the auxiliary fund, if any, also vest in the employees upon discontinuance of the plan, but the vesting may follow a system of successive preferential classes of employees rather than a pro rata formula. It should be understood, of course, that any sums in the auxiliary fund attributable to employee contributions would be returned to the proper employees, either in cash or as deferred pension credits.

Any undistributed employer withdrawal credits or dividends arising after the date of discontinuance are usually distributed in the form of paid-up benefits among the active employees who were covered under the plan at the time of its discontinuance. The distribution may be made on any equitable basis, the most common one being in proportion to the reserves.

Deferred Group Annuity Plan.[16]—In terms of coverage, the deferred group annuity is the most important contract developed by the life insurance companies to underwrite pension plans. At the end of 1953, 2,285,000 employees were covered under 3,280 deferred group annuity contracts.[17]

The contract is relatively free from statutory controls. Only four

16. For a comprehensive discussion of group annuities, see Kenneth Black, Jr., *Group Annuities* (Philadelphia: University of Pennsylvania Press, 1955).
17. *Life Insurance Fact Book*, 1954, p. 31.

states—New York, Massachusetts, North Carolina, and Louisiana—have statutes specifically directed at group annuities. None of these statutes prescribes a minimum number of lives, although the New York law has been interpreted to require a minimum of two lives. At one time a few states ruled that their group insurance laws applied to group annuities, thus requiring a minimum of 25 lives, but all such administrative rulings have now been rescinded. In all states other than New York, therefore, the number of lives to be covered is a matter of insurance company underwriting practice.

Most companies require a minimum of 25 lives, but there is a trend toward reducing the minimum in order to reach the small case market. At least one large company has no published minimum, while another is extending its group annuity services to employers with as few as ten eligible employees. Virtually all companies require 100 per cent participation if the plan is noncontributory, and 75 per cent participation if contributory.

Apart from the number of lives required, most companies have either a minimum premium requirement or levy a special administrative charge on cases developing a premium below a specified minimum. The minimum annual premium may be expressed in terms of an aggregate, e.g., $10,000, or in terms of an average premium per covered employee, such as $250. With respect to administrative charges, one company assesses a charge of $750 on all contracts with an annual premium of less than $50,000, while another levies a charge of $600 on all contracts producing premiums of less than $200,000. There is no upper limit to the number of lives that can be covered under a group annuity contract.

The underlying legal document is the master contract which, along with the application, if attached, constitutes the entire contract between the employer and the insurance company. The provisions of the pension plan are incorporated in the master contract, and each employee receives a certificate which contains those clauses of the master contract which directly affect his rights or those of his beneficiary. Legally, this certificate is merely evidence of participation in the plan and is not a contract between the employee and the insurance company. Nevertheless, the employee is considered to be a third party beneficiary under the master contract and, as such, can enforce his rights created thereunder. As is true with all group plans, no trust arrangement need be used.

Since no mortality risk is involved, no evidence of insurability is required for participation in the plan.

A. Benefit Structure of the Plan.—The group annuity contract is designed for the payment of retirement benefits. Any other benefits that may be provided under the contract are incidental to and, perhaps, even inconsistent with the main objective. The mechanism by which the basic benefits—those payable at retirement—are provided is described in the following section.

(1) Retirement Benefits.—The group annuity contract can be used to finance any type of retirement benefit, but it is best suited to a formula which provides a unit of benefit for each year of service. The benefit may be expressed as a flat amount for each year of service or as a percentage of earnings. The typical group annuity contract provides a specified percentage of current earnings for each year of service. For purposes of administrative convenience, a schedule of salary classes is frequently established, and the percentage is applied to the midpoint of the appropriate salary bracket.

The benefits are provided through the medium of a deferred life annuity. This is a type of annuity under which the income payments do not commence until a specified period has elapsed. The typical period of deferment extends from the date of purchase to the attainment of a specified age by the annuitant. A *pure* deferred life annuity refunds no part of the purchase price if the annuitant should die before reaching the specified age, the sum thus released being used by the insurance company, as is implicitly provided in the rate structure, to increase the annuity payments of those who survive. The *refund* deferred life annuity, on the other hand, returns the purchase price, with or without interest, if the annuitant should die before the annuity payments commence. In a typical group annuity plan, the employer's contributions are used to purchase pure deferred annuities, inasmuch as it is not intended that the estate of the deceased employee should receive the employer's contributions. In a contributory plan, however, the employee's contributions are used to purchase refund annuities, since the employee must be assured that his estate will recover his contributions in the event that he should die before retirement. If the employer's contributions are to vest upon death, the same type of contract would be purchased with the employer's contributions.

These annuities are purchased on a single premium basis.[18] In other words, each unit of benefit is purchased in full for the employee in the year in which it is earned. If an employee earns a retirement credit of $45 in a particular year, there will be purchased for his account, in the same year, a single premium deferred annuity that will provide him with an annual income of $45 at normal retirement age. Each year that he participates in the plan an additional paid-up deferred annuity in the appropriate amount will be purchased for his account. At retirement, the employee will be entitled to the income from a series of paid-up deferred annuities purchased for him over the entire period of his participation, the cumulative income from which will equal the total credits granted by the pension formula.

With respect to an individual employee, the premium outlay per dollar of retirement income increases from year to year as the employee approaches retirement. For example, the single premium for a pure deferred life annuity that will provide an income of $1 per year at age 65 is only $3.80 at age 30, but by 35 it has increased to $4.36 and at 45, 55 and 60, the premium is $5.83, $8.22 and $10.10, respectively.[19] Moreover, the earnings of an employee normally rise over the years, which further inflates the cost of providing his retirement benefits. From the standpoint of the entire employee group, however, turnover and deaths will normally have the effect of leveling out the over-all outlays for future service benefits. The prime consideration is the age composition of the employee group.

Past service benefits may likewise be purchased with a lump sum payment, but, for tax reasons, or because of the burdensome financial obligation involved, the accrued liability of a pension plan is normally liquidated over a period of years. In order to prevent the liquidation of this obligation during the most favorable tax period, the tax laws permit the employer to deduct in any one taxable year only 10 per cent of the *initial* past service liability.[20] Since the initial

18. It is possible to fund a group annuity plan on a level premium basis but, with the exception of money purchase plans, it is not customary to do so.

19. Rates are based on the 1937 Standard Annuity Table, 2½ per cent interest, and loading of 8 per cent of gross premium.

20. Section 404(a)(1)(C), I.R.C. and Section 29.23(P)-7, Regulations 111. Actually, the limitation stated above is only one of three tests applied by the Treasury authorities to gauge the reasonableness of employer contributions to pension plans. See pp. 134-36 of this volume.

past service liability is an interest-bearing item, representing a discounted value, liquidation at the rate of 10 per cent per year requires between 11 and 12 years, depending upon the rate of interest assumed. Apart from the statutory limitation, many companies, in an effort to regularize their premium income and to protect themselves against adverse financial selection, will not permit an employer to pay off more than 10 per cent of the initial past service liability in any one contract year. Such companies are fearful that, without such a limitation, the employers might make large past service payments in a period of low investment yields. Furthermore, with no restrictions, if the insurance company should give notice of an impending rate increase, the employer might pay off all or a large part of the past service liability before the change becomes effective.

As a matter of fact, however, liquidation of the past service liability at too slow a rate is a more serious problem than the reverse. As a consequence, most companies require that such accrued liability be completely amortized within a specified period of time. Except in unusual circumstances, no company would compel an employer to amortize the past service liability over a shorter period than that permitted by Federal tax regulations and, in practice, most companies allow the past service payments to be spread over a period of twenty years or more.

Since all past service credits are normally not purchased at one time, a policy must be established to govern the allocation of past service contributions to the purchase of individual annuities. A fundamental consideration in this respect is the fact that virtually all insurance companies require that the retirement benefits of an employee be purchased in full before the employee retires. To implement this requirement, most group annuity contracts stipulate that, should an employee reach retirement before his past service annuity has been fully purchased, the contributions to complete the purchase are due immediately.[21] In view of this, the customary practice is to allocate past service contributions to the purchase of

21. If the average age of the covered employees is higher than normal, this requirement may force the employer to liquidate more than 10 per cent of the initial past service liability each year. This would not penalize the employer tax-wise, since under such circumstances the payments would undoubtedly be deductible under the straight-line rule.

individual annuities in the order of nearness to retirement. In other words, the past service credits of those employees who are within one year of retirement would be purchased first, those for employees within two years of retirement next, and so on.

Occasionally, a plan will specify that past service credits shall be purchased in the order of seniority in order to protect the rights of employees with the longest periods of service. While this method may be equitable, it permits an employee with a shorter period of service than normal to reach retirement before his past service credits have been purchased, thus requiring an additional contribution from the employer.

Finally, a group annuity contract may provide that each past service contribution will be applied to the purchase of a pro rata share of the unpurchased past service credit of each employee. The advantage of this method is that each employee who is entitled to past service benefits is credited with an appropriate share of the employer's past service contributions each year, so that if the plan should be discontinued, all employees would have the same proportion of their past service annuities purchased for them. The principal disadvantage of this arrangement is that until the past service liability has been completely liquidated employees will reach retirement with a portion of their past service annuities unpurchased, and the employer will have to make supplemental payments for them. Consequently, this method is frequently modified to provide that past service contributions paid during a particular contract year shall be first applied to the purchase of any remaining unpurchased past service credits of employees who are retiring within the year, after which any balance is applied, on a pro rata basis, to the purchase of past service annuities for the other employees. Administratively, the pro rata method is burdensome, since each employee must be credited with a portion of the past service contribution, but the work is reduced to some extent by accumulating, with interest, all payments during a contract year to the end of the year and crediting them at one time.

(2) Withdrawal Benefits.—The rights of an employee to the annuities purchased by the employer's contributions upon termination of his employment depend upon the vesting provisions of the plan. The employee may be entitled to all or none of such annuities. In

some plans, he may be permitted to retain the annuities purchased by a portion but not all of the employer's contributions.

In a contributory plan, the employee is assured of a return of his contributions with or without interest. If interest is allowed, the rate is usually 2 per cent compounded annually. It is not customary to credit the contributions with any interest in the contract year in which they are made. In the year of termination, however, interest on the contributions of all prior years is credited for all completed months.

The employee usually is given the alternative of withdrawing his contributions in cash, in which event the annuities which have been purchased for his account would be cancelled, or leaving his contributions with the insurance company and retaining the paid-up deferred annuities which they have purchased along with the vested portion of the paid-up benefits, if any, purchased by employer contributions. If the amount of the paid-up benefit is less than a specified minimum, normally $10 per month, the insurance company usually has the right to make a cash settlement. Some companies permit the election of the paid-up annuity option for benefits as small as $40 per year, but where the annual amount is less than $120, payments are made quarterly rather than monthly. If the employee elects a paid-up deferred annuity, he nevertheless retains the right to withdraw its cash value at any time prior to his normal retirement date. A few group annuity contracts permit an employee, usually subject to employer consent, to withdraw his contributions without terminating his employment, but most contracts contain prohibitions against this practice.

(3) Death Benefits.—At the death of an employee before retirement, any contributions which he may have made are payable to his estate or designated beneficiary. It is customary to credit such contributions with interest, although a slightly higher retirement benefit or, conversely, a lower cost to the employer, may be obtained if the contributions are returnable without interest. Interest credits are calculated in the same manner as for withdrawal benefits, which means no interest on a contribution during the contract year in which made, with interest thereafter on completed portions of any year.

As in the case of withdrawal from employment, the disposition of the employer's contributions depends upon the vesting provisions of the plan. It is not customary to grant death benefits with respect to employer contributions under a group annuity contract, although such benefits could be provided by the purchase of refund deferred life annuities with the employer's contributions.

Most group annuity contracts permit the use of settlement options. The optional settlement may be arranged in advance by the employee or elected by the beneficiary after the employee's death. In either event, it is customary to provide that the death benefit will be paid in a lump sum if it is less than a specified minimum, usually $1,000.

Death benefits after retirement depend upon the type of annuity elected. Under noncontributory plans, the normal form of settlement is usually the straight life annuity with no death benefits. The normal form of annuity for contributory plans is typically the modified cash refund annuity, under which the deceased's estate or designated beneficiary will receive at his death a sum equal to the difference between the accumulated value of his contributions, with interest, at retirement and the aggregate amount of income payments received by the employee before his death. Virtually all group annuity contracts permit the employee to elect an option, on an actuarially equivalent basis, which provides a death benefit, or a larger benefit, as the case may be, but such election must be made at a specified time prior to retirement, such as one, two, or five years, or else must be accompanied by evidence of insurability. This is to protect the insurance company, and, indirectly, the employer, against adverse selection.

(4) Disability Benefits.—Disability benefits are available under group annuity contracts only in the form of early retirement provisions, which have been previously discussed. The employer, of course, may provide such benefits on a pay-as-you-go basis, but it is not the policy of life insurance companies to underwrite the permanent disability hazard in connection with a group annuity contract.[22]

22. Disability benefits were available under early group annuity plans, and the claims experience was not unfavorable. The coverage was eliminated from group annuity contracts in the interest of uniform underwriting practices when, with few exceptions, the life insurance companies, in the face of extremely adverse loss experience, eliminated permanent disability coverage from their individual life insurance contracts. See R. A. Hohaus, "Further Remarks on Group Annuities," *Record of the American Institute of Actuaries*, Vol. XXIII, 1934, p. 338.

B. Premiums and Rates.—Premiums for deferred group annuity contracts reflect only three factors: mortality, interest, and expenses, including an allowance for contingencies. Contrary to the practice in some plans, notably self-administered plans, the rate structure does not take into account withdrawal rates and anticipated increases in salary, since these two variables are not reliably predictable. Moreover, they are subject, to some extent, to the control of the employer and his employees.

(1) Rate Factors.—Early group annuity contracts were generally written on the basis of the American Annuitants Table and the Combined Annuity Table, in that order, but since 1939 practically all new plans have been based on the 1937 Standard Annuity Table. Continued improvement in mortality, with the consequent narrowing of safety margins, has caused some companies to rate the 1937 Standard Annuity Table down one year.[23] Female lives are normally set back five years, which means that if male ages are set back one year, female ages are set back six years. Recent studies of annuitant mortality indicate that the margins in the table, adjusted in this manner, may not be adequate to absorb anticipated improvement in mortality.[24] Consideration is currently being given to the development of group annuity tables that will make an allowance for future improvement in mortality.

The interest assumption used in connection with group annuity rates is usually 2 or 2¼ per cent. A few companies use a rate as high as 2½ per cent. This is in contrast to the 4 per cent rate used in group annuity contracts issued before 1934. Declining yields on investments compelled the companies to lower their interest assumption time after time until the present low rates were reached.

The interest assumptions currently being used for group annuity contracts are generally lower than those used for life insurance contracts. The rates were deliberately made conservative in order

23. When an annuity table is rated down one year in age, the mortality rate at Age x in the rated table is the same as the mortality rate at age x-1 in the unrated table. In simple terms, it means that the annuitants at all ages are assumed to be one year younger than their actual age, which produces a lower rate of expected mortality than that of the unrated table.

24. See W. A. Jenkins and E. A. Lew, "A New Mortality Basis for Annuities," *Transactions of the Society of Actuaries*, Vol. I, November 1949, pp. 369-466, and Ray M. Peterson, "Group Annuity Mortality," *ibid.*, Vol. IV, June 1952, pp. 246-307.

to hedge against adverse mortality experience, which, in the case of annuities, means excessive longevity. The trend toward greater longevity which has been so evident during the last half-century has had the effect of gradually reducing the safety margins included in the static annuity tables used by the life insurance companies.[25] The 1937 Standard Annuity Table, for example, was outdated at some younger ages almost as soon as it was published. Rather than adopt a new table, the companies have preferred to use a considerably lower rate of interest than they expect to earn. In this connection, it has been estimated that an interest margin of ¼ per cent will absorb a general improvement in mortality of 6 to 7 per cent. Any interest margins that are not needed to cover improvements in longevity are available for dividends or experience credits.

The loading factor in group annuity rates is generally 5 to 8 per cent of the gross premium. This factor is designed to cover not only the expenses connected with the contract but also an allowance for contingencies. As a matter of fact, the proportion of the loading charge that is allocated to expenses is much smaller than that allocated to the accumulation of a contingency reserve. Studies have indicated that, on the average, expenses absorb about 2½ or 3 per cent of the gross premium, while the remainder of the loading charge is applied toward the accumulation of a contingency reserve or released through the dividend formula.[26] Furthermore, approximately one-third of the expenses are accounted for by taxes, primarily premium taxes. A portion of the expense allowance is set aside as a reserve for future expenses since the annuities are purchased with single premiums.

In order to protect themselves against excessive longevity of annuitants, a possible decline in investment yields below the rate of interest assumed in actuarial calculations, capital losses, new taxes, and other unforeseen developments, the insurance companies feel that it is necessary to maintain a fund over and above the statutory reserves. In some states, a contingency fund is required by law. At

25. A static annuity table is one which purports to reflect the death rates among annuitants as of a fixed date or for a designated period in the past. It is to be contrasted with a table which by means of projection factors would attempt to anticipate future improvement in mortality. The use of annuity tables with mortality projection factors is presently being considered.

26. An analysis of group annuity expenses is presented in Chapter V of this volume.

any rate, most companies attempt to accumulate a contingency reserve of the order of 4 to 6 per cent of the group annuity statutory reserves. As experience unfolds and the reserve is revealed to be redundant, a portion can be released to the employer as a credit against future contributions.

(2) Rate Guarantees.—Many of the group annuity contracts issued before 1935 were underwritten with a lifetime guarantee. Such a guarantee usually provided that rates could be changed on or after the fifth anniversary of the contract but that no change in rates would apply to annuities purchased for employees covered under the plan prior to the date of the change. Some contracts with lifetime guarantees provided that rates could not be changed more often than every five years. A few such contracts stipulated that the rates could be increased by not more than a certain percentage of the original rates within any five- or ten-year period.

The lifetime guarantee in group annuity contracts was an obvious extension of the familiar lifetime guarantee under individual insurance policies. It subsequently became evident that such a guarantee is inappropriate for a group annuity contract. In the first place, improvements in mortality, while favorable to life insurance contracts, are decidedly unfavorable to annuity contracts. Since the obligation assumed under a group annuity contract may extend over a period of seventy-five years or longer, continued improvement in annuitant mortality could prove extremely embarrassing. Secondly, the margin in participating group annuities is much smaller than the margin in participating individual insurance policies. This was particularly true when the group annuity contracts were being written on a 4 per cent interest basis. Finally, the benefit formula of a deferred group annuity contract usually bases the benefits on the current earnings of the employee. Unpredictable increases in salary, particularly during a period of inflation, may result in the ultimate purchase of benefits much larger than those anticipated in the lifetime guarantee. In individual insurance contracts the premiums are guaranteed only as to benefits which are fixed at the time the policy is issued.

Since 1935, the practice has been to guarantee the rates initially used in the contract only for premiums received during the first five contract years. Thereafter, the insurance company can specify a new set of rates which will apply to all premium payments, including those applied to the purchase of annuities for employees covered under the plan before the date of the rate change. No change in rates, however, can apply retroactively to annuities purchased before the date of change. After the fifth contract year, guarantees usually run from year to year, except that some contracts provide a longer guarantee after a change in rates or a change in the benefit formula.

Premiums for past service benefits are subject to the same rate conditions that govern future service benefits. Only those benefits which are purchased during the first five contract years receive the protection of the rate guarantee. In order to extend the protection of the initial rate guarantee to all past service benefits, some insurance companies permit the employer to "purchase" all past service benefits on the effective date of the contract by means of a "loan" from the insurance company. The "loan" is repaid in level annual instalments over a period of years, sometimes as long as twenty. If an employee retires or dies during the repayment period, payments for his past service benefits must be continued until the end of the period. The same procedure applies when an employee retires because of ill health or when a terminating employee has a vested interest in his past service credits. Otherwise, in the event of termination, the employer is entitled to the original single premium, plus interest, less a surrender charge to cover expenses, and less the present value of the past service payments which have not been made.

C. Employer Credits.—The group annuity contract, like other plans, provides certain credits to the employer, which, because of statutory restrictions, cannot be paid in cash but must be applied against future premiums under the contract.

(1) Withdrawal Credits.—Since employer contributions are ordinarily applied to the purchase of pure deferred life annuities, in which mortality has been discounted, no refund is usually made to the employer in the event of the death of an employee before retirement. On termination of employment other than by death or retirement, however, the employer is entitled to a credit on account of any annuities cancelled.

Under noncontributory plans the employer's future service withdrawal credit is typically 96 per cent of the future service contributions accumulated at interest. Under contributory plans, the future service withdrawal credit is normally 96 per cent of the employer's contributions with interest, less 4 per cent of the cash value payable to the employee, whether or not he avails himself of the cash option. In other words, the employer absorbs the surrender charge for both sets of contributions, and the employee recovers his contributions in full. If the contract provides for the return to the employee of his contributions without interest and the employee has participated in the plan for a minimum period of three to five years, depending upon the plan, the 4 per cent deduction is not made. The employer's past service withdrawal credit is the greater of 96 per cent of the past service contributions with interest or 100 per cent of such contributions without interest.[27]

This 4 per cent surrender charge is admittedly an approximation. The original loading in the rates is intended to cover all expenses allocable to any given premium payment from the date of payment to the date of the employee's death. When an annuity is cancelled before the employee's death, the unused portion of the loading can be released. The longer the annuity has been in force, the smaller the unused portion of the loading or, conversely, the larger the surrender charge should be. The inference might be drawn that the 4 per cent charge is based on the assumption that, on the average, terminations will occur at that point in time when one-half of the loading has been expended. There is no such statistical foundation, however, for the precise amount of the charge, particularly since a portion of the loading is earmarked for contingencies. Moreover, some companies which load their premiums by only 5 per cent still levy a 4 per cent surrender charge.

There are other respects in which the withdrawal credit formula does not attempt precision. For example, reserves for pure deferred annuities increase from year to year because of benefit of survivorship, while the withdrawal credit makes no allowance for such factor. Furthermore, the interest rate used in the determination of withdrawal credits is usually lower than the rate assumed in premium calculations. Finally, with respect to withdrawal values, in-

27. If an employer takes his withdrawal credit in cash, the amount is reduced by 5 per cent of the sum otherwise available. The extra charge is levied to protect the insurance company against the possibility of having to liquidate some of its investments in a poor market. The employer may also suffer tax penalties since Treasury regulations prohibit the taking of credits in cash.

terest is normally allowed only from the end of the contract year in which contributions are made, while in the calculation of premium rates interest is credited from the date of payment. It is not essential that the employer's withdrawal credit be calculated precisely, since adjustments will automatically be effected through the dividend formula.

The employer's withdrawal credit is payable only if the employee was in good health at the time of his termination. The reason for this is that the employer's contributions are calculated in the first instance on the assumption that any premiums paid on behalf of an employee who dies before retirement shall be retained by the insurance company and used to provide benefits to those employees who survive to retirement. In other words, employer premiums are discounted for mortality. Therefore, if an employee withdraws from employment because of an impairment that would have certainly caused his death before the normal retirement age, the contributions represented by his annuities should be treated in the same manner as they would have been had the employee died while in service. In the absence of this restriction, an employer could terminate the employment of a seriously ill employee just prior to death and secure a credit that would not be available had the employee died in service. It is only the extra mortality that occurs among terminated employees as a result of health impairments at date of termination that the good health clause seeks to include in the mortality experience under the group annuity contract.

In most cases, the insurance company will rely upon the employer's statement regarding the health of the terminating employee. Where the value of the annuity is unusually large, the company may require a medical examination of the employee. In lieu of this, the employer's withdrawal credit may be used to purchase a pure endowment running for five years. If the employee survives the endowment period, the endowment is then credited to the employer. This arrangement introduces the problem of keeping track of a former employee, as well as the complication of death during the endowment period from a cause unrelated to the impairment at date of termination.

The financial importance of the ill-health provision is revealed by the fact that, in the recent experience of male employees, there has been one ill-health termination for each three deaths among active employees, and all these ill-health terminations were needed to produce an aggregate mortality experience approximating that expected by the 1937 Standard Annuity Table.[28]

To the extent that employer contributions vest in the employee, there will, of course, be no cancellation of annuities and no employer credits.

(2) Deferred Retirement Credits.—As was pointed out previously, various arrangements can be worked out to effect an equitable financial arrangement when an employee continues to work beyond normal retirement age. A procedure which is commonly used in connection with group annuity contracts is to defer the payment of the retirement benefits until the employee actually retires, at which time benefits in the same amount as would have been paid at the normal retirement date are commenced. In this case, the retirement income payments which would have been paid from the normal retirement age to the date of actual retirement are returned to the employer in the form of credits against future premiums under the contract. If the plan provides a death benefit after retirement, however, the credits are retained by the insurance company in a suspense account, on which interest is allowed, to be applied to the payment of the death benefits, if necessary. Once the employee has received retirement benefits equal to the guaranteed death benefit, the sum in the suspense account is credited to the employer. Or if the employee should die before receiving the equivalent of the death benefit, any balance in the account after the death benefit has been paid is released to the employer.

(3) Dividends or Premium Rate Adjustments.—All group annuity contracts make provision for an adjustment in the contributions of the employer if experience warrants it. In a mutual life insurance company such an adjustment is described as a dividend, while in a stock company it is referred to as a rate credit. Except for the smallest plans, the amount of the refund depends primarily upon the experience of the plan in question. This is accomplished through the maintenance of a separate account, called the Experience Account, or Experience Fund, for each group annuity contract.

During any particular contract year, including the first, this indi-

28. Society of Actuaries, *1949 Report of the Committee on Group Mortality and Morbidity*, pp. 46-47.

vidual account is credited with all premium payments under the contract for that year. The accumulated balance, including premiums for the current year, is credited with the net rate of interest earned on the total investment portfolio of the insurance company, or in some companies, the net rate of interest earned on all investments other than policy loans. The account is charged with benefit disbursements under the contract during the current year, as well as with all expenses allocable to it under accepted cost accounting techniques. It is credited or charged, as the case may be, with a "mortality adjustment" which has the effect of smoothing mortality fluctuations (1) over the years for the particular contract, and (2) among all group annuity contracts written by the company. If the mortality under the contract is lighter than the average for all group annuity contracts during the period, it will be entitled to a credit. If its mortality is heavier than the average, it must share a portion of its "savings" with the less fortunate cases in the form of a charge. The extent to which the mortality experience of a particular contract is modified to reflect the experience of other contracts depends upon the size of the case. Virtually no cases receive 100 per cent credibility for the first year, but after a few years the larger cases receive practically full recognition of their experience. On the other hand, the initial averaging on a small case is strong, or to state it differently, the credibility of the experience of the small case is low. As the years go by, however, the averaging grows weaker, and progressively greater recognition is given to the experience of the particular contract.

At the end of the contract year, the insurance company calculates the present value of the benefits that are payable under the annuities that have been purchased and are still in force. The minimum basis for this valuation may be specified in the contract, but the actual valuation may be more stringent than the minimum. Nevertheless, whatever basis is used is normally applied to all group annuity contracts, regardless of when they were issued. For the purposes of the valuation, the unpurchased portion of past service credits is not considered to be a contract liability.

The difference between the cash balance in the account and the contractual liabilities, as revealed by the periodic valuation, reflects the gain or loss under the contract. After appropriate amounts have been allocated to the contingency reserve, and, in some companies, to the reserve for future expenses, the gain, if any, may be returned to the employer in the form of a dividend or rate reduction. The company is under no contractual obligation to pay a dividend, if earned, and the employer has no legal right to demand an accounting.

As a matter of fact, few companies have been in a position to pay substantial dividends under group annuity contracts. The group annuity business has developed in a period of significant improvement in mortality and declining investment yields, both of which increase the cost of providing retirement benefits. Many, if not most, of the early contracts were written at rates which subsequent developments have demonstrated to be inadequate. As a result, many companies have had to divert funds which normally would have been available for dividend distribution to the strengthening of the reserve bases of contracts issued in earlier years. With the upturn of investment yields, the completion of reserve strengthening programs, and a general boosting of group annuity rates, the future should offer reasonable prospects for dividends.

D. Modification of the Contract.—The group annuity contract can be modified at any time by the mutual consent of the employer and the insurance company. If a bargaining unit is involved, consent of union representatives may also be required. No modification or change in the contract can alter or affect adversely the amount and terms of payment of any annuities which have already been purchased. Some insurance companies also reserve the right unilaterally to modify any terms of the contract at any time at which the rates may be changed, although certain types of changes may require employee consent in any event. Such modifications would normally be confined to those provisions which would be affected by a change in rates.

E. Cessation of Contributions.—The employer has the right to discontinue premium payments under the group annuity contract at any time. Discontinuance can be effected by a mere notice to the insurance company or by failure to pay a premium when due. The insurance company, on the other hand, can discontinue the contract only under the following conditions: (1) failure of the employer to pay premiums within the grace period; (2) reduction in number of employees covered under the contract below a specified number, such as 25 or 50, or, in the case of contributory plans, below 75 per cent of those employees eligible for coverage; (3) failure of the employer to consent to a new set of rates and conditions which the insurance company may promulgate under the terms of the contract.

Under the procedure of most companies, if a contract is discontinued, the annuities which have already been purchased automatically vest in the employees, except that if all past service benefits have not been purchased, any employer credits that might arise on termination of employment are applied to the purchase, under a prescribed procedure, of past service annuities for the employees remaining in the service of the employer. The contracts of some companies, however, state that vesting will not occur if the plan continues with another insurance company or trustee.

Most group annuity contracts contain a provision which permits reinstatement of the contract if application is made within a specified time, usually one year, after discontinuance. Some contracts go further and permit temporary suspensions of payments by mutual agreement between the employer and the insurance company, or even at the option of the employer. Under a Treasury ruling, employer contributions can be suspended only if the benefits to be paid under the contract are not affected at any time by the suspension and the unfunded past service does not exceed the initial past service liability.[29] In other words, any contributions or premiums which are suspended must be paid later. The significance of the requirement relating to the unfunded past service liability will be clear after the discussion of funding methods in the next chapter.

Strictly speaking, a group annuity contract is not terminated until the insurance company has fulfilled all its obligations under the contract. Therefore, in the usual circumstances, a group annuity contract will not be terminated until many years after discontinuance of premium payments. If a situation arises, however, under which there is no party to carry out the duties of the employer under the contract, the contract may be terminated, and thereafter the insurance company's obligations for the benefits purchased to the date of termination will be to the covered employees directly.

Deposit Administration Plan.—Deposit administration is a form of group annuity contract under which the contributions or premiums

29. P.S. No. 57, August 5, 1946.

are not applied to the purchase of annuities for individual employees until date of retirement or, in some plans, until the vesting requirements have been met. While the contract has been used on a limited scale for the last quarter-century, it has achieved new popularity in recent years as the insurance company's answer to the self-administered trusteed plan. It permits much greater flexibility in plan provisions than the rigid deferred group annuity, and the employer enjoys somewhat greater control over his contributions. It is usually confined to groups of 200 or more, although a few companies will write it on a group as small as 10. It has been widely used to underwrite negotiated pension plans which typically require a fairly high degree of flexibility.

A. Basic Features.—Under the deposit administration group annuity plan, all employer contributions are paid into an undivided fund which is variously described as the "deposit fund," "active life fund," or "deposit account." The monies paid in are commingled with the general assets of the insurance company, and the fund exists only as a bookkeeping account, based, however, on the contract guarantees. The fund is credited with a guarantee rate of interest specified in the contract. An immediate annuity in the appropriate amount is purchased for each employee as he reaches retirement, the required single premiums being transferred from the deposit fund. Some deposit administration contracts, however, provide for the purchase of a paid-up deferred annuity for all accrued benefits on the date that the employee satisfies the vesting requirements, with additional single premium deferred annuities being purchased each year thereafter until the employee retires. Another variation provides for the purchase of deferred annuities for future service credits upon completion of the vesting requirements and the purchase of an immediate annuity for past service credits at retirement.

Under contributory plans, annuities may be purchased with employee contributions as they are received, or at the time the vesting requirements are met, or at retirement. If either of the last two methods is used for employee contributions, the same method is normally used for the employer's future service contributions in order to simplify administrative procedure.

B. Benefit Structure.—The deposit administration contract can be used to finance a pension plan whose benefit structure follows the pattern of deferred group annuity contracts, but its real significance lies in its adaptability to plans which require a higher degree of flexibility than that which could be afforded by the deferred group annuity contract.

(1) Retirement Benefits.

(a) Eligibility for Participation.—To cope with the problem of high turnover among young and short-service employees, most insured pension plans provide that no employee may become a member of the plan until he has attained a specified age or performed a minimum period of service, or satisfied both conditions. This problem does not exist in noncontributory deposit administration plans, since no funds are allocated to individual employees prior to retirement or the completion of vesting requirements. No individual accounts are established, and, consequently, no annuities have to be cancelled when an employee withdraws from employment. Contributions can be discounted for expected turnover through the use of a turnover table or through a fixed policy of not contributing for short-service employees. For this reason it is possible to dispense with the conventional eligibility requirements in pension plans underwritten by a deposit administration contract. This may be an important advantage from the standpoint of employee relations.

Under contributory plans this flexibility is sacrificed when employer contributions are applied immediately to the purchase of deferred annuities.

(b) Benefit Formula.—The deposit administration contract may be readily used with any type of benefit formula, and need not be restricted to a plan which provides a unit of benefit for each year of service. It can be easily adapted to a final salary type of plan, since the annuity is normally not purchased until the employee has reached retirement and his benefit is definitely ascertainable. Social Security benefits may be included directly in the benefit formula, which creates serious administrative difficulties in the case of deferred group annuities. Early retirement benefits need not be limited to the actuarial equivalent of the benefits accrued up to the time of early retirement. Similarly, minimum benefits may be determined independently of the basic benefit formula.

(c) Retirement Age.—The deposit administration contract lends itself to a variable retirement age, whereas other types of insured plans are dependent on a fixed retirement age. Contributions can be based on an assumed distribution of retirements which, of course, should bear a reasonable relationship to past experience. It might be assumed, for example, that 5 per cent of the employees will retire at each age from 60 through 64, 40 per cent at age 65, 5 per cent at each age from 66 through 69, and 20 per cent at age 70. Annuities in the appropriate amounts are then purchased for the employees on the date of actual retirement.

(d) Annuity Forms.—In common with all other plans, the deposit administration contract assumes that the retirement benefits will be paid in accordance with a specific annuity form. The form specified is usually the life annuity with no guaranteed payments. Optional annuity forms are ordinarily made available except in plans which require an adjustment in the amount of an employee's annuity payments in the event there should be a change in his Social Security benefits after retirement. In that case, the benefits must be paid under a life annuity with no guaranteed instalments. The rules governing the election of an optional form are, in general, the same as those pertaining to deferred group annuity contracts.

(2) Withdrawal Benefits.—In contributory plans, the withdrawing employee is entitled to a return of his contributions, with or without interest. If individual deferred annuities have been purchased with employee contributions as they were received, with the resultant administrative expense, the insurance company will assess a 4 per cent surrender charge against the employee withdrawal value. The charge will be deducted from the deposit fund, however, and the employee will receive the full withdrawal value. No surrender charge is levied when the withdrawal does not involve cancellation of annuities.

(3) Death Benefits.—Death benefits are available on the same basis as under a deferred group annuity contract. Employee contributions are refunded, with or without interest, while employer contributions, not having been allocated to any particular individual, remain in the fund to provide benefits for employees who survive to retirement.

(4) Disability Benefits.—Disability benefits can be provided more readily under a deposit administration plan than under a deferred group annuity contract. If the plan promises disability benefits, the customary procedure is for the employer to make payments prior to the normal retirement age on a pay-as-you-go basis. At the normal retirement age, an immediate annuity for the benefits accrued up to the date of disability is purchased for the disabled employee by a withdrawal from the deposit fund as for any other employee. If the number of cases justifies it, some insurance companies will make the disability payments directly from the deposit fund. Under such an arrangement, the employer usually makes actuarially calculated contributions to the deposit fund for the payment of disability benefits.

Another manner in which disability benefits are sometimes provided is through the purchase of a temporary annuity running from date of disability to the normal retirement date or date of recovery, whichever is earlier. In the event that the employee recovers before normal retirement age, the value of the temporary annuity at date of recovery is credited to the deposit fund. If the disability continues to the normal retirement age, an immediate annuity is purchased for the employee from the deposit fund.

C. Premiums and Rates.

(1) Rate Factors.—Strictly speaking, the only premiums involved in a deposit administration contract are those applicable to the immediate annuities purchased at retirement. After the initial guarantee has expired, the premium rates charged for immediate annuities under a deposit administration contract are usually on the same basis as those charged for deferred group annuity contracts. The annuities are purchased on a gross single premium basis, which means that the premium contains an allowance for expenses. The loading is usually the same as that in a deferred group annuity premium—5 to 8 per cent.

Contributions to the deposit fund bear no fixed relationship to the premiums charged for the immediate annuities. The only requirement is that the contributions in the aggregate be sufficient to purchase an immediate annuity in the appropriate amount for each employee as he reaches retirement. The assumptions underlying the contributions need not be the same as those used in the calculation of insurance company premiums. It is feasible to assume rates of mortality that reflect actual experience more accurately than the rates assumed in premium calculations. The contributions can be discounted at a rate of interest approximately equivalent to that which the insurance company is actually crediting to group annuity funds for dividend purposes. Expense assumptions that reflect probable expenses under the particular contract can be used in lieu of the standard loading factor. Finally, allowance may be made for turnover, disability, early and delayed retirements, and salary changes. The calculations may be made by the insurance company or by an independent actuary retained by the employer.

Contributions are not made according to a fixed schedule set forth in the contract. They are initially based on estimated cost assumptions and thereafter are adjusted in accordance with actual experience. If experience under the contract indicates that the deposit fund is being built up at too slow a rate, the employer, as a matter of prudence, should step up his rate of contribution. If the experience is more favorable than the underlying assumptions, the rate of funding can be reduced and any excess funds applied against future contributions. The contract may specify maximum and minimum amounts which the employer may contribute in any contract year, or the amount of contribution may be determined by mutual agreement from year to year; but the employer, not the insurance company, is wholly responsible for the adequacy of the deposit fund.

(2) Rate Guarantees.—Every dollar paid to an insurance company under a deposit administration contract is given a permanent guarantee as to the rate of interest which will be credited to it annually and the schedule of annuity rates that will be applied to it. That is, the minimum rate of interest and the rate schedules that are in effect at the time a dollar is received apply to that dollar regardless of the time it is used to purchase an annuity.

Early deposit administration contracts guaranteed that the original set of annuity rates and the minimum rate of interest would apply to all contributions used to purchase annuities for employees covered under the contract during the first five years of its existence. Contracts issued currently, however, follow the pattern of the deferred group annuity contract and guarantee the initial annuity and interest rates only for contributions paid during the first five years of the contract. Thereafter, the guarantee runs from year to year.

In order to assure contributing employees the full protection of the guarantee, employee contributions are permanently allocated to the employees by whom they were made, either by the purchase of a single premium deferred annuity or by an earmarking process. With respect to employer contributions, however, the guarantee operates on the first-in, first-out principle. In other words, the contributions, with accumulated interest, are applied to the purchase of annuities in the order in which they were received by the insurance company.

D. Employer Credits.

(1) Withdrawal Credits.—Since employer contributions are never allocated to a specific individual prior to vesting or retirement, no employer credits would arise on termination of employment. Turnover is normally estimated, however, in determining the employer's contributions to the deposit fund, so, in effect, credit for withdrawals is taken in advance.

(2) Deferred Retirement Credits.—Under noncontributory deposit administration contracts, there are normally no employer credits for delayed retirement in the conventional sense, inasmuch as the annuity is not purchased until the employee retires. As was indicated earlier, however, employer contributions may be reduced initially in anticipation of a certain percentage of delayed retirements. Under contributory plans, and noncontributory plans which provide for purchase of annuities at point of vesting, the employer may receive credits for delayed retirements.

(3) Dividends or Premium Rate Adjustments.—The deposit administration contract provides for the payment of dividends, which are calculated in substantially the same manner as those under a deferred group annuity contract. Dividends are payable only with respect to those elements of cost which are guaranteed, i.e., interest on the deposit fund and purchased annuities, mortality among retired employees, and expenses for both active and retired employees. Variation of actual from assumed experience with respect to the nonguaranteed elements of cost, such as turnover, mortality among active employees, and rate of retirement, is reflected directly in adjustments to employer contributions. As a matter of fact, excess

interest may be credited directly to the deposit fund rather than through the dividend formula.

E. Discontinuance of the Contract.—The discontinuance of a deposit administration contract does not affect the annuities which have already been purchased. A definite procedure must be set forth, however, as to the disposition of the deposit fund. Any employee contributions in the fund are returned to the employees, either in cash or in the form of paid-up annuities. Employer funds can be disposed of in accordance with one of two basic methods. The first is to continue the operation of the plan until the deposit fund is liquidated. That method obviously provides full benefits for accrued credits for the employees nearest retirement and no benefits for some employees. The other general procedure is to apply the fund immediately to the purchase of deferred annuities on a pro rata basis. Some plans specify that the deposit fund is first to be applied to the purchase of all future service benefits, if possible, the balance being used to purchase a pro rata portion of the past service benefits for each employee. If the fund is not adequate to purchase all future service benefits credited to date of discontinuance, only a pro rata portion of the future service benefits is purchased. Other plans provide for the purchase of a pro rata portion of the future and past service benefits combined.

Many deposit administration contracts permit the deposit fund to be "cashed out" under certain circumstances.[30] It may be that the plan has become overfunded as a result of a change in the benefit formula or as a result of an increase in Social Security benefits which have been integrated in the benefit formula;[31] or the plan may be transferred to another agency, either at the request of the insurance company or on the petition of the employer. Under negotiated plans, it is common for the insurance company to reserve the right to discontinue the contract and transfer the deposit fund to another agency if the plan should subsequently be amended in such a manner as to render it impracticable to provide the benefits under a

30. See D. C. Bronson, et al., "Discussion of Pensions," Transactions of the Society of Actuaries, Vol. II, 1950, pp. 476-484.
31. The insurance company might prefer to return the excess funds to the employer rather than credit them against future contributions, inasmuch as the funds would enjoy the protection of a rate guarantee which the insurance company might not want to perpetuate.

deposit administration contract. Some contracts make no reference to a transfer of funds to another agency but, if the occasion should arise, a transfer can be worked out on a negotiated basis.

A 5 per cent liquidation charge is levied against the cashing out or transfer of the deposit fund. This charge is intended to cover not only the expenses incident to the liquidation and disbursement of money from the deposit fund but also all expenses, including commissions and premium taxes, which have been incurred on amounts paid into the fund. A portion of the charge is intended to reimburse the insurance company for the loss which it would sustain if the withdrawal should come at a time when the yield on its portfolio is less than that which can be obtained on new investments. Such a loss could be brought about through the forced sale of investments at less than their book value or, if the withdrawal were met by the use of premium income, through a reduction in the funds available for investment at the higher yields. In addition to the liquidation charge, the company usually reserves the right to pay the funds out over a ten-year period, with guaranteed interest, although the right may not be exercised.

Immediate Participation Guarantee Contract.—The immediate participation guarantee contract is a form of group annuity which has been developed within the last few years for the sole purpose of meeting the competition of the self-administered trusteed plan. It represents an attempt to combine in one contract the flexibility of the self-administered plan and the security of the insured plan. As might be expected, each of these attributes had to be compromised to some extent in the final product.

As has been indicated, the deposit administration contract permits almost complete flexibility in the coverage and benefit features of a pension plan; the only area in which more flexibility might be afforded is that of financing. While the cost of a pension plan underwritten by either a deferred group annuity or a deposit administration contract will, in the long run, be determined solely by its own experience, the insurance company, as a hedge against the guarantees provided under the contract, builds up a contingency fund from employer contributions which it administers free of employer control. Moreover, any savings that accrue from experience more favorable than was assumed with respect to the basic cost factors are credited to the employer only through the operation of the dividend formula, which is also under the exclusive jurisdiction of the insurance company. Many employers whose employee groups are large enough to experience average results relative to the basic cost factors would like to avail themselves of the insurance company's investment facilities and rate guarantees but object to the maintenance of a contingency reserve by the insurance company and, to a lesser extent, the insurance company's discretion as to dividends. Such employers would prefer to retain in their business the funds which the insurance company would place in the contingency reserve and offset any adverse fluctuations through future contributions.[32] It is toward this group of employers that the IPG contract is directed.

The IPG contract is still in the formative stage and is not written by all companies. It is normally restricted to employee groups of 2,000 or more, but at least one company will write it on much smaller groups. It is generally written on a noncontributory basis, although some companies will accept employee contributions.

In its structure, the IPG contract is merely an extension of the deposit administration contract and in the following sections only its distinctive features will be discussed.

A. Basic Features.—As under the deposit administration plan, a fund is established for each contract into which all employer contributions are deposited. The fund is credited annually with the net rate of interest earned by the insurance company on its total investment portfolio, adjusted for capital gains and losses. The fund is charged directly with all insurance company expenses allocable to the contract in accordance with established cost accounting techniques. Under some plans all benefit payments, including retirement benefits, are charged directly to the fund. Under other plans the fund is debited, as each employee reaches retirement, with the gross single premium needed to purchase the retirement benefits due the

---

32. It has been argued that contingency reserves are not as vital in the field of pensions as in life insurance, since no one grows old suddenly. Since contingency reserves in connection with retirement plans are for the purpose of meeting adverse experience that develops over a long period of time, the argument goes, the contingency fund could be dispensed with and the increased cost shifted to the employer on a current basis. This argument overlooks the fact that a substantial portion of the contingency reserve is for the purpose of protecting the company against capital losses.

employee. Under this arrangement, all annuities are cancelled, for accounting purposes, at the end of each contract year, and all sums not paid out as benefits during the year are returned to the fund, with interest equal to the net rate earned by the insurance company. At the beginning of the next contract year, new annuities are purchased for each retired employee still living, the premium being based on the attained age of the employee but on rates in effect at the time of his retirement. Irrespective of the procedure used to record benefit payments, the fund is automatically credited each year with any savings resulting from a higher death rate among the retired employees than that anticipated. In fact, the fund participates immediately in all savings arising out of more favorable experience than was anticipated, which, under a deposit administration contract, is true only of the unallocated fund and even then excess interest is sometimes credited only through the dividend formula. Moreover, except as noted below, no contingency reserve is maintained by the insurance company.

One of the few underwriting restrictions imposed by the insurance company—but a crucial one, nevertheless—requires the employer to maintain the fund at a level sufficient to provide full benefits to all employees who have retired. To implement this requirement, the insurance company sets up a reserve equal to the present value of all benefits payable to retired employees, calculated on the basis of the rate schedule in effect at the time the employees retired. The valuation is on a gross premium basis in order to assure that the annuities will be self-sustaining in the event that the contract should be discontinued. In this case, as with all group annuities, the loading would not only take care of expenses but would provide a margin for contingencies. Furthermore, the contract provides that if the fund should ever shrink to the point where it is just equal to the amount needed to provide benefits to retired employees, annuities will be purchased for such retired employees and the contract will revert to a conventional deferred group annuity contract. Thus, the retired employees have the insurance company's guarantee that they will receive the benefits to which they are entitled. The active employees have no such guarantee and occupy essentially the same position as active employees under the deposit administration contract.

B. Premiums and Rates.—The employer is granted wide latitude in making contributions to the IPG fund. The insurance company fixes a lower and upper limit to the annual contributions, but within those limits the employer can adapt his deposits to his financial circumstances and his estimate of future costs of the plan. The employer normally retains an actuarial consultant who determines the rate of funding on the basis of his judgment as to future mortality, interest earnings, expenses, turnover, rate of retirement, and other pertinent factors. Any deviations from the projected experience of the plan are reflected immediately in the condition of the fund. The employer, of course, is solely responsible for the adequacy of the fund and must make good any deficiency that might arise.

In general, annuities are "purchased" at whatever rates are in effect at the time the employe retires.[33] Some contracts, however, provide that all monies, with accumulated interest, deposited during the first five years of the contract shall be applied to the purchase of annuities at rates guaranteed in the contract. Year-to-year guarantees apply thereafter. One large company guarantees an initial schedule of rates for all annuities provided from the fund during the first ten contract years. This is quite different, obviously, from a guarantee that all monies deposited during the first ten years will be applied in accordance with a particular rate schedule.

Contrary to the practice under deposit administration plans, no minimum rate of interest is guaranteed on the IPG fund. It is credited with the actual rate earned by the insurance company.[34] Neither is the fund guaranteed against investment losses; it is charged with its pro rata share of capital losses and credited with its share of capital gains.

C. Discontinuance.—All IPG contracts provide for the automatic discontinuance of the plan when the fund falls to that level which the insurance company has actuarially determined to be necessary to provide benefits to all employees who have retired.

33. Annuities are not actually purchased under the IPG plan, but the same effect is obtained through the valuation of reserves on the basis of the rates in effect at the time the employee retires.
34. Some companies credit the fund with 1/40 per cent less than the earned rate in order to accumulate a small contingency reserve.

The contract thereupon ceases to provide for automatic adjustments to reflect actual experience under the plan and becomes, in effect, a closed annuity contract, participating as to dividends in the regular manner. The active employees would receive no part of the fund, and the future financing of their retirement credits would be a matter for the employer to resolve.

The employer, however, has the right under the contract to discontinue his contributions at any time. In such event, the plan might operate in the normal manner until the unapplied funds are exhausted, at which time it would become a closed annuity contract. An alternative procedure would be to apply the unallocated balance in the fund to the purchase, on some equitable basis, of deferred annuities for the active employees.

Some companies permit the employer, as a matter of contract, to transfer the IPG fund to another funding agency. Such a transfer would be subject to a surrender charge and possible restrictions on the rate at which the money could be withdrawn. Other companies will not guarantee the right of transfer but are willing to negotiate a transfer if the circumstances should justify it.

SELF-ADMINISTERED TRUSTEED PLAN

A self-administered trusteed plan is an arrangement under which contributions to provide pension benefits are deposited with a trustee, normally a trust company, who invests the money, accumulates the earnings, and pays benefits directly to eligible employees. The plan is to be distinguished from the type of self-administered plan which operates on the pay-as-you-go basis, without the services of a trust company. The self-administered trusteed plan is extensively used to underwrite the benefits of negotiated pension plans, although it is by no means restricted to that type of plan. Contributory as well as noncontributory plans are written on this basis.

The trust indenture is the formal document under which the plan operates. This is a written agreement between the employer and the trustee setting forth the terms under which the trust fund will be created and administered. The indenture must either include all the terms and conditions of the pension plan or incorporate it by reference, since the benefit payments are made from the trust fund in accordance with the provisions of the plan. The assets of the trust fund are not commingled with other assets of the trust company.

BENEFIT STRUCTURE

Retirement Benefits.—The self-administered plan, like the deposit administration group annuity, lends itself to any type of benefit formula. The plan may provide a unit of benefit for each year of service, expressed as a percentage of earnings or as a fixed dollar amount; or it may provide a flat benefit, unrelated to either earnings or service. A fairly common procedure is to express the benefit as a fraction, such as 1/60 or 1/70, of the final average earnings for each year of service. Formulas which provide for direct offsetting of Social Security benefits, disability benefits, variable retirement ages, and other such features, can be underwritten with no difficulty. The reason for this, of course, is that the benefits are paid by the employer—through the medium of the trust—and it is not essential that the cost of such benefits be determined as precisely as would be required if they were being purchased from a third party, i.e., an insurance company.

If the plan is contributory, employee contributions are frequently administered on a money-purchase basis. For accounting purposes, an individual account is established for each employee. The account is credited with the employee's contributions, plus a rate of interest equal to the average rate earned on the entire fund. At retirement, the balance in the employee's account is used to provide an annuity on an actuarial basis established for that purpose.

The plan may provide for a normal retirement age, or it may permit an employee who has satisfied the minimum service requirements to retire at any age within a specified range of ages. In the latter case, assumptions would have to be made, for funding purposes, as to the number of employees who will retire at the different ages within the permissible range.

The normal form of annuity used under a self-administered plan is the straight life annuity which, it will be recalled, makes no provision for a refund at the time of the employee's death. Most plans, however, provide the same optional forms of annuity as are available under insured plans, particularly the joint and survivorship annuity. Practice varies as to whether optional forms of annuities must be elected a specified time prior to retirement or else supported by evidence of insurability. When such a requirement is not invoked, the trust fund is exposed to adverse selection.

Some plans provide that the trustee shall purchase an immediate annuity of the appropriate amount for each employee as he reaches retirement. Such an arrangement is sometimes called *terminal reinsurance*. The purpose of this procedure may be twofold. As an administrative matter, it may be more economical for the insurance company to send out the pension checks than for the employer or trustee to do so. More important, however, particularly when the number of pensioners is small, is the fact that the employer avoids the hazards and uncertainties of providing lifetime benefits to his employees out of his own funds. Under such a procedure, the annuities are purchased at current rates.

Withdrawal Benefits.—On termination of employment, the employee will receive a return of his contributions, with or without interest. Vesting of employer contributions in the event of withdrawal is far less common among self-administered plans than among insured plans. This is partly due to the lack of adequate facilities for keeping track of persons with vested benefits.

Death Benefits.—Death benefits after retirement are a function of the annuity form under which the retirement benefits are paid. Death benefits before retirement depend upon the provisions of the plan. If the plan is contributory, there will always be a death benefit equal to the total accumulations in the employee's account at the time of his death. Employer contributions, however, rarely vest at the employee's death. Self-administered plans resemble deferred group annuity plans in that no death benefits, other than return of the employee's contributions, are generally made available as an integral part of the plan, such benefits being provided, if at all, in the form of a separate group life insurance plan.

Nevertheless, if the employer should so desire, death benefits in any amounts can be provided directly from the trust fund. This involves an element of risk, however, that is not present in the underwriting of retirement benefits. Abnormally heavy mortality may be experienced during a short period of time, creating a serious drain on the fund, whereas any adverse mortality among annuitants is, by the very nature of the arrangement, spread over a long period of time. This risk is lessened as the size of the employee group increases. Furthermore, the loss occasioned by heavy mortality is offset to a substantial extent by the release of funds that were being accumulated for the payment of retirement benefits, particularly at the higher ages where the heavier mortality generally occurs.

Disability Benefits.—Disability benefits, other than those inherent in early retirement provisions, are generally not provided under self-administered plans, with the exception of negotiated plans which frequently include a special disability benefit. Employer attitudes toward disability benefits are undoubtedly influenced by the generally unfavorable experience of insurance companies with *personal* disability income coverage. There is general agreement, however, that an employer, because of his peculiar relationship to his employees, is in a position to administer a disability benefit more effectively than an insurance company.[35] Neverthelesss, most employers have shown little disposition to offer direct disability benefits under self-administered plans.

PREMIUMS AND RATES

The self-administered plan is a form of self-insurance, with a trustee providing investment services and performing such administrative functions as may be agreed upon between the employee and the trustee. There are no premiums in the conventional sense, only deposits with the trustee. The magnitude of the deposits is determined by a consulting actuary who is retained and paid by the employer.

In general, the contributions to the trust fund are based on the consulting actuary's estimate as to the "most probable" cost of the pension plan. Whereas insurance company actuaries utilize assumptions that contain recognized margins of safety, the consulting actu-

35. It should be observed that an eminent actuary, with wide experience in the field of group annuities, has stated that under an insured plan employers view the disability provision as a means of ridding themselves of inefficient employees who are not old enough to retire and yet are not permanently and totally disabled in the medical sense. R. A. Hohaus, "Further Remarks on Group Annuities", *Record of the American Institute of Actuaries,* Vol. XXIII, 1934, p. 338. The employers might be expected to take another view of the provision if they must pay the benefits directly.

ary uses assumptions with much smaller margins or, in some cases, no margins, in order to keep the employer's initial outlay for pensions as low as possible.

Employer contributions are almost invariably discounted for anticipated mortality, disability, and turnover. This is accomplished through the use of a so-called "Experience Table," which reflects not only the death rate for each age represented in the eligible group of employees but also the disability and turnover rates.[36] These three sets of rates are applied to a hypothetical group of employees coming under the plan at the youngest permissible age in order to forecast the number of such employees who will remain with the employer until retirement. The death and disability rates may be taken from annuity and disability tables developed by life insurance companies, modified by the consulting actuary if desired, but the withdrawal rates should properly reflect the past and prospective experience of the employer involved. The table which reflects the number of employees out of the original group who are assumed to be with the employer at the various possible ages is called a "Service" table. A combination Experience and Service Table which is representative of those used in connection with self-administered plans is presented in Table 5.

It will be noted from the Service Table that at each age the various rates of death, withdrawal, and disability may be combined and applied to the number of employees in that age group in order to determine the attrition for the year. At age 30, for example, the combined rates produce a total decrement of 2,537 employees, withdrawals accounting for all but 37. According to the table, only 1,735 employees out of an original group of 10,000 who began their service at age 30 will remain with the employer until retirement. For each higher age group a larger percentage of the employees will remain with the employer until retirement. It is assumed that no employee over 50 would voluntarily leave the service of the employer.

The application of a table of this nature to an actual group of employees will provide an estimate as to the number of employees to whom retirement benefits will have to be paid. If no other benefits

---

36. Some experience tables also contain a column showing the estimated salary progression from age to age. Such a salary scale merely sets forth *average* salaries for each age group and does not purport to reflect the actual salary that a particular employee might receive.

TABLE 5

COMBINED EXPERIENCE AND SERVICE TABLE

	Experience Table		

Age	Mortality Rates[*]	Withdrawal Rates	Disability Rates[†]
30	.00207	.25	.0016
31	.00221	.17	.0016
32	.00238	.13	.0017
33	.00256	.09	.0018
34	.00276	.07	.0018
35	.00298	.05	.0019
36	.00322	.04	.0020
37	.00347	.04	.0021
38	.00374	.03	.0022
39	.00404	.03	.0023
40	.00436	.03	.0024
41	.00470	.02	.0025
42	.00507	.02	.0026
43	.00547	.02	.0028
44	.00590	.02	.0030
45	.00636	.02	.0031
46	.00686	.01	.0034
47	.00740	.01	.0037
48	.00798	.01	.0040
49	.00861	.01	.0044
50	.00929	.01	.0048
51	.01002		.0052
52	.01081		.0057
53	.01165		.0061
54	.01257		.0068
55	.01355		.0076
56	.01461		.0086
57	.01576		.0098
58	.01699		.0113
59	.01832		.0131
60	.01975		.0152
61	.02130		.0179
62	.02296		.0211
63	.02475		.0253
64	.02668		.0300
65			

[*] This column reflects the rates of the 1937 Standard Annuity Table.

[†] This column is used only if disability benefits are to be provided; otherwise, terminations from disability would be combined with withdrawals.

TABLE 5—Continued

COMBINED EXPERIENCE AND SERVICE TABLE

	Service Table				
Age	Number Remaining in Service	Number With-drawing From Service	Number Disabled in Service	Number Dying in Service	Total Number Terminat-ing Service
30	10,000	2,500	16	21	2,537
31	7,463	1,269	12	16	1,297
32	6,166	802	10	15	827
33	5,339	480	10	14	504
34	4,835	338	9	13	360
35	4,475	224	9	13	246
36	4,229	169	8	14	191
37	4,038	162	8	14	184
38	3,854	116	9	14	139
39	3,715	111	9	15	135
40	3,580	107	9	16	132
41	3,448	69	9	16	94
42	3,354	67	9	17	93
43	3,261	65	9	18	92
44	3,169	63	10	19	92
45	3,077	61	10	20	91
46	2,986	30	10	20	60
47	2,926	29	11	22	62
48	2,864	29	11	23	63
49	2,801	28	12	24	64
50	2,737	27	13	26	66
51	2,671		14	27	41
52	2,630		15	28	43
53	2,587		16	30	46
54	2,541		17	32	49
55	2,492		19	34	53
56	2,439		21	36	57
57	2,382		23	38	61
58	2,321		26	40	66
59	2,255		30	41	71
60	2,184		33	43	76
61	2,108		38	45	83
62	2,025		43	46	89
63	1,936		49	48	97
64	1,839		55	49	104
65	1,735				

are provided under the plan, this is the only figure that has significance for the employer. By the use of a salary progression table, the dollar value of the benefits to be paid out can be determined. Then the employer can set aside only such sums, improved at an assumed rate of interest, as will be needed to provide the promised benefits.

It can be seen that by this procedure an employer's initial outlay is much smaller than it would be if he assumed that every employee on his payroll at a particular time would, barring death, remain in his service until retirement. This is one of the strong appeals of the self-administered plan. In the long run, of course, the cost would be equalized, since under those plans which do not discount contributions for withdrawals the employer is credited with the sums released as the actual withdrawals occur. Some self-administered plans, however, follow the conventional insurance approach of discounting for only mortality and interest, while it is quite common for contributions under deposit administration and IPG contracts to be discounted for withdrawals and adjusted in accordance with salary progression tables.

The experience under the plan is reviewed periodically, perhaps annually, but no less frequently than every five years, and appropriate adjustments are made in future contributions. The employer assumes the obligation of making up any losses resulting from the cost assumptions used and reaps the advantages of any gains.

There are no guarantees of any sort under the self-administered plan. The trustee agrees only to invest the sums deposited with it in accordance with the trust agreement and applicable statutes, using due care in the process. Neither the principal nor the investment return is guaranteed by the trustee. Nor does the consulting actuary guarantee to indemnify the fund for any losses arising out of erroneous actuarial assumptions. On the other hand, the larger trust companies have investment facilities comparable to those of the largest life insurance companies, and those facilities are equally available to all pension trusts administered by the trust companies. Furthermore, the great majority of actuarial consultants are competent technicians who are presumably making their cost calculations on a reasonably conservative basis.

DISCONTINUANCE

Whenever a self-administered plan is discontinued, the balance in the trust fund can be allocated among active and retired employees in any manner that does not violate the regulations of the Internal Revenue Service. Successive preferential classes of employees similar to those found in insured plans are usually established.

The self-administered plan, however, is faced with a problem in the event of discontinuance that is not present in an insured plan. The fund must be liquidated over a period of time and the latter stages of this process may involve the forced sale of assets and other investment difficulties. Furthermore, the employer must continue to meet the expenses of the plan or else charge them to the fund, thereby diminishing the benefits that can be paid. These problems can be avoided by the purchase of annuities from an insurance company at the time of discontinuance.

COMBINATION PLAN

When it is desired to provide substantial death benefits as an integral part of a pension plan, a combination of insurance and a trust fund may be used. The insurance contracts provide the death benefits and a portion of the principal sum needed to provide the retirement benefits. The additional sums needed to purchase the retirement benefits are accumulated in an auxiliary fund, administered by a trust company under the terms of a trust.[37] The insurance policies contain a provision which permits them to be converted to an annuity contract on or immediately prior to the employee's retirement.

Any type of life insurance contract which provides protection to the time of retirement and accumulates a cash value can be used. As a matter of practice, an ordinary life contract, or a modified version thereof, is usually used. The coverage may be made available through individual contracts, if the number of employees is small, or through a group permanent contract, if the number of employees is large enough to qualify for group coverage.

37. As was pointed out on p. 78, the additional sums may be accumulated through an auxiliary fund administered by a life insurance company on the deposit administration principle.

TABLE 6

ACCUMULATED VALUES IN AUXILIARY TRUST FUND
FOR EACH $10 UNIT OF RETIREMENT INCOME*

Age at Entry	Annual Contribution	Accumulation in Trust at End of Year:		
		1	2	3
Males:				
25	$ 10.25	$ 10.25	$ 20.79	$ 31.62
35	17.46	17.46	35.44	53.96
45	34.93	34.93	71.04	108.41
55	100.19	100.19	204.78	314.26
Females:				
25	12.28	12.28	24.92	37.90
35	20.73	20.73	42.08	64.08
45	40.96	40.96	83.29	127.12
55	115.38	115.38	235.81	361.89

BENEFIT STRUCTURE

The benefits under a combination plan are essentially the same as those under an individual contract or group permanent plan. Retirement benefits are payable only in multiples of $10 per month, the payments being guaranteed for ten years. Optional annuity forms are available. Unlike the death benefits under those plans, however, which for a few years prior to retirement may exceed the face of the policy, the death benefits under the combination plan remain equal to the face amount up to the date of conversion. Conversion normally takes place at date of retirement, or, as required by some companies, on the policy anniversary one year prior to retirement.

The termination values under this type of plan are also available on a slightly different basis from those of individual contract and group permanent plans. Depending upon the vesting provisions of the plan, the withdrawal benefits may consist of the cash values of the applicable insurance contracts and a supplemental amount from the auxiliary fund. Employee contributions, if any, are normally applied as premiums on the insurance contracts, with any excess, and the employer's contributions, going into the auxiliary fund. It is not customary for the employer's contributions to vest in the employees.

TABLE 6—Continued

ACCUMULATED VALUES IN AUXILIARY TRUST FUND
FOR EACH $10 UNIT OF RETIREMENT INCOME*

Age at Entry	Annual Contribution	Accumulation in Trust at End of Year:		
		5	10	Age 65†
Males:				
25	$ 10.25	$ 54.22	$ 116.83	$1,043.79
35	17.46	92.75	201.60	1,103.61
45	34.93	187.39	415.89	1,200.36
55	100.19	550.37	1,283.91	1,365.98
Females:				
25	12.28	64.98	140.00	1,250.82
35	20.73	110.15	239.41	1,310.64
45	40.96	219.71	487.62	1,407.39
55	115.38	633.78	1,478.50	1,573.01

* Payments guaranteed for ten years.

† The sums in this column supplement the cash value at age 65 of a Life Paid-Up at 85 policy, calculated on the basis of the C.S.O. Table and 2½ per cent interest.

PREMIUMS AND RATES

The life insurance policies under this plan are purchased on a level premium basis at the regular rates of the insurance company. The company guarantees the rates only for the policies which have already been purchased. Contracts to be purchased in the future for either old or new employees are subject to the rates in effect at time of purchase.[38]

Rates for the immediate annuities to be purchased at retirement are likewise guaranteed only as to the policies which have been issued. In other words, the guarantee is limited to the number of retirement units represented in the life insurance policies in force. This means, however, that the conversion cost of each insurance policy is guaranteed.

With respect to the auxiliary fund, the insurance company usually furnishes a table of valuation factors which shows the amount which

38. When the life insurance coverage is provided under group permanent policies, the company may guarantee the rates, including those for immediate annuities at retirement, for coverage effective within the first three to five years after the inauguration of the plan.

should be in the fund at the end of each year for each unit of retirement income. Such a table assumes a certain rate of mortality among the active employees and a certain rate of interest earnings. Although entirely practicable, no allowance is normally made for turnover, credit being taken whenever it occurs. From this valuation table can be determined the aggregate amount which should be in the fund at the end of any particular year. The difference between such sum and the actual balance in the fund is the amount which the employer should contribute in that year if the plan is to remain fully funded. If this procedure is followed, the employer is credited directly and immediately for any gains and charged with any losses relative to the basic assumptions.

This valuation process may be more easily grasped by reference to Table 6, which is an extract from the table of valuation factors used by one of the leading life insurance companies. The table shows the level annual contribution that would be required at the selected ages at entry for each $10 of monthly income at age 65, if the assumed experience under the plan is exactly realized in practice. Automatic adjustments for deviations from assumed experience may be accomplished by the use of the other columns. For example, at the end of three years, the trustee should be holding $53.96 for each $10 of retirement income due a male employee who entered the plan at age 35. If the trustee is actually holding $56.00 at the end of the third year because of turnover, higher interest earnings than assumed, or more deaths than were expected, the employer can contribute $2.04 less the following year. If, however, the trustee is holding a smaller sum than the table prescribes, the employer must make up the deficit, in addition to contributing the regular deposit.

The sum shown under "Age 65" for any age at entry is the amount by which the cash value of each $1,000 of life insurance coverage must be supplemented in order to provide $10 of monthly income at age 65. According to the actuarial assumptions of this particular company, $1,624 must be on hand at age 65 for each $10 unit of monthly life income payable to a male employee, with payments guaranteed for ten years. For a female employee, $1,825 is required because of her longer life expectancy. The cash value per $1,000 of insurance coverage on a male employee who entered the plan at age 35, for example, amounts to $552.53 at age 65. The difference between this sum and $1,624, increased by a 3 per cent conversion charge, equals $1,103.61, the amount in the auxiliary fund. The same procedure applies at all ages.

An employer need not follow the rigid funding pattern prescribed in the table of valuation factors prepared by the insurance company. The table is only a guide, and the employer is free to adopt any funding pattern which suits his circumstances. The insurance company has no responsibility for either the accumulation or the management of the auxiliary fund. The insurance company merely agrees to provide annuities on a stipulated price basis; the employer, with the advice of a consulting actuary, must schedule his contributions in such a manner as to accumulate the necessary funds.

Methods of Financing 4

THE foregoing chapter outlined the basic features of the various contractual arrangements under which the benefits of a pension plan may be provided. This chapter will describe and illustrate the various techniques by which the sums required to provide the benefits of a pension plan can be accumulated or budgeted. These budgeting arrangements are usually referred to as *funding methods*, while the legal instruments, such as a group annuity contract, under which the funding arrangements operate, are properly called *funding media*. The ultimate true cost of a pension plan is in no wise affected by the choice of funding method. Yet, the funding method determines how much of the ultimate cost of a plan is to be met during any particular period of time.

Underlying the funding process are certain concepts which should be clearly understood. The most basic, perhaps, is that of *normal cost* which may be defined as that level of contributions that would currently be required under a particular funding method if the plan had been in effect and contributions had been made in accordance with such funding method from the earliest date of credited service and all actuarial assumptions had been exactly realized. The normal cost varies as between funding methods, particularly during the early years of a plan, but as the years go by and the employee group (including pensioners) matures, the normal cost will, in theory, stabilize at a level which is identical under several of the conventional funding methods.

The *accrued liability* of a pension plan, as of any given time, represents the difference between the present value of future benefits and the present value of future normal costs.[1] It reflects not only the present value of benefits credited for service prior to the effective

1. Accrued liability may be viewed retrospectively as the accumulation of all past normal costs incurred under the plan.

126

date of the plan but also the present value of all benefits credited for service subsequent to the effective date of the plan, up to the date of valuation. It follows, therefore, that the accrued liability grows with the passage of time, attaining its ultimate level only when the plan has matured and benefits to retired employees have reached their peak.

The accrued liability on the effective date of a pension plan is commonly referred to as the *initial accrued liability*. While originating in credited past service, the initial accrued liability is precisely equal to the present value of past service benefits only under the single premium method of funding, which makes a clear-cut distinction between past service and future service benefits. In connection with the latter method of funding, it is customary—and proper—to speak of the initial accrued liability as the *initial past service liability* and accrued liability as past service liability, meaning all service prior to the date of valuation.

The essence of the funding process is the accumulation of assets, in a segregated fund, to offset the liabilities arising under the pension plan. The sums set aside may be adequate, with future interest earnings, to pay all benefits which have accrued at a particular time, which might be designated as full funding, or, a more common situation, they may be adequate to meet only a portion of the accrued liability, which reflects a condition of only partial funding. That portion of the accrued liability of a pension plan which is not offset by assets is termed the *unfunded accrued liability*.

DISBURSEMENT APPROACH

All budgeting arrangements do not contemplate the accumulation of a pension fund. The simplest approach and, historically, the traditional one is for the employer to disburse the benefits as they become due. This is sometimes referred to as the pay-as-you-go approach or, derisively, as the owe-as-you-go approach. Under this plan, retirement benefits are treated as payroll costs and are paid directly to the superannuated employees by the employer. Such benefits, if reasonable in amount, are deductible from the employer's gross income as a necessary business expense and are taxable to the recipient as ordinary income. No distinction is made between past service and future service benefits since under this arrangement such a distinction would be meaningless.

The cost of providing retirement benefits under this method is normally low during the early years of a company's existence, since the number of retired employees is relatively small and no provisions are being made to meet the accruing benefits of those employees who are still working. As the employee group matures, however, a constantly increasing number of persons are added to the retired rolls until eventually retirement benefits constitute a significant percentage of the total payroll costs. In fact, for reasons which will be evident later, the annual outlay under this arrangement, expressed as a percentage of payroll, ultimately reaches a level that is considerably higher than that of any other financing method. Not infrequently the contributions become so burdensome that the pension plan must be abandoned or drastically modified.

In order to anticipate the heavy drain on cash resources that this method ultimately entails, some companies set up a balance sheet reserve for pensions. This action may involve the earmarking of specific assets for the payment of pension benefits, or it may be limited to a restriction against surplus, similar to a reserve for depreciation. In either case it does not place any assets beyond the control of the employer and fails, therefore, to insulate the pension benefits against the financial vicissitudes of the employer. Moreover, the reserve may not be established nor maintained on the basis of actuarial estimates of the liabilities of the pension plan. A final weakness of the balance sheet reserve from the standpoint of the employer is that the sums transferred to the reserve are not deductible as an ordinary and necessary business expense. To be deductible, such sums would have to be placed beyond the control of the employer as by transfer to a trustee under a suitably drawn trust agreement or payment to an insurance company for the purchase of benefits. The benefits, nevertheless, are deductible in the tax year in which paid.

Though once dominant, the disbursement method of pension financing is used only on a limited scale among larger employers today.

TERMINAL FUNDING

There is no funding in the proper sense of the term in connection with the disbursement method. The employer underwrites the bene-

fits and pays them out of current operating income. The receipt of
benefits by the employees is completely dependent upon the employer's willingness and ability to pay them. The employees can look
to no earmarked fund, irrevocably committed to the payment of
pension benefits and administered by an impartial third party, for
the satisfaction of their claims. Retired employees, however, can
be provided with a high degree of security through an arrangement
known as terminal funding.

Terminal funding is a compromise between no funding and full
funding. Under this arrangement, the benefits payable to retired
employees are funded in full, while the benefits standing to the
credit of the active employees are completely unfunded. This funding may be accomplished through the purchase of an immediate
annuity in the appropriate amount for each employee as he reaches
retirement or by the transfer to a trust company of a principal sum
actuarially estimated to be sufficient to provide the benefits promised. The principal sums required for such transactions normally
come out of the operating income of the employer, since by definition the employer makes no advance provision, other than through
the possible creation of a balance sheet reserve, for the accumulation
of the sums needed. If otherwise eligible, such sums are deductible
for Federal income tax purposes at such time as they are transferred
to the insurance company or the trust company.[2]

The terminal funding device is frequently used among negotiated
pension plans, a trust company usually serving as the funding
agency. Under most of these plans the employer is legally obligated
to provide retirement benefits only to those employees who retire
during the term of the labor agreement. The benefits, nevertheless,
must be continued throughout the lifetime of such employees even
though the pension plan should be terminated. Although the pre-
sumption exists that the plan is a permanent venture and will be
extended by mutual agreement to provide benefits to those employees who retire beyond the term of the current contract, many
employers prefer not to fund for any employees who cannot qualify
for benefits during the current agreement. In other cases, the financial commitment to which the employer agreed is no more than

2. The conditions under which contributions under the terminal funding
arrangement are deductible for tax purposes are set forth in PS No. 67, April
26, 1951.

adequate to provide benefits on a completely funded basis to those employees who have retired.[3] The terminal funding plan meets the demands of either situation.

ADVANCE FUNDING

The term "advance funding" may be applied to any arrangement under which sums intended for the payment of retirement benefits are set aside under proper legal safeguards in advance of the date of actual retirement. It does not necessarily imply full funding, since it is usually many years after a plan has been established before the accrued liability is fully funded. In fact, the initial accrued liability may never be funded, a practice which is referred to as "freezing" the initial accrued liability.[4] It usually implies, as a minimum, that sufficient funds are set aside each year to meet the pension obligations created in that year, plus an amount equal to the interest on the unfunded past service liability. As a matter of practice, virtually all plans which follow the advance funding approach set aside each year enough funds to pay the benefits credited during that year, plus a portion of the initial past service liability, with a view toward having all obligations fully funded at the earliest practicable date. The advanced funding approach is the conventional financing technique used in pension plans today.

Arguments for and Against Advance Funding

There are several arguments in favor of advance funding, the most persuasive undoubtedly being the financial advantage. The out-of-pocket cost of providing pensions is much smaller under the advance funding method of financing than under either of the other two methods. For example, an employer would pay out $17,200 on the pay-as-you-go basis if he were to provide $100 a month to an employee who retires at age 65 and lives out the life expectancy

3. In the case of several negotiated welfare and retirement funds, current disbursements are approximately equal to current contributions. In effect, these plans are on a pay-as-you-go basis. Many negotiated plans are silent as to funding provisions, the emphasis being on the benefits to be paid.

4. See p. 144. If the initial accrued liability is frozen, contributions to the plan may well be smaller than those under a terminal funding arrangement. In fact, under a mature plan such a funding policy would, in theory, produce contributions precisely equal to those required under a pay-as-you-go plan.

accorded him under the 1937 Standard Annuity Table. Under the terminal funding arrangement, however, with the cost calculated on the basis of the 1937 Standard Annuity Table, 2½ per cent interest, and no allowance for expenses, the employer would need to set aside at the employee's age 65 only $13,766. Finally, if the sum required to provide the benefits were to be accumulated through a series of level annual instalments, extending from age 30 to age 65, discounted for interest but not for mortality, the cost would aggregate only $8,558, or approximately 50 and 62 per cent, respectively, of the cost under the disbursement and terminal funding methods.

The difference in the out-of-pocket cost under the three methods of financing is, of course, wholly attributable to the interest factor. Under the disbursement plan, the employer's contributions obviously earn no interest, and the total cost is the sum of the individual payments. In the case of the immediate annuity, the benefits are discounted for interest, and the employer, in effect, is credited with 2½ per cent interest on the unliquidated portion of the single premium. Under the advance funding scheme, each annual instalment earns 2½ per cent interest from date of payment until the time it is disbursed as a retirement benefit. Over the period of years, the sums which the employer contributes are credited with $8,642 in interest.[5]

These interest earnings should properly be viewed as a part of the cost of the pension plan. They represent money which presumably would have been earned if the sums transferred to the plan had been invested elsewhere. In fact, the counter argument for nonfunding is that such funds will earn more in the employer's business than in the hands of a separate funding agency. While this may be true on a gross yield basis, it should be remembered that under a pension plan which meets Treasury specifications interest earnings are not taxable. Therefore, at current tax rates a corporate employer would have to have an earnings rate, before taxes, at least double that of the funding agency in order to net the same rate. Furthermore, the funding agency credits the pension accumulations with the actual rate of interest earned, which is normally in excess of 3 per cent, rather than with the 2½ per cent assumed in the illustration.

5. The employer's outlay would be reduced by another $2,018 if his contributions were discounted for mortality prior to age 65 in accordance with the 1937 Standard Annuity Table. His outlay could be reduced by another $2,321 by applying a moderate discount for turnover.

A second argument for advance funding is the higher degree of security afforded the participants in the pension plan. Under the disbursement or pay-as-you-go arrangement, the employees are completely dependent upon the solvency of the employer. Under the terminal funding approach, retired employees can look to a separate agency for payment of their benefits, but the active employees enjoy no such protection and are just as dependent on the continued existence of the business as are the employees under a disbursement arrangement. Under the advance funding scheme, however, all employees, active and retired, enjoy the added measure of security afforded by a segregated fund dedicated to the payment of their retirement benefits. If the plan is fully funded, on the basis of conservative assumptions, all benefits which have accrued as of a particular time can be paid without further contributions from the employer. If the plan is only partially funded, the employees obviously enjoy a lesser degree of security.[6]

A third argument, which is closely related to the foregoing, is that advance funding facilitates the vesting of employer contributions, which is considered to be socially desirable. A vesting provision is basically inconsistent with either the disbursement or terminal funding method of financing. There is an inherent assumption under these two arrangements that no benefits will be disbursed until the employee reaches retirement, although benefits naturally could be provided earlier. It is generally assumed, however, that if employer contributions vest prior to retirement, the funds necessary to meet the accrued obligations should be accumulated by the earlier date. Certainly, the security attached to such vested benefits is greatly enhanced by advance funding.

A final argument in favor of advance funding is that it forces each generation of workers to pay for its own pensions.[7] This argument is fraught with economic ramifications but, in essence, it rests on the assumption that if the cost of pensions is added to the cost of production, and presumably to the price of the commodities produced,

6. It is interesting to observe that the concept of advance funding is based on the assumption that the pension plan will eventually terminate. If it could be assumed that a plan would continue in perpetuity, no reserves would be necessary. They might still be desirable, however, as a source of tax-exempt earnings and as a device for the leveling of costs.

7. See Arthur H. Dean, "Accounting for the Cost of Pensions," *Harvard Business Review,* Vol. XXVIII, No. 5, September, 1950, pp. 102-22.

in the year in which the benefits accrue, the increased prices will cause the generation of active workers to consume less than they would otherwise, thus conserving economic resources for their old age. The argument is complicated by the fact that there is no general agreement among economists as to the manner in which pension costs are borne by the employer, the employees, and the consuming public. In any case, the argument is valid only if the funds set aside for pensions are invested in capital improvements that will increase the flow of consumer goods in the future. Otherwise, the generation of retired workers would still be subsisting on the production of the younger generation.

The arguments against advance funding are few. The most serious one is that the funding process removes and segregates increasingly large sums of corporate funds which might be retained to better advantage for use as venture capital. From the standpoint of one employer, it involves the question of whether it would be more profitable to retain the funds in the business than to have them invested by a separate agency. From the standpoint of the economy as a whole, however, it raises the issue as to whether venture capital is being drained away from corporate enterprises more rapidly than it is being returned through investment channels.

A less serious argument against advance funding is that it involves a loss of flexibility and maneuverability. An unfunded plan can be operated without Treasury interference, whereas a funded plan, if it is to qualify for tax deductions, must meet the specifications of the tax laws.

STATUTORY LIMITATIONS ON ADVANCE FUNDING

In order to prevent the employer from funding his pension obligations in a manner that would afford him the greatest tax advantage, the Congress has imposed certain maximum limitations on the rate at which a plan can be funded. These limitations are set forth in Subparagraphs (A), (B), and (C) of Section 404(a)(1) of the Internal Revenue Code and are applied as alternative tests. As a general rule, however, the employer must select the basis under which he will seek deductions and adhere to it. He cannot shift freely from one basis to the other in an effort to obtain maximum tax deductions.

The first test laid down in the law is known as the Five Per Cent Rule. Under this rule the employer is presumptively entitled to deduct annually an amount not in excess of 5 per cent of the compensation paid to employees covered under the plan. The law requires the Commissioner of Internal Revenue to audit the financial operations of the plan at not less than five-year intervals, and empowers him to reduce the permissible deduction if it appears from the actuarial evidence that the cost of the plan is less than 5 per cent of compensation. The annual cost of a pension plan, of course, will normally be considerably in excess of 5 per cent of compensation, particularly during the period that the past service liability is being liquidated. This provision would have been rather restrictive, therefore, if relief had not been afforded through the other two tests.

The second test, or Straight-Line Rule as it is usually called, permits the employer to deduct any amount in excess of 5 per cent of compensation "necessary to provide with respect to all of the employees under the trust the remaining unfunded cost of their past and current service credits distributed as a level amount, or as a level percentage of compensation, over the remaining future service of each such employee . . ." This simply means that an employer can deduct each year such sum as is needed to provide on a level contribution basis the total benefits payable under the pension plan. The calculation can be made with respect to each individual employee or on an aggregate basis, but the actuarial assumptions must meet the approval of the Treasury authorities. Under this rule, there is no limitation as to the minimum number of years over which the cost of an employee's benefits must be spread, except "if such remaining unfunded cost with respect to any three individuals is more than 50 per centum of such remaining unfunded cost, the amount of such unfunded cost attributable to such individuals shall be distributed over a period of at least 5 taxable years . . ." In other words, if more than half of the cost of a pension plan is attributable to the benefits payable to any three employees, who in the normal case would be officers of the company, the contributions would have to be spread over at least five taxable years.

The third, or Past Service Rule, states that the employer may deduct, in lieu of the amounts allowed under the two previous rules, a sum equal to the normal cost of the plan, plus 10 per cent of the initial past service liability.[8] Referred to as the "standard 10 per cent base," this sum can be increased only through a retroactive increase in benefits or through correction of an actuarial error.[9]

The last mentioned rule is the one that regulates employer contributions under most pension plans. In most cases, the initial past service liability is of such magnitude that its liquidation requires financial management of the highest order. In the absence of restrictive legislation, an employer could be expected to liquidate his past service liability in a manner that would yield the greatest tax savings. If possible, the liquidation would be concentrated during a few years of unusual profits, when the costs could be charged off against income taxes, and in recent years against the excess profits tax. To forestall this loss of tax revenue, the law provides that no more than 10 per cent of the initial past service liability may be deducted in any one tax year. Since the initial past service liability is an interest-bearing item, representing a discounted value, liquidation at the rate of 10 per cent per year requires between eleven and twelve years, depending upon the rate of interest assumed.

The enactment of this limitation created a possible conflict with the second rule discussed above. Specifically, the question was whether the benefits of a particular individual could be financed on the straight-line basis, if such method resulted in the liquidation of the past service liability at a faster rate than 10 per cent per year. By regulation the Treasury ruled, in effect, that the straight-line method could not be used if it would violate the Past Service Rule.

8. The law and regulations use the expression "initial past service liability," but the initial accrued liability produced by other funding methods, particularly the entry age normal method (discussed later), may also serve as the 10 per cent base.

9. A special 10 per cent base may be substituted for the initial past service liability in order to fund increases in such liability arising out of (1) net losses arising from experience in previous years less favorable on the whole than that assumed in the estimated costs for such years, (2) changes in valuation assumptions or contract premium rates to a basis more conservative than that on which the original cost estimates were based, and (3) failure to fund the full normal costs and interest on unfunded past service costs in one or more years. See Paragraph 38 of Treasury Bulletin on Section 23(p)(1)(A) and (B), dated June 1, 1945.

The ruling was contested, and the Tax Court overruled the Commissioner of Internal Revenue, thus permitting the straight-line method to be used in any situation.[10]

It should be noted that any amounts contributed by the employer in excess of those permitted by the foregoing limitations may be carried over to future tax years and deducted in accordance with prescribed procedures.

The preceding rules impose limitations on the maximum amounts that may be deducted by an employer in any one tax year; the minimum amount that may be contributed to a pension plan is likewise the subject of regulation. This limitation, however, is couched in terms of total contributions to the plan, rather than employer contributions. Broadly stated, the contributions must be adequate to meet the normal costs of the plan plus interest on the initial past service liability.[11] That is, the contributions must be large enough to purchase all benefits that accrue after inception of the plan and at the same time prevent an increase in the initial past service liability. Since this latter sum is a discounted value, failure to contribute an amount equal to the assumed rate of interest would produce an increase in the total liability. Such an increase in the initial past service liability would be equivalent to unfunding a portion of the future service benefits which, by regulation, must be paid up at all times. After a portion of the initial past service liability has been funded, contributions for any particular year may be less than the amount needed to provide the benefits for that year, or may be omitted entirely, so long as, in the aggregate, contributions have been adequate to provide in full all future service benefits.

Apart from the exception noted in the preceding sentence, it may be said that the annual rate of funding can range from a minimum of the normal cost plus interest on the initial past service liability to a maximum of the normal cost plus 10 per cent of the past service liability.

10. *Saalfield Publishing Co.* v. *Commissioner,* 11 TC 756, November 1, 1948. The Commissioner appealed the decision to the Circuit Court of Appeals for the 6th Circuit but later acquiesced. See Internal Revenue Bulletin, No. 21, October 13, 1952, p. 1.

11. Paragraph 9(d), Mimeograph 5717, July 13, 1944; P.S. No. 64, November 9, 1950; and Paragraph 4, P.S. No. 67, April 26, 1951.

Factors Affecting Pension Costs

Advance funding, by definition, involves the setting aside of funds for the payment of pension benefits in advance of their due date. This means that the cost of providing the benefits must be estimated years in advance. Each factor that has a bearing on the cost must be analyzed and its influence evaluated. The factors that are normally taken into account are (1) mortality, (2) interest, (3) expenses of operation, (4) turnover, (5) age of retirement, and (6) changes in rate of compensation.

Mortality.—Mortality is one of the most important determinants of the cost of benefits. The rate of mortality among active employees, along with the rate of withdrawal, determines the number of employees who will become entitled to benefits. If death benefits are available before retirement, the rate of mortality will directly determine the cost of such benefits. The rate of mortality among retired employees is even more crucial than that among active employees, since it determines how long the benefits will be paid. The higher the death rate among both active and retired employees, the lower will be the cost of the pension plan.

Mortality among retired employees is estimated according to an annuity table, frequently the 1937 Standard Annuity Table, while mortality before retirement may be estimated according to an annuity, insurance or other type of table, depending upon the nature of the death benefits, if any. Contributions under virtually all plans, whether insured or uninsured, are adjusted to take account of the anticipated mortality before retirement. This process is referred to as discounting for mortality. In the interest of conservatism, a lower rate of mortality is usually assumed than that which is actually expected, the employer being credited with any gains as they accrue.

Interest.—Interest must be taken into account since the dollars that are set aside are invested and earn interest until they are paid out as benefits. This is particularly important during the period before retirement, or the accumulation period. In this connection it is interesting to observe that a dollar invested at 2 per cent compound interest will double itself in 35 years, while a dollar invested at 3 per cent interest will double itself in less than 24 years. Thus, annual contributions on behalf of an individual who enters a pension plan at age 40, if invested at 3 per cent compound interest until age 65, would, in the aggregate, increase by 50 per cent from interest earnings.

Contributions under all plans are likewise discounted for interest, with the actual rate earned being credited to the funds.

Expenses of Operation.—Under insured plans an arbitrary allowance is made for anticipated expenses. This allowance is designed to take care of all expenses incurred before and after retirement. An allowance is also made for contingencies, the two items being combined into a composite increment to the net premium called loading. In group annuities the usual loading is 5 to 8 per cent of the gross premium, the major portion of which is for contingencies.[12] Under other insured forms, the loading is somewhat higher. Under all types of insured plans, except individual contracts issued by stock companies, if expenses are less than anticipated, the savings are credited to the employer, either as a dividend or as a premium credit.

Under self-administered plans, the employer is permitted by Treasury regulations to make advance provision for expenses of operation, but no deductions may be taken for contributions to the trustee for the purpose of accumulating a reserve for contingencies. As a general rule, however, expenses are handled on a pay-as-you-go basis.

Turnover.—Turnover among employees has the same effect on pension costs as mortality before retirement—it reduces the number of persons to whom retirement benefits must be paid. Under many plans turnover is a more important factor than mortality and interest combined. Most plans, however, attempt to exclude high turnover employees through the imposition of age and service requirements, which tends to lessen the influence of the turnover factor. Its influence is further modified in plans which vest the employer's contributions in the employees either immediately or after certain requirements have been met.

Contributions under self-administered plans are frequently discounted for turnover. In other words, no contributions are made on behalf of the employees who are expected to terminate their em-

12. See pp. 93-94.

ployment before date of retirement. The number of employees who will terminate their employment is generally estimated from a turnover table, which may reflect the actual or projected experience of the employer or may represent the turnover rates applicable to a broader segment of industry. A turnover table indicates the percentage of employees who may be expected to withdraw at each age, and it is applied in the same manner as a mortality table to determine the number of employees who should survive to retirement. In fact, the turnover table is usually combined with the mortality or annuity table to show the total decrements from employment age by age. Occasionally, the turnover table is on a select basis, which means that turnover rates are shown not only by age but also by duration of service. In such event, it would not generally be combined with the mortality table. In some cases, the contributions are not discounted in the technical sense, the employer, rather, simply failing to make contributions on behalf of employees known to be subject to high turnover.

Premiums under the usual forms of insured plans are never discounted for turnover. The insurance companies consider turnover to be uninsurable in that the risk is partly under the control of the employer and, in addition, is influenced by such broad economic forces as to be essentially unpredictable. For purposes of funding, the assumption is made that each employee who becomes a member of the plan will remain with the employer until retirement, and in the event that an employee withdraws before date of vesting or retirement, the employer is credited with the contributions he has made on behalf of the terminating employee.

Under the deposit administration and immediate participation guarantee forms of group annuity contracts, in connection with which employer contributions are not allocated to individual employees before retirement, contributions may be discounted for turnover at the discretion of the employer. If actual turnover should turn out to be less than that anticipated, the employer would have to contribute the additional sums needed. If, on the other hand, turnover should be greater than that estimated, future contributions of the employer could be reduced.

Age of Retirement.—For purposes of funding, it is necessary to make an assumption as to the age or ages at which employees will retire. In the majority of cases, it is assumed that retirement will occur at the normal retirement age. In such cases, the normal retirement age fixes the date by which the funds for the employee's pension must be accumulated in full and, furthermore, determines the principal sum which will be needed. The lower the age at which retirement is permitted, the more costly the pension plan will be. Other things being equal, a plan with a normal retirement age of 60 will cost about 50 per cent more than one with a retirement age of 65, and the latter in turn will cost about 50 per cent more than a plan which provides for retirement at age 70.

The great majority of plans specify 65 as the normal retirement age, although a few plans permit female employees to retire at age 60. Retirement at an age younger than the normal retirement age, when permitted, generally does not increase the cost of the plan, since the employee usually receives only the actuarial equivalent of the benefit which would have been paid had he retired at the normal age. Retirement at an age later than the normal retirement age, however, may decrease the cost since, if the employee continues to draw his full salary, a common arrangement, the employer may be credited with the benefits which would normally have been paid to the employee.

Conventional insured plans must fund for a normal retirement age. Self-administered and deposit administration plans may and often do assume an average retirement age or a distribution of retirements over a range of ages.

Changes in Rate of Compensation.—This factor need be considered only in those plans whose benefits are directly related to compensation. Among such plans the type whose benefits are based on the compensation of the final years of service, presents the greatest complications in funding.

Self-administered plans usually attempt to anticipate the effect of increases in compensation through the use of an assumed or projected salary scale which reflects the rate of earnings for each age to retirement. In general, insured plans do not attempt to anticipate salary changes. The assumption is made that the rate of compensation for each employee will continue at its current level until retirement, and any changes, when they occur, are also deemed to be permanent. Under the deposit administration and immediate participation guarantee plans, however, salary projections may be used by the employer if desired.

Methods of Advance Funding

Several methods of advance funding are in general use, but they may be broadly classified, as to approach, into three basic types: single premium, level annual premium, and aggregate.[13] The structure of these methods and the manner in which they influence the cost of a pension plan can be described most effectively by reference to concrete figures, but it seems advisable to preface such an analysis with a description of the general characteristics of the methods.

Single Premium Method.—This method, also known as the "unit credit" method, involves the setting aside, in one sum, of the amount of money needed to fund in full one unit of benefit. Theoretically, this unit of benefit could be defined in various terms, but in practice it is almost invariably related to a year of service. In other words, it is the benefit earned during one year of service. Thus, if in his first year of coverage, an employee age 25 should earn an annual benefit at age 65 of $30, a paid-up annuity in that amount would be funded for the employee at a cost, under one set of actuarial assumptions,[14] of $99.90. Each year thereafter that such employee participates in the plan, a paid-up annuity in the appropriate amount is funded for the employee at a constantly increasing cost per dollar of benefit. At retirement, his income is derived from a series of paid-up deferred annuities funded over the entire period of his participation in the plan.

13. This classification differs sharply from that developed by Charles L. Trowbridge in his paper entitled "Fundamentals of Pension Funding," *Transactions of the Society of Actuaries,* Vol. IV, 1952, pp. 17-43. Trowbridge derived a highly logical but rather complex classification of funding methods based on the magnitude of the ultimate fund that would be accumulated under the assumption of an initially mature population. Six classes were set up in ascending order of size of the ultimate fund, ranging from pay-as-you-go, under which the fund is zero, to *complete* funding, under which the fund would be of such size that interest on the fund would be adequate to meet the benefit payments.

14. 1937 Standard Annuity Table, 2½ per cent interest, and loading of 8 per cent of gross premium.

Under this method of funding, current and past service benefits are treated separately. The current service benefits of each employee are funded in full as they accrue, and the current service or normal cost of the plan is the sum of the single premiums required to fund the benefits of all employees covered under the plan. The past service cost is the sum of the single premiums required to fund in full all benefits credited to the employees for service prior to the effective date of the plan. These benefits need not be funded at the inception of the plan and as a rule are funded over a period of years. If the plan is insured, however, all benefits to which a particular employee is entitled, regardless of the period during which they were earned, must be purchased in full before retirement.

The single premium method of funding is virtually always used in connection with deferred group annuity contracts and may be used with other types of plans. It is equally appropriate for a benefit formula which provides a definite benefit and one which utilizes the money purchase concept. It is not suitable for a plan which provides a flat benefit or benefits based on the earnings of a future period, such as the last five years of service, or one which provides for the deduction of OASI benefits. Under such benefit formulas, it is extremely difficult, if not impossible, to determine the unit of benefit to be funded each year.

Level Annual Premium Method.—Contrasted with the method under which each unit of benefit is funded in full in the period during which it is earned is one under which the total benefits to be paid to an employee are estimated and the sum required to provide the benefits is accumulated through uniform increments over the remaining years of service. This latter method is known as the level annual premium method, of which there are two principal forms.

Perhaps the most familiar form of the annual level premium method is the "individual level premium" method which is employed in connection with individual and group permanent insurance contracts. The contract for a particular employee is written in an amount exactly adequate to provide the benefits that would be payable to the employee if his rate of compensation remains unchanged to normal retirement age, and the payment of premiums on the contract meets the funding requirements. As is true of all insurance contracts, the premium is calculated as of the attained age of the employee.

If the rate of compensation increases, with an attendant change in benefits, an adjustment in the amount of insurance is made in the manner described earlier, and the funding of the increase in benefits is accomplished by a separate and additional level premium, payable from the date of increase.

Inasmuch as the insurance contracts are written in amounts designed to provide benefits for the entire period of credited service, no distinction is made between past and current service costs. The sums necessary to amortize the past service liability are merged indistinguishably into the annual premium and are not identifiable as past service contributions. The total amount funded each year is simply the sum of the premiums on all contracts issued under the plan.

This method of funding, which is frequently referred to as "attained age level premium" funding, is not confined to individual and group permanent insurance contracts or to insurance contracts in general. It can be and frequently is used to fund self-administered plans. It lends itself to any type of benefit formula, being especially adaptable to formulas which provide a flat benefit or one expressed as a flat percentage of salary.

The other principal form of level annual premium funding is the so-called "entry age normal" method.[15] This method differs from the individual level premium approach in that the contribution on behalf of an individual employee is that level amount, or percentage of payroll, which would have been required to fund all the benefits of the employee if the plan had been in effect, and contributions had been made, from the beginning of the employee's credited service. In other words, it is assumed for purposes of funding that contributions have been made for the duration of the employee's credited service, and that a reserve equal to such contributions, plus interest and the benefit of survivorship,[16] is standing to the credit of the employee as of the effective date of the plan. Obviously, the

15. Some actuaries regard entry age normal as a separate funding method, since only the normal cost is calculated as a level amount or level percentage of payroll. It is further differentiated from the individual level premium method in that both normal and past service costs are frequently calculated on a collective basis, without reference to individual employees.

16. Benefit of survivorship is an actuarial concept meaning in this instance that those employees who are assumed to survive to normal retirement age share pro rata in the contributions, plus interest, made on behalf of those employees assumed to die before normal retirement age.

longer the period of prior service, the larger is the "reserve" or deficiency. For the plan as a whole, the sum of the individual "reserves," including those for retired lives, constitutes the past service liability, a definitely identifiable entity. Thus, it may be seen that the entry age normal method effects a separation between past service and current service costs. In fact, its very name denotes that the periodic contributions are designed to fund only the normal cost of the plan. The expression "entry age" refers to the age at entry into employment or membership in the plan if there are age or service prerequisites.

The deficiency produced by this method of funding can be liquidated in the same manner as any other accrued liability. Insurance companies, however, usually require that the accrued liability be funded at such a rate that benefits for retired lives are completely funded at all times. If the deficiency is completely liquidated, the distinction between the entry age normal and the attained age methods disappears when the last employee with prior service is removed from the payroll. At that point, the "entry age" and "attained age" are the same for all employees.

If the employer prefers, the past service liability need not be liquidated or even reduced, in which case it is said to be "frozen."[17] In other words, it will never be paid off. This can be managed by financing the past service benefits of retired employees out of the current service contributions for active employees, the process being continued ad infinitum. It is based on the assumption that the plan will exist in perpetuity. The concept is not confined to the entry age normal method of funding, but it cannot be applied under a funding instrument which allocates contributions to specific employees during their period of employment.

The entry age normal device may be used with any type of funding instrument which does not allocate contributions to individual employees before retirement. It is widely used to fund deposit administration, IPG and self-administered plans.

17. The expression "frozen initial liability" may also refer to a method under which funding of the accrued liability is contemplated but in accordance with which the initial accrued liability remains fixed, as the 10 per cent base, any adjustments for gains or losses being reflected in future normal costs. See Charles L. Trowbridge, op. cit., pp. 38-39. See also Paragraph 55 of Treasury Bulletin, dated June 1, 1945.

Aggregate Cost Method.—This method is analogous to the individual level premium or "attained age" method of funding except that the benefits and contributions are calculated on a collective basis. The portion of the cost which is to be met each year is generally expressed as a percentage of annual covered payroll, which percentage is called the "accrual rate" or the "aggregate cost ratio." The precise manner in which the accrual rate is determined can be more easily illustrated than described, but, in essence, the present value of estimated future benefits, less any funds already accumulated, is divided by the present value of estimated future compensation of all covered employees. The rate must be recalculated periodically.

The aggregate cost method calculates past service and future service benefits together and is considered by the Treasury to be a Straight-Line method. The accrued liability is paid off rather rapidly in the beginning but at a progressively diminishing rate, so that it is completely paid off only at infinity.

This method of funding has found its widest use among self-administered plans, although it is adaptable to the deposit administration and immediate participation guarantee forms of group annuity. Once widely used, its popularity has declined in recent years.

Combination Methods.—There are two other significant forms of funding which can best be described as combination methods, since they possess some of the characteristics of more than one method. The first is a rather complex method going under the designation "attained age normal," not to be confused with the individual level premium method which is sometimes referred to as the "attained age" method. It is applicable only to the type of benefit formula associated with the single premium funding method, which is to say a definite unit of benefit for each year of service. The procedure consists of sealing off the past service liability as derived by the single premium funding method and funding future service or normal costs on the aggregate basis. The past service liability can be liquidated in any manner permitted by the funding agency or frozen at its original level.

The money purchase plan also has the characteristics of more than one funding method. The contribution rate is a level percentage of compensation, which would seem to place the method in the level premium category, except that the contributions are usually applied as single premiums. Inasmuch as there is no real distinction between a series of equal single premiums and a level annual premium, a strong case can be made for classifying money purchase as a level premium method.

ILLUSTRATION OF ADVANCE FUNDING TECHNIQUES[18]

The impact of the foregoing funding techniques on the initial cost of a pension plan can be more clearly visualized in connection with a specific set of pension data. For purposes of illustration, a hypothetical but typical pension case has been formulated, with each of the major funding methods demonstrated. The case is presented in a series of integrated tables with the columns numbered consecutively. The illustration is applicable to both insured and self-administered plans.

The assumptions underlying the cost calculations of the case are as follows:

Employee Data.—The age distribution, average earnings, and average length of service, are based upon the data for an actual group of salaried employees. The characteristics of this group appear to be fairly typical of that class of employees. In order to simplify the computations, all employees are assumed to be males.

Mortality.—The mortality assumptions before and after retirement are based on the 1937 Standard Annuity Table with no setback.

Interest.—An interest rate of 2½ per cent was assumed. This is higher than the 2¼ per cent assumed by most insurance companies in their annuity premium calculations and somewhat lower than the rate commonly assumed in the valuation of self-administered plans.

Expense Loading.—No allowance was made for expenses. This seemed advisable in view of the divergent treatment of expenses as between insured and self-administered plans.

18. The cost calculations presented in this section were prepared for the author by the firm of Towers, Perrin, Forster, and Crosby, Inc., under the direction of Mr. John K. Dyer, Jr., Vice-President and Actuary.

Turnover.—No discount for future turnover was included. Since this is a major determinant of cost, the modifications in the cost figures that would be produced by inclusion of a turnover factor will be pointed out later.

Salary Increases.—No allowance was made for future salary increases. This factor exerts an influence on costs exactly opposite to that of the turnover factor, so that the two omissions cancel out to some extent.

Age of Retirement.—The normal retirement age was assumed to be 65, and no allowance was made for delayed retirement in individual cases. This is the customary procedure under both insured and self-administered plans, with credit being taken for postponements as they actually occur.

It is emphasized that these cost figures have been developed primarily to illustrate the effect upon costs of the use of the different funding methods, and the most significant comparisons, therefore, are those relating to relative costs and payments under the different methods.

Basic Data.—The basic data for the hypothetical pension case are presented in Table 7. The age distribution of the employee group is

TABLE 7

BASIC DATA FOR HYPOTHETICAL PENSION PLAN

Age Bracket	Age Assumed for Computations	Number of Employees	Total Annual Earnings	Average Annual Earnings	Average Years of Past Service
(1)	(2)	(3)	(4)	(5)	(6)
15-19	17	30	$ 60,000	$ 2,000	1
20-24	22	110	253,000	2,300	2
25-29	27	160	464,000	2,900	4
30-34	32	130	455,000	3,500	6
35-39	37	110	451,000	4,100	9
40-44	42	100	460,000	4,600	13
45-49	47	90	459,000	5,100	17
50-54	52	80	448,000	5,600	21
55-59	57	70	434,000	6,200	26
60-64	62	60	390,000	6,500	31
65 & over	65	60	378,000	6,300	33
Totals	39.7(Av.)	1000	$4,252,000	$4,252(Av.)	12.8(Av.)

shown by quinquennial age groups, with the median age in each group used for premium computations. The average age of the group, which numbers 1,000, is 39.7, while the average period of service is 12.8 years. The average annual earnings range from $2,000 to $6,300, the average for the group being $4,252. All funding calculations are based on the assumption that the plan is in its first year of operation.

Single Premium Method.—The cost calculations for single premium funding are shown in Table 7a. The plan provides an annual benefit at age 65 of 1 per cent of earnings for each year of service, past and current. For any particular age bracket, prospective benefits for the current year of service are derived by multiplying the total annual earnings of that group by 1 per cent, and benefits for past service are found by multiplying 1 per cent of total earnings for the entire period of credited service. For the 30-34 age bracket, for example, current service benefits total $4,550, while the benefits credited for the six years of past service aggregate $27,300. At age 32, the median age of the group, each $1.00 of benefit at age 65

TABLE 7a

COST CALCULATIONS FOR SINGLE PREMIUM FUNDING

Age Bracket	Total Prospective Benefits Upon Which Costs Are Based		Single Premium Cost Factors	Normal Cost (Col. 7 × Col. 9)	Accrued Liability (Col. 8 × Col. 9)
	Current Service (1% of Col. 4)	Past Service (1% of Col. 4 × Col. 6)			
(1)	(7)	(8)	(9)	(10)	(11)
15-19	$ 600	$ 600	2.488	$ 1,493	$ 1,493
20-24	2,530	5,060	2.834	7,170	14,340
25-29	4,640	18,560	3.231	14,992	59,967
30-34	4,550	27,300	3.693	16,803	100,819
35-39	4,510	40,590	4.239	19,118	172,061
40-44	4,600	59,800	4.899	22,535	292,960
45-49	4,590	78,030	5.717	26,241	446,098
50-54	4,480	94,080	6.768	30,321	636,733
55-59	4,340	112,840	8.181	35,506	923,144
60-64	3,900	120,900	10.196	39,764	1,232,696
65 & over	–	124,740	11.360	–	1,417,046
Totals	$38,740	$682,500		$213,943	$5,297,357

requires a single premium of $3.69. Therefore, the cost of the benefits credited for the current year of service, or normal cost, is $16,803, or $4,550 times $3.69. By the same token, the cost of past service benefits, or the accrued liability, for the 130 employees in the 30-34 age category amounts to $100,819. The 1,000 employees, as a group, earn benefits of $38,740 in the current year, at a cost of $213,943. The accrued liability for the plan as a whole aggregates $5,297,357.

Level Annual Premium Method.—The cost data for the individual level premium and entry age normal forms of funding are set forth in Table 7b.

The first step in the calculation is common to both methods and entails the determination of the total benefits that will be credited to the employee group during their entire period of service, including service to be performed in the future. In this calculation the assumption is made that each employee will continue to earn his current salary until retirement, so that column 12 is derived by taking 1 per cent of the current earnings of each employee multiplied by the total prospective years of service. In the case of employees 65 and over the benefits have already been earned, since it is assumed that all such employees are at the point of retirement.

Column 13 is used in connection with the individual level premium or attained age form of funding. The factors in this column represent the sums which must be set aside each year from the attained age of the employees to normal retirement age for each $1.00 of annual benefit to be provided. For example, 17.5 cents set aside each year from age 32 to age 65 will, with interest and the benefit of survivorship,[19] amount to $11.36 at age 65, the sum required at that age to provide a life income of $1.00 per year. The initial annual cost of the plan is obtained by multiplying the prospective annual benefits at each attained age by the level premium cost of $1.00 of benefits at that age. The results in this particular case are distorted by inclusion of the single sum liability of $1,417,046 for employees age 65 and over.

The normal cost under the entry age normal method of funding is derived from the same set of prospective benefits and in the same

19. See p. 143, fn. 16. In this instance, the concept refers to the fact that the sums paid with respect to those employees who are assumed to die before age 65 are needed to provide the average accumulation of $11.36 for each of those assumed to survive to age 65.

TABLE 7b

COST CALCULATIONS FOR LEVEL ANNUAL PREMIUM
AND AGGREGATE FUNDING

Age Bracket	Prospective Benefits Upon Which Costs Are Based [1% of Col. 4 × (Col. 6 + Yrs. to 65)]	Level Premium Cost Factors for Attained Age	Initial Annual Cost on Attained Age Level Premium Method (Col. 12 × Col. 13)	Level Premium Cost Factors for Entry Age[*]	Normal Cost on Entry Age Normal Method (Col. 12 × Col. 15)
(1)	(12)	(13)	(14)	(15)	(16)
15-19	$ 29,400	.093	$ 2,734	.089	$ 2,617
20-24	113,850	.113	12,865	.104	11,840
25-29	194,880	.139	27,088	.118	22,996
30-34	177,450	.175	31,054	.133	23,601
35-39	166,870	.226	37,713	.146	24,363
40-44	165,600	.302	50,011	.152	25,171
45-49	160,650	.426	68,437	.159	25,543
50-54	152,320	.654	99,617	.167	25,437
55-59	147,560	1.187	175,154	.167	24,643
60-64	132,600	3.568	473,117	.167	22,144
65 & over	124,740	11.360	1,417,046	–	–
Totals	$1,565,920		$2,394,836		$208,355

[*] Based on assumed entry ages: Col. (2) - Col. (6).

general manner. Under this method, however, the level premium factors, listed in column 15, are based on the assumption that contributions on behalf of any employee have been made from the inception of his credited service. At each age bracket, therefore, the factor is lower than the comparable one under the "attained age" method. The factor for the 30-34 age bracket, for instance, is the level premium required at age 26 to fund a life income of $1.00 per year at age 65. The factor for the 50-54 age bracket, in which the employees have an average length of service of 21 years, is the level premium for age 31. No factor is shown for age 65 and over, since it is assumed that the benefits for such employees have been fully funded.

Column 16 reflects only the normal cost of the plan, or the cost of current benefits. The accrued liability under the entry age normal method is derived by subtracting the present value of future normal

TABLE 7b—Continued

COST CALCULATIONS FOR LEVEL ANNUAL PREMIUM
AND AGGREGATE FUNDING

Age Bracket	Present Value Factors	Present Value of Prospective Benefits (Col. 12 × Col. 17)	Temporary Annuity Factors	Present Value of Future Normal Costs (Col. 16 × Col. 19)	Present Value of Future Earnings (Col. 4 × Col. 19)
(1)	(17)	(18)	(19)	(20)	(21)
15-19	2.488	$ 73,147	26.779	$ 70,081	$ 1,606,740
20-24	2.834	322,651	25.089	297,054	6,347,517
25-29	3.231	629,657	23.192	533,323	10,761,088
30-34	3.693	655,323	21.083	497,580	9,592,765
35-39	4.239	707,362	18.763	457,123	8,462,113
40-44	4.899	811,274	16.221	408,299	7,461,660
45-49	5.717	918,436	13.433	343,119	6,165,747
50-54	6.768	1,030,902	10.354	263,375	4,638,592
55-59	8.181	1,207,188	6.894	169,889	2,991,996
60-64	10.196	1,351,990	2.858	63,288	1,114,620
65 & over	11.360	1,417,046	—	—	—
Totals		$9,124,976		$3,103,131	$59,142,838

costs (column 20) from the present value of prospective benefits (column 18). The present value of prospective benefits is obtained by multiplying the dollar amount of annual prospective benefits (column 12) by the present value of each $1.00 to be paid (column 17). Column 17 is identical with column 9 and shows the sum that must be set aside at each of the attained ages for each $1.00 of benefit at age 65. In other words, column 18 represents the single sum that would have to be set aside in the current year to provide, without further contributions, all benefits that will be earned by the present group of employees. The present value of future normal costs (column 20) is found by multiplying the contribution toward normal costs that is required in the current year (column 16) by the present value of $1.00 per annum for the number of years between the respective attained ages and age 65 (column 19). For example, if the present value of $1.00 per annum payable from age 32 to age 65 is $21.08, a series of annual payments of $23,601 from age 32 to

TABLE 7c

SUMMARY OF COST CALCULATIONS

Type of Funding	Basic Elements of Cost	
Single premium Method	Normal Cost (Total of Col. 10)	$ 213,943
	Accrued Liability (Total of Col. 11) 5,297,367	
Level Annual Premium Method— Attained Age	Initial Level Annual Premium (Total of Col. 13) 2,394,836 Note: This includes single sum liability of $1,417,046 for employees age 65 and over	
Level Annual Premium Method— Entry Age	Normal Cost (Total of Col. 16) 208,355 Accrued Liability (Total Col. 18 minus Total Col. 20) 6,021,845	
Aggregate Cost Method	Initial Annual Cost 656,041 $\frac{\text{Col. 18}}{\text{Col. 21}} \times \text{Col. 4}$	

* Trends indicated assume organization of constant size and character and actual experience in conformance with interest and mortality assumptions.

age 65 is worth $497,580 at the present time. The difference between that sum and $655,323, the present value of future benefits of employees in the 30-34 age category, is the accrued liability for that age category. For the entire employee group, the accrued liability under the entry age normal method of funding is $6,021,845.

Aggregate Method.—The initial annual cost under the aggregate funding method can be easily ascertained from the foregoing tables. It will be recalled that the annual contribution under this method bears the same ratio to covered annual earnings that the present value of future earnings bears to the present value of future benefits,

TABLE 7c—Continued

SUMMARY OF COST CALCULATIONS

Initial Funding Contributions		Trend of Funding Contributions*
Minimum—Normal Cost plus 2½% of Accrued Liability	$ 346,377	Gradual increase in normal costs until group reaches stable age distribution. After accrued liability is paid off contributions reduced to normal cost only
Maximum—Normal Cost plus 10% of Accrued Liability	743,679	
Fixed amount, assuming cost for employees 65 and over is paid in lump sum	2,394,836	Decreasing year by year, ultimately reaching cost level equal to normal cost on level premium entry age method
Fixed amount, assuming cost for employees 65 and over spread over 11 years	1,119,495	
Minimum—Normal Cost plus 2.5% of Accrued Liability	358,901	Approximately level until accrued liability is paid off, then reducing to normal cost only
Maximum—Normal Cost plus 10% of Accrued Liability	810,540	
Fixed amount, equal to initial annual cost	656,041	Decreasing year by year, ultimately reaching cost level approximately equal to normal cost on level premium entry age method

less any accumulated funds. In simpler language, the "accrual rate" is multiplied by the covered payroll. In this case, since there is no accumulated fund, the accrual rate is obtained by dividing the present value of prospective benefits (column 18) by the present value of future earnings (column 21), which yields a percentage of 15.43 per cent. Applied to the total annual earnings of $4,252,000 (column 4), this percentage produces an initial annual cost of $656,041.

Summary of Cost Calculations.—A summary of the costs developed under each of the foregoing funding methods is presented in Table 7c. Under the single premium method, the normal cost is

$213,943, and the accrued liability is $5,297,357. If the plan is to qualify under Federal income tax laws, the normal cost plus 2.5 per cent of the accrued liability, or a total of $346,377, must be funded each year. In addition to the normal cost, 10 per cent of the accrued liability, or $529,736, may be funded each year and deducted as an ordinary and necessary business expense. Contributions equal to normal cost plus 10 per cent of the accrued liability would amount to $743,679, or 17.5 per cent of covered payroll. The normal cost will increase gradually until the age distribution of the employee group stabilizes. After the accrued liability is paid off, the contributions will be reduced to those necessary to meet only the normal cost.

The initial contribution required under the attained age method is $2,394,836, if the single sum liability of $1,417,046 for employees age 65 and over is liquidated in the first year. If the liquidation of such liability is spread over eleven years, the initial contribution will be $1,119,946, or 26.3 per cent of covered payroll. The cost will decrease year by year, ultimately reaching the normal cost level of the entry age normal method.

The normal cost under the entry age normal method of funding is $208,355, and the accrued liability is $6,021,845. As under the single premium method, the contributions may equal only the normal cost plus 2.5 per cent of the accrued liability, or a portion of the accrued liability may be paid off each year in addition to the funding of the normal cost. The normal cost plus 10 per cent of the accrued liability would equal $810,540, or 19.1 per cent of payroll. The contributions would continue at an approximately level rate until the accrued liability is liquidated, after which they would drop to the level of normal cost only.

Finally, the initial annual cost under the aggregate method is $656,041, with no distinction between normal cost and accrued liability. As previously indicated, this is 15.43 per cent of payroll. The contributions will decrease each year, ultimately reaching a cost level approximately equal to the normal cost under the entry age normal method of funding.

In considering these cost comparisons, it is important to realize that any differences in first year costs among the various funding methods must necessarily be made up in the future. The present value of all future costs is identical under all methods. Although it may appear so from a comparison of first year costs, no method in the long run is "cheaper" than another.

Modifications of Actuarial Assumptions.—The effect on the cost projections of a pension plan produced by changes in certain basic assumptions can be observed in Table 8. The cost projections in this table are based upon the same set of data used in the construction of Tables 7-7c and, with the exceptions noted, on the same set of actuarial assumptions.

Section A of the table reflects the results of using a 3 per cent interest assumption in lieu of 2½ per cent, the other assumptions remaining the same. In other words, the cost projections are based on the 1937 Standard Annuity Table with interest at 3 per cent, no allowance for expenses or salary increases, and no discount for turn-over. The table reveals that under the single premium method of funding, the normal cost of the pension plan in question is reduced by about 11 per cent while under the entry age method of funding such cost is reduced by about 14 per cent. The accrued liability under the foregoing methods of funding is lowered to a somewhat smaller extent, 7.7 and 6.6 per cent, respectively. Decreases among the other cost projections in Section A range from 5 to 9 per cent.

The substitution of the 1951 Group Annuity Table for the 1937 Standard Annuity Table has the opposite effect on costs, as Section B discloses. This follows from the fact that the more recent table, whose derivation and characteristics are described at a later point,[20] shows a lower rate of mortality at all ages below 73 than the widely used 1937 Standard Annuity Table, and at the younger ages the divergence is significantly great. Nevertheless, only the normal cost under the single premium and entry age methods of funding registers any significant change, the increase being 5.3 and 6.6 per cent, respectively. Only slight upward changes are recorded in the other cost categories.

The effect of introducing a moderate turnover factor into the cost calculations is shown in Section C of the table. Substantial reductions are reflected in virtually every type of cost expression, the most significant being those produced in the normal cost under the single premium and entry age methods of funding, 36 and 50 per

20. Appendix D.

TABLE 8

COST PROJECTIONS UNDER VARIOUS ACTUARIAL ASSUMPTIONS[a]

	A			
	1937 Standard Annuity Table, 3% Interest, No Turnover			
	Basic Elements of Cost		*Initial Funding Contributions*	
Type of Funding	*Normal Cost*	*Accrued Liability*	*Minimum*	*Maximum*
Single Premium	$189,010	$4,891,901	$335,767[c]	$678,200[d]
Level Annual Premium— Attained Age	*Initial Level Annual Premium* $2,273,496[b]		$1,048,225[e]	$2,273,496[f]
Level Annual Premium— Entry Age	$179,395	$5,616,445	$347,888	$741,040
Aggregate Cost	*Initial Annual Cost* $617,545		$617,545	

a The supporting calculations, arranged in columns identical in nature and sequence with those of Tables 7a and 7b, are presented in Appendices A, B, and C.

b Includes single sum liability for employees age 65 and over of $1,361,412, $1,406,069, and $1,417,046, for Sections A, B, and C, respectively.

c Normal cost plus 3% (2½%) of accrued liability.

d Normal cost plus 10% of accrued liability.

e Based on the assumption that the cost for employees age 65 and over is spread over 11 years.

f Based on the assumption that the cost for employees age 65 and over is paid in lump sum.

cent, respectively. The impact of turnover is lighter on accrued liability under any funding method than on normal cost, since the employees who give rise to the bulk of the accrued liability are in the age brackets least affected by turnover. Even so, the accrued liability projection under the single premium and entry age methods is reduced 18 and 14 per cent, respectively, by recognition of the turnover factor. Exclusive of the single sum liability for employees age 65 and over, which sum would obviously be unaffected by turnover, the initial level premium under the attained age method of funding is reduced 15 per cent. Annual costs under the aggregate cost method are affected only to a minor extent by introduction of the turnover factor, since both benefits and wages are pushed down-

TABLE 8—Continued

COST PROJECTIONS UNDER VARIOUS ACTUARIAL ASSUMPTIONS[a]

	B			
	1951 Group Annuity Table, 2½% Interest, No Turnover			
	Basic Elements of Cost		Initial Funding Contributions	
Type of Funding	Normal Cost	Accrued Liability	Minimum	Maximum
Single Premium	$225,272	$5,425,973	$360,921	$767,869
Level Annual Premium— Attained Age	Initial Level Annual Premium $2,400,590[b]		$1,135,128[e]	$2,400,590[f]
Level Annual Premium— Entry Age	$222,085	$6,137,002	$375,510	$835,785
Aggregate Cost	Initial Annual Cost $667,970		$667,970	

TABLE 8—Continued

	C			
	1937 Standard Annuity Table, 2½% Interest, Moderate Turnover			
	Basic Elements of Cost		Initial Funding Contributions	
Type of Funding	Normal Cost	Accrued Liability	Minimum	Maximum
Single Premium	$136,478	$4,334,704	$244,846	$569,948
Level Annual Premium— Attained Age	Initial Level Annual Premium $2,247,458[b]		$972,117[e]	$2,247,458[f]
Level Annual Premium— Entry Age	$102,191	$5,156,064	$231,093	$617,797
Aggregate Cost	Initial Annual Cost $643,514		$643,514	

ward and to approximately the same degree. In fact, it is a peculiarity of the aggregate method that the assumption of withdrawal rates, or heavier withdrawal rates, as the case may be, sometimes leads to a higher initial contribution.

In connection with all the modifications considered in this section, and particularly with respect to turnover, it should be borne in mind that the sums in question are cost *projections* and that the true costs that finally emerge are neither increased nor decreased by the assumptions that enter into the projections.[21]

21. The true costs are affected to the extent that the cost projections influence the rate of funding and, hence, the magnitude of investment earnings.

Choice of
Funding Medium

5

IN IMPLEMENTING his decision to install a funded pension plan, arrived at unilaterally or in response to union demand, an employer must exercise his judgment with respect to several fundamental aspects of the plan. The decisions which he must make in this situation are interdependent and should be made in proper sequence and with an awareness of the interrelationships involved.

The first decision in point of time should relate to the benefit structure of the plan. The benefit pattern may rule out certain funding methods and media, thus narrowing the area of choice with respect to the latter.

Once the benefit pattern is established, a choice should be made between allocated and unallocated funding methods. This decision, which is greatly influenced by the benefit structure and the desire for flexibility in funding, determines whether or not contributions are to be allocated to individual employees prior to retirement. Allocated funding is an inherent feature of individual, group permanent, and deferred group annuity contracts, while unallocated funding is normally followed under deposit administration, immediate participation guarantee, and self-administered trusteed plans. Throughout this Chapter, unless otherwise indicated, allocated funding media will refer to individual, group permanent, and deferred group annuity contracts, whereas unallocated funding media will refer to the other three forms of financing.

The final broad decision, which should be made only after the foregoing issues have been settled, is whether to fund through an insurance contract or through a trust.

The purpose of this Chapter is to discuss in a general fashion each major factor that has a bearing on the choice of a funding medium and then to indicate the impact of that factor on each specific medium. The combination plan, whether in the form of an individual contract pension trust plus a trusteed auxiliary fund, or a group permanent contract plus an auxiliary fund on a deposit administration basis, is not treated as an independent funding medium for the purpose of this critique. Whatever is said about the basic forms applies to the combination plan to the extent that the principles of the former are embodied in the latter.

COST

Of critical importance to the employer in the adoption of a pension plan, and the choice of a funding medium, is the cost that will be incurred. The basic determinant of the cost, of course, is the benefit structure of the plan. As is generally recognized, the gross cost of a pension plan in the long run is equal to the benefits paid out, plus the costs of administration, less the earnings on any funds set aside for the payment of the benefits. This is an obvious oversimplification in that it ignores the factors that determine the magnitude of benefit disbursements and makes no allowance for possible differences in administrative expenses and fund earnings that might be traceable to the use of a particular funding mechanism. To arrive at the net or "true" cost of a pension plan, consideration would have to be given to the economic gains accruing to the employer from reduced labor turnover, retirement of inefficient employees, improved morale, and other factors. Because of the difficulty of measuring these indirect but nonetheless tangible benefits of a pension plan, the net financial outlay is generally assumed to represent the cost of the plan.

The factors that determine the net financial outlay under a pension plan, with a given set of benefits, are analyzed in the following sections.

MORTALITY

Effect of Mortality.—The mortality that will be experienced by the group of covered employees is a most significant determinant of the cost of a pension plan. The rate of mortality among active employees, in combination with the rate of withdrawal, determines the number of employees who will become entitled to benefits. The lower the death rate among the active employees, the higher, other things being equal, will be the cost of the retirement benefits. This does not necessarily mean, however, that the over-all cost of the plan would be increased. If the plan provides death benefits prior to retirement, the savings in death benefits resulting from lower mortality might more than offset the added cost of retirement benefits. The net effect of an improvement in mortality would depend upon the relative magnitude of death and retirement benefits and the relative improvement at the various ages.

The rate of mortality among retired lives is even more significant than that among active employees, since it determines the average period over which benefits will be paid. The impact of improved longevity is direct, and there are no significant offsetting factors. Every year that is added to the life expectancy of a retired employee produces a substantial increase in the cost of his pension. A period of guaranteed installments would lessen, to some extent, the consequences of such an improvement in mortality, but in many cases the benefits would be extended beyond the period of the guarantee.

Assumptions as to Mortality.—The rate of mortality varies among different types of lives, and an organization whose operations are concerned with life contingencies must utilize that body of mortality experience which appears to be most appropriate for its purpose. It has been found, for example, that the mortality among individuals who purchase life insurance tends to be higher, age for age, than that of persons who purchase annuities. This impels the insurance companies to adopt a mortality table for the underwriting of annuities different from that used for the writing of life insurance. This practice is dictated not only by the lower death rates among annuitants but by the necessity or desirability of providing a margin of safety in the mortality assumptions. Such a margin is provided in a life insurance mortality table by the use of death rates which are higher than those that are likely to be experienced, while the converse is true with respect to an annuity mortality table. That is, a conservative annuity mortality table shows lower death rates than those actually expected. Thus, the same table cannot be conservative for both life insurance and annuity purposes.

It has also been found that the mortality among employee groups is lower than that experienced by the general population.[1] This is attributable to the fact that the general population embraces persons in varying conditions of health, including many in an impaired state of health, while a minimum standard of health is required for participation in the active labor force. This superior vitality presumably carries over into retirement, which suggests that an annuity mortality table used for the underwriting of a private pension plan should lean heavily on the mortality experience of employed lives and those retired from active employment.

Finally, it is a matter of common knowledge that females live longer, on the average, than males. This superior longevity appears to flow from a better biological heritage,[2] but it may be due, in some measure, to the relatively greater stresses and strains to which the male population is exposed. The superiority of the female has been so pronounced in recent years that the death rates among female lives has conformed rather closely to that of male lives four to five years younger. As a result, it has been possible to use the same annuity table for male and female lives by assuming that the female is four or five years younger than her actual age, a device known as a setback or "rating down."

In the recent past, the mortality table most frequently used as a basis for pension cost projections has been the 1937 Standard Annuity Mortality Table. In the process male ages have sometimes been set back one or two years, depending upon the judgment of the actuary, and female ages an additional five years. At ages below sixty, this table is based on the experience of clerical employees covered under group life insurance contracts during the period 1932-36, while the death rates at ages 60 and above reflect the mortality among individual annuitants for the same period. No margin of safety was provided other than that implicit in the use of individual annuitant experience, which is assumed to be subject to a high degree of adverse selection, and group life clerical experi-

1. Ray M. Peterson, "Group Annuity Mortality," *Transactions of the Society of Actuaries,* Vol. IV, 1952, p. 255. See also, Louis O. Shudde, *ibid.,* Vol. III, 1951, p. 202.

2. Dublin, Lotka, and Spiegelman, *Length of Life,* Revised Edition (New York: Ronald Press Co., 1949), pp. 129-34.

ence, which reflects a sizable proportion of female lives.[3] Apart from this margin, no specific provision was made for future improvement in mortality.

Trend of Annuitant Mortality.—Substantial improvement in mortality has taken place since the construction of the 1937 Standard Annuity Table, particularly at the younger ages. This, of course, is only a continuation of the secular trend toward lower death rates which has produced such a striking extension in life expectancy during the last half-century. Studies of the mortality experience of various groups of the population point up the magnitude of the improvement. The experience of three representative groups for the approximate period 1940 to 1948 is presented in Table 9. Limitations of data restrict the exhibit to ages 25-64.

TABLE 9

AVERAGE ANNUAL RATE OF DECREASE IN MORTALITY AT AGES 25-64
(GEOMETRICAL BASIS)

Age Group	Intercompany Group Life (Clerical) From 1939-40 to 1946-47	White Industrial Policyholders (Metropolitan Life Ins. Co.) From 1939-40 to 1948		United States White Population From 1939-40 to 1947	
	Male and Female Combined	Male	Female	Male	Female
25-34	4.8%	4.6%	5.9%	3.6%	5.9%
35-44	3.3	2.6	4.0	2.2	3.9
45-54	1.4	1.3	3.0	0.9	2.9
55-64	1.6	1.3	3.1	0.6	2.8

Source: Jenkins and Lew, "A New Mortality Basis for Annuities," *Transactions of the Society of Actuaries,* Vol. I, 1949, p. 383.

The table shows the average annual rates of decrease that were registered in the death rates of the three groups between the dates indicated. The percentages were derived on a geometrical basis, i.e., with a new base each year, but the over-all decrease for the periods under consideration can be ascertained fairly accurately by multiplying the annual rate of decrease by the number of years

3. It is generally assumed that a minimum of 25 per cent of the employees in a typical clerical group are females, with the percentage ranging as high as 50 per cent in some groups.

involved. Thus, the total decrease in the death rates among the 25-34 age group of group life insurance policyholders between the two periods of observation was roughly 28 per cent. The greatest improvement was shown at the younger ages, specifically 25-34, which undoubtedly reflects the increasing control over infectious diseases, with the percentages declining with advancing age. Females display a greater percentage of improvement than males, which means that the divergence between male and female mortality is growing wider. The experience for group life insurance policyholders was not tabulated separately for males and females.

Similar studies of earlier experience indicate that mortality has been improving since 1920 at approximately the same rate as that shown in Table 9.[4]

This improvement in mortality has not been confined to ages below 65. All available evidence indicates that the improvement has extended into the more advanced age groups. The evidence from three important areas of experience is presented in Table 10.

The rates in Table 10 display some erratic behavior, which in the case of group annuity female experience is undoubtedly attributable

TABLE 10

AVERAGE ANNUAL RATE OF DECREASE IN MORTALITY AT AGES 66-85
(GEOMETRICAL BASIS)

Age Group	Intercompany Group Life (Clerical) From 1939-40 to 1946-47	Federal Civil Service Retirement Plan From 1935-40 to 1945-50		Intercompany Group Annuity From 1938-40 to 1946-50	
	Male and Female Combined	Male	Female	Male	Female
66-70	2.3%	−0.2%*	2.4%	1.0%	6.1%
71-75	2.3	1.3	1.9	2.4	−1.5*
76-80	2.0	1.3	2.8	1.7	2.7
81-85	2.0	1.6	2.4	−0.2*	− †

* Increase in mortality.
† No data available.
Source: Ray M. Peterson, "Group Annuity Mortality," *Transactions of the Society of Actuaries,* Vol. IV, 1952, p. 266.

4. Jenkins and Lew, "A New Mortality Basis for Annuities," *Transactions of the Society of Actuaries,* Vol. I, 1949, p. 399.

to the meagerness of the data and which with respect to male ages 66-70 of the Federal Civil Service Retirement Plans reflects changes in retirement policy. In general, the picture is one of significant decreases at all ages, with females again exhibiting a greater rate of decrease than that of males. Studies of the experience of the United States white population, the white industrial policyholders of the Metropolitan Life Insurance Company, and certain large self-administered pension plans, during the same general period substantiate the evidence of Table 10.[5]

As a result of these decreases, the 1937 Standard Annuity Table no longer portrays accurately the mortality among annuitants. The table overstates the mortality of annuitants at all ages up to 70 or 75 and understates it beyond that point. The extent and pattern of the divergence may be observed by reference to Table 11.

Table 11 presents a comparison between the death rates per 1,000 of the 1937 Standard Annuity Table and the Group Annuity Table for 1951. The latter table, whose construction and characteristics are discussed in Appendix D, is regarded as conservatively representative of the mortality rates among group annuitants during the year 1951. Separate rates are shown for males and females, with the rates for females under the 1937 Standard Annuity Table being those of males five years younger. Rates at the two extremities are not shown since such rates were derived by a mathematical formula, a process known as extrapolation, and do not necessarily represent the actual death rates at those ages.

Perhaps the most striking feature of the table is the great disparity between the male and female death rates in the Group Annuity Table for 1951. Nevertheless, the disparity between the death rates of the same sex in the two tables is almost as striking. At some ages the death rates of the 1937 Standard Annuity Table are more than double those of the Group Annuity Table for 1951. In general, the overstatement of female mortality is more pronounced than that of males, even with female ages set back five years in the earlier table. The male death rates of the 1937 Standard Annuity Table are higher than those of the Group Annuity Table for 1951 up to age 73,

5. *Ibid.*, pp. 383 and 393; Society of Actuaries, "Report of Special Committee on Experience Under Self-Administered Retirement Plans," 1953.

Table 11

Comparison of Mortality Rates of the 1937 Standard Annuity
Table and Group Annuity Table for 1951*

	Males		Females	
Age	1937 Standard Annuity	1951 Group Annuity	1937 Standard Annuity †	1951 Group Annuity
25	1.56	0.76	1.33	0.50
30	2.07	0.99	1.56	0.67
35	2.98	1.37	2.07	0.93
40	4.36	2.00	2.98	1.34
45	6.36	3.58	4.36	1.99
50	9.29	6.48	6.36	3.07
55	13.55	10.44	9.29	4.65
60	19.75	15.56	13.55	7.84
65	28.75	24.42	19.75	13.60
70	41.76	39.30	28.75	23.10
75	60.46	62.43	41.76	44.31
80	87.16	99.68	60.46	74.15
85	124.84	146.85	87.16	112.32
90	177.14	200.59	124.84	164.33
95	248.06	268.03	177.14	241.34

* Mortality rates are rates per 1,000.
† Female rates are those of male ages five years younger.

whereas the female death rates converge around age 71. Above those ages, the more recent table shows higher death rates for both males and females.

Not only does the 1937 Standard Annuity Table overstate mortality at the present time, except for the older age brackets, but if recent mortality trends continue, the disparity will become even greater. With respect to future mortality behavior, there seems to be general agreement that the rate of decrease in mortality at the younger ages, under 45 for example, must inevitably slacken since the area for improvement is constantly shrinking. On the other hand, medical and population authorities expect further significant reductions in death rates at ages over 45. Such a development can be expected from not only future advances in the treatment and prevention of disease, but also more intensive application of existing knowledge.[6]

6. For a detailed survey of medical and scientific opinion of this subject, see Jenkins and Lew, op. cit., pp. 407-13.

The inference to be drawn from these mortality developments is that the cost of providing any given set of retirement benefits can be expected to increase in the future. Not only will more employees survive to normal retirement age, but the survivors will live longer after retirement.[7] While there are some factors that may lessen the impact of this reduction in mortality, particularly during the period prior to retirement, it has been authoritatively predicted that a pension plan with a fixed retirement age of 65 should experience, solely by reason of mortality improvement, a 5 per cent increase in costs every ten years.[8]

There is a belief in some quarters that such increase in costs will be offset by a gradual extension in the age at which retirement occurs. Some have even predicted that plans in the future will prescribe an age beyond 65 at which retirement with full benefits will be permitted. In this connection, it is interesting to note that an increase in the normal retirement age from 65 to 66, with no increase in benefits, is generally assumed to reduce the over-all cost of a typical plan by about 8 per cent. A normal retirement age of 67 is assumed to cost approximately 15 per cent less than one of 65. If the prolongation of service results in higher benefits, the saving to the employer would be reduced and under certain types of benefit formula might be completely offset. The feasibility of this approach depends upon many factors, including nature of the industry, economic conditions, vitality of older workers, and employee attitudes.

Significance of Funding Medium.—It hardly seems necessary to point out that the various forces which are operating to lengthen the life expectancy of the American population are not influenced by the financial or legal arrangements adopted to provide retirement benefits to a particular segment of that population. The rate of mortality among a specific group of employees will be the same, whether their retirement benefits are to be provided through the intermediacy of an insurance company or a trust company. If the facilities of a trust company are used, the entire cost of the increased benefits resulting from greater longevity will inevitably fall upon the employer—and employees, if the plan is contributory—

7. See Appendix D.
8. Ray M. Peterson, *Proceedings of the Equitable Society Pension Forum,* The Equitable Life Assurance Society of the United States, 1953, p. 23.

since no possibility exists for the transfer of a portion of the costs to another agency. If, on the other hand, the plan is underwritten by an insurance company, a possibility exists that a portion of the cost can be shifted to the insurance company, the likelihood depending upon the size of the group and the type of contract chosen.

In this connection, it is pertinent to observe that the mortality among a group of employees may vary from that on which cost calculations were based either because the group is too small to develop an average experience or because the general level of mortality has shifted. The larger the group of employees, the greater the probability that the actual mortality experience will conform to the average. The small employer cannot be sure of an average experience. In order to protect himself against the risk that his particular employees will live longer than average, the small employer can avail himself of the rate guarantees of the insurance company. The plan of insurance normally appropriate for such circumstances is the individual contract which provides a lifetime guarantee for any given set of benefits and, if issued by a mutual company, pays dividends on the basis of company-wide experience. The premiums may prove to be more than adequate to provide the benefits under the plan or they may turn out to be inadequate. In the latter instance, the employer, in effect, transfers a portion of his costs to the insurance company. The insurance company, through the pooling technique, spreads such a loss over the contracts that develop a favorable experience and expects to break even on its total volume of business. The lifetime guarantees protect the employer not only against the possibility of fluctuations from average experience but also against the financial consequences of future improvement in mortality. In the case of the small employer, the former is the paramount consideration. The group permanent contract also provides a lifetime guarantee of rates for any given set of benefits but is usually experience rated.

With respect to the larger insured plans—those utilizing some form of group contract—the expectation is that each plan will in the long run pay its own way. If the plan continues in perpetuity, there is no question that it will bear the entire cost of its benefits. This conclusion is based on the fact that group annuity rates, after the expiration of the original five-year guarantee, are subject to revision at periodic intervals, as a rule annually, and, in addition, the dividend formula functions in such a manner that the insurance com-

pany can recoup any losses that may have developed, or are anticipated, under earlier rate guarantees. Should a group plan terminate,
there is a possibility that the insurance company might sustain a loss
as the experience of the plan emerges. The probability that this
would happen depends upon the safety margin in the rates, the size
of the contingency reserve, and the pattern of future mortality. With
the development of more reliable estimates of the trend of future
mortality and the increasing attention devoted to methods of coping
with the trend, the prospects that a large employer can shift any part
of his ultimate pension burden to the insurance company are becom-
ing increasingly remote.

INTEREST

A second factor that exerts a fundamental influence on the cost
of a pension plan is the interest rate earned on funds set aside for
the payment of future benefits. Any earnings on such funds naturally
reduce the amout of money that would otherwise be necessary to
provide a given set of benefits. From the employer's standpoint, the
savings thus made possible constitute one of the prime advantages
of advance funding.

Effect of the Interest Factor.—The significance of the interest
factor can be appreciated from the fact that a dollar invested at
3 per cent compound interest will double itself in 24 years. Thus,
at that rate, past service benefits could be purchased for an employee
age 40 at only half the cost that would be entailed if the interest
earnings were not available. Furthermore, sums set aside at a uniform rate over the next 25 years for the purchase of future service
benefits would increase by 50 per cent because of interest, or, conversely, the benefits would cost one-third less. Even greater discounts would be available at ages younger than 40. Lower interest
yields would produce smaller discounts, but a dollar invested at
2½ per cent interest will double itself in 35 years.

The impact of the interest factor in a particular plan depends
upon the age distribution of the employees and the degree of
advance funding. In a typical plan, however, a variation of one-
fourth of 1 per cent in the rate of interest could be expected to
produce a differential of 6 or 7 per cent in the long-run cost of the
plan. It can be seen, therefore, that the choice of a financing medium
may well hinge on the prospects for future interest earnings.

Earnings Potential of Insurance and Trust Companies.—It seems to be a fair generalization that if insurance and trust companies place their funds in the same general types of investments their over-all investment results should be roughly similar, inasmuch as no basis exists for assuming significant differences in the quality of the investment staffs of the two institutions. The only way that any substantial difference could arise would be for the two agencies to invest consistently in different channels or under significantly different circumstances. It would seem desirable, therefore, to inquire as to any differences that might exist between the two agencies in those respects.

In the first place, there is a difference with respect to the manner in which the pension funds are held by insurance and trust companies. All funds held by a life insurance company, regardless of their source, are pooled and invested as a unit. This means that each insured pension plan owns a fractional interest in the *total* portfolio of the insurance company and will share on a pro rata basis any gains or losses that may flow from the company's investment activities. It means also that the funds of each pension plan, irrespective of size, enjoy the same degree of diversification that exists in the entire investment portfolio.

In contrast, trust companies operate under the principle of segregation. The assets of each trust are set apart and administered as a unit. There is no sharing of experience, each trust enjoying the full and immediate benefit of favorable investment of its funds and, by the same token, bearing alone the full effect of unfavorable developments. In some states, at the direction of the grantor, trust funds not in excess of a specified sum, typically $50,000 or $100,000, can be pooled with other small trusts and administered as a common trust, thus providing the basis for greater diversification. Virtually all pension plans accumulate funds in excess of such limits, however, so that, for all practical purposes, a trusteed pension fund will enjoy only the degree of diversification that can be obtained through the investment operations of that particular fund.[9]

9. The Girard Trust Corn Exchange Bank of Philadelphia, with special permission from supervisory authorities, recently (November, 1954) established a common trust fund, called the Girard Diversified Pension Fund, for the exclusive use of pension plans, with no limit on the extent of participation. Thirty per cent of the Fund is to be invested in common stocks. Other banks may be expected to establish such funds.

A second difference exists with respect to the latitude with which the funds can be invested. In this connection, it should be observed that the funds of life insurance companies are invested within the framework of strict statutory regulation. The insurance codes of the various states not only specify the types of investments which are legal for insurance companies but also prescribe certain qualitative standards which must be met. Investment in common stock is severely restricted, being prohibited altogether in a few states and permitted only on a very limited scale in the other states. The New York insurance code, for example, permits a company to invest in common stock to the extent of 3 per cent of its admitted assets or one-third of its surplus, whichever is the lesser. Less restrictive limitations are imposed on preferred stock. Investment in real estate has traditionally been restricted to that required for the conduct of the company's business or that acquired in foreclosure proceedings, the company being under obligation to dispose of the latter within a reasonable period of time. In recent years, however, many states have liberalized their laws to permit limited investment in income-producing real estate under carefully prescribed conditions.

The bulk of insurance company investments is in government bonds (Federal, state, and local), high-grade corporate bonds, and real estate mortgages, with lesser amounts in real estate, policy loans, and stocks, preferred and common. The companies rely on real estate mortgages, privately-placed corporate securities, and income-producing real estate to raise the yield on their portfolios above that obtainable on governments and public issues of high-grade corporate bonds. Stocks account for only 3.6 per cent of insurance company investments, common stock comprising about a third of the total.

The funds of trusteed pension plans may also be subject to statutory investment restrictions. Statutes have been enacted in all states to govern the investment of fiduciary funds, and in the absence of a provision in the trust agreement to the contrary, such statutes apply with full force to trusteed pension plans. Under the fiduciary investment statutes of a few states, the trustee is limited to a list of government and corporate bonds promulgated by the banking commissioner or comparable official or to bonds and mortgages that can meet the qualitative standards prescribed by statute. A large number of states have adopted the Prudent Man type of statute which requires only that the trustee observe the principles that govern a prudent man in the investment of his own funds when his objective is a reasonable income and the preservation of his capital. In any state, however, the grantor, by an express provision in the trust agreement, can exempt the trust from the operation of the governing investment statute and give the trustee broad latitude in the investment of the trust assets. In practice, the investment provisions of the pension trust agreement are generally drafted jointly by the employer and trustee to fit the circumstances of the case, and it is customary for the trustee to be granted considerable discretion. Under such circumstances, the amount of statutory control is nominal.

With or without statutory restraints, trustees until recently have generally followed traditional practices in the investment of pension funds. Primary emphasis has been placed on government obligations and high-grade corporate debt securities. Real estate mortgages and privately placed securities, which are major and highly attractive outlets for life insurance funds, have played minor roles in trust company investment operations. In recent years, common stocks have attracted considerable attention as an outlet for trusteed pension funds. Investment in equities has been urged on the grounds that (1) it permits wider diversification, since many strong companies, including virtually all banks and insurance companies, have no securities outstanding other than common stock, and (2) it offers the possibility of a higher yield than that of fixed-income investments, particularly when dividends and capital gains are combined. The latter prospect has been viewed as a partial hedge against secular increases in the price level. As a result, trusteed pension funds are flowing into equities in increasing quantities. Many trusteed plans have adopted programs calling for equity investments to the extent of 25 to 35 per cent of the portfolio.

A final matter that has a bearing on the relative earning capacity of insurance and trust companies is the income tax status of the investment earnings. The Internal Revenue Code of 1954 provides that "A trust . . . forming part of a stock bonus, pension, or profit-sharing plan of an employer for the exclusive benefit of his employees or their beneficiaries shall be exempt from the Federal income tax."[10] Therefore, if a trusteed pension plan meets the general standards of qualification prescribed by Section 401(a) of the

10. Sections 501(a) and 401(a).

Code, its investment earnings are not subject to Federal income taxation.

Insured pension plans do not enjoy this exemption. Life insurance companies pay a special Federal income tax of 6½ per cent on their net investment earnings,[11] including that portion attributable to the investment of pension reserves. At the current level of insurance company investment earnings, the tax reduces the yield on pension reserves by about 0.20 per cent, with the practical effect of increasing the cost of an insured pension plan by roughly 5 per cent.[12] This difference in tax treatment of trusteed and insured pension reserves, stemming from a technical distinction between a trust and an insurance contract which has not been observed in Section 404 of the Code or, for that matter, throughout Section 401(a), seems to represent a definite discrimination in the application of the tax laws. There is a strong likelihood that future legislation will equalize the tax status of insured and trusteed plans, through either the imposition of a tax on trust earnings or, what is more likely, the exclusion of insurance company investment earnings attributable to pension reserves.

Advocates of the insured and trusteed approaches to pension funding disagree as to the implications of the differences just described. Insurance partisans see unique advantages in the principle of commingling. They point out that the insurance company need not be concerned with the liquidity of an isolated pension plan but can integrate the requirements of that plan with those of other pension plans and, in fact, of the company's entire business. Since an insurance company's total income, including premiums, investment earnings, and maturing investments, normally exceeds its disbursements by a large margin,[13] the company enjoys an unusual degree of liquidity. The company is in a position to place the

11. More accurately, the companies pay a Federal income tax of 3¾ per cent of the first $200,000 of net investment income and 6½ per cent on amounts in excess of $200,000.

12. Statement of D. N. Warters before the Subcommittee on the Taxation of Life Insurance Companies of the Committee on Ways and Means, House of Representatives, 82nd Congress, December 13, 1954, pp. 2-3.

13. In 1932, the year of heaviest withdrawals, the aggregate income of the life insurance companies exceeded their disbursements, including cash surrenders, by approximately $655 million. This figure does not reflect funds made available through maturing investments. *Proceedings of the National Association of Insurance Commissioners*, 1952, p. 240. Individual companies, of course, may have suffered a shortage of cash resources.

bulk of its funds in long-term investments, thus taking advantage of the higher yields associated with the longer maturities. The liquidity requirements of a segregated trusteed plan are pictured as much higher than those of the typical insurance company. A single trust, it is argued, cannot depend on a flow of new money, adequate under all circumstances to meet cash demands, particularly in the case of a contributory plan which is subject to the hazard of heavy withdrawals of employee contributions during periods of unemployment. To avoid the possibility of having to liquidate securities in an unfavorable market, the trustee must hold substantial sums in short-term securities, thus reducing the yield on the over-all fund.

The pooling technique is conducive to higher investment returns in another respect, according to insurance advocates. The regular—and predictable—flow of new money enables the insurance company to invest its funds with a minimum lag, thus narrowing or eliminating altogether the spread between gross and net yields stemming from investment delays. The irregular flow of new money into a trusteed pension fund is alleged to complicate the trustee's job and make more difficult the avoidance of delays.

In addition to promoting higher yields, the pooling principle enhances the safety of the funds, say the insurance proponents. The funds of the smallest insured pension plan are invested with the same degree of diversification as that obtaining in the composite portfolio of the insurance company. Comparable diversification is found only among the largest trusteed plans. Investment losses, which are inevitable under both types of funding agency, are spread pro rata over all interests, including pension plans, in the case of an insurance company, while in the case of a trust company they fall on the particular interest or interests involved.

Partisans of the trusteed approach deny that the liquidity requirements of a trusteed plan are greater than those of a plan underwritten by a life insurance company. They argue that, to the contrary, the demand nature of surrender values, loan values, and certain deposits held by life insurance companies require them to place greater emphasis on liquidity, repayment features, and early maturities than is found necessary under the typical pension trust. Any advantage gained by mingling insured pension funds is lost, trust adherents claim, by merging the funds with other insurance company assets and exposing them to the uncertainties of the company's other business. As to investment delays, trust officers point out that contributions are received monthly from the large majority of pension trusts, enabling the trustee to estimate with precision the amount of money to be invested and minimizing the possibility of lags.

Trust advocates see no virtue in commingling from the standpoint of capital preservation. They point to the obvious fact that the quality of the assets determines the amount of losses and rest their case on the claim that the quality of pension trust assets is superior to that of life insurance company assets. Moreover, they assert, it is a matter of individual preference whether an employer wishes to bear only the losses that are sustained by his particular trust fund or whether he wishes to have a share in all losses, including those arising from the investment of assets accumulated for purposes unrelated to pensions. While conceding that small trust funds cannot be adequately diversified and, hence, should be pooled, trust company spokesmen hold that the great majority of trusteed pension funds are large enough to permit of adequate diversification.

More controversial than the issue of pooling versus segregation is the growing trend toward inclusion of substantial amounts of common stock in the investment portfolio of trusteed pension funds. Trust companies have advocated the inclusion of common stock as a means of raising the yield on the portfolio and thereby reducing the cost of the pension plan to the employer. They have pointed to the favorable performance of common stocks in recent years, as well as to the hypothetical results that could have been obtained by adherence to a long-run program of common stock investment. They argue that a pension fund, with a steady flow of new money and relatively low liquidity requirements, particularly during the early years of its existence, is in an ideal position to realize the maximum potential of common stock earning power. The peculiar adaptability of pension funds to common stock investment has been described by a proponent in the following terms:

Employee Pension Funds will steadily expand in size over a period of years. Payments into the fund, whether contributory or noncontributory, may be expected to far exceed benefit payments until such time as a large percentage of the employees entitled to benefits has retired.

As a result, the ability to liquidate the bulk of the investments of a pension fund without loss at a specific time is not an important objective.

Unlike banks and like life insurance companies, pension funds do not require a high degree of liquidity in their investments.

Moreover, employee pension funds will receive money for investment in moderate amounts year after year. Hence, in the acquisition of investments they automatically resort to "dollar averaging"; that is, investing about the same number of dollars year after year so that they acquire more of a security when prices are low than when they are high. The "dollar averaging" principle results in reducing the average cost of an investment well below its average selling price over a period of years.[14]

Those who oppose the inclusion of common stock in the portfolio of pension funds regard equities as too speculative for pension purposes. They cite the potentially higher yield of common stock as proof that they are inherently more risky than the fixed income type of investment. They assert that there is not only greater uncertainty that the anticipated yield will materialize but also less certainty that the principal will remain intact. They caution against hedging a fixed dollar obligation with assets that promise neither definiteness of yield nor return of the purchase price.

The same skeptics warn against overly optimistic assumptions regarding common stock performance. Virtually all pension trust equity investment programs have been initiated within the last few years, under the most favorable economic conditions, and have shown generally good results. The long-run success of such a program, however, will depend to a great extent on (1) the liquidity requirements that arise under less favorable economic conditions, and (2) the ability of the trustee, acting on behalf of and under instructions from the employer, to ignore the current behavior of the stock market and adhere unwaveringly to a fixed policy of common stock investment, such as that represented by the principle of dollar averaging. The merits of a common stock investment program can be evaluated only in retrospect, it is argued, not on the basis of expectations.

The Record to Date.—Statistics are available as to the performance of the insurance companies. As a group, the life insurance companies domiciled in the United States earned 3.36 per cent on their mean ledger assets in 1953.[15] This figure represents the net investment income, after deducting all expenses allocable to investment

14. Jules I. Bogen, Editorial in the *Journal of Commerce,* May 5, 1950, p. 4.
15. Institute of Life Insurance, *Life Insurance Fact Book*, 1954, p. 53.

operations but before deduction of Federal income taxes. The yield after taxes was 3.15 per cent. Neither figure reflects capital gains and losses.

The yield after taxes was about 38 per cent less than the companies were able to earn during the 1920's and early 1930's. The average earning rate for the decade of the 1920's was 5.07 per cent, but with the decline in the general level of interest rates the yield dropped to 4.10 per cent in the 1930's and to 3.16 per cent in the 1940's.[16] The low point was reached in 1947 when the yield declined to 2.88 per cent, and the upturn which began in 1948 has continued to the present. The reversal of the trend has been due partly to portfolio changes and the development of new outlets for funds and partly to a general rise in interest levels since the end of World War II.

A statistic which is more meaningful for pension purposes is the net rate of interest credited to funds held by life insurance companies under group annuity contracts. Fortunately, a composite rate is available on an annual basis for the twelve-year period 1942-1953 for the seven companies writing the bulk of the group annuity business. That information is presented in Table 12.

The rates shown in Table 12 were derived from investment data that were tabulated on a comparable basis and weighted according to the investment income of the companies involved. They represent net earnings after taxes. Capital gains and losses are reflected, which accounts for the wide fluctuations from year to year and the fact

TABLE 12

COMPOSITE RATE OF INTEREST CREDITED TO GROUP ANNUITY
ACCOUNTS BY SEVEN LEADING COMPANIES 1942-1953

Year	Rate Credited	Year	Rate Credited
1942	3.14%	1948	2.93%
1943	3.86	1949	3.03
1944	3.99	1950	3.12
1945	4.08	1951	2.95
1946	3.08	1952	3.11
1947	2.90	1953	3.10

Source: Kenneth Black, Jr., *op. cit.*, p. 172.

16. *Ibid.*, p. 54.

that in some years the rate of interest credited to annuity reserves greatly exceeded the yield on mean ledger assets for the industry as a whole.

Information on trust company performance is fragmentary. Trust companies are under no obligation to report the earnings of the trusts administered by them, and most are reluctant to divulge such data even on a confidential basis. Nevertheless, one large firm of pension consultants has compiled the earnings experience of a number of trusteed plans of various sizes and ages and has kindly made the exhibit available, with company identification withheld. Excerpts from the exhibit are presented in Table 13.

Only plans with assets of $1 million or more are included in the table, the plans being classified into four categories by size and listed in the order of yield in 1953—the last year for which information is available. The assets represented by these thirty plans aggregate more than $2 billion or about 20 per cent of the estimated $10 billion held under all trusteed plans, which should provide a fairly reliable sample of trust fund performance in the recent past. In general, the earnings rate for trusts with fewer than $1 million in assets is lower than that of the larger trusts.

The earnings reflect capital gains and losses but, in accordance with trust company accounting practice, have not been adjusted for trustee fees. The reduction in yield because of trustee fees will amount to as much as ¼ per cent in the case of the smaller funds and to as little as 1/20 per cent in the case of the largest funds. In the case of extremely small funds (under $100,000, for example), trustee charges may equal ½ per cent of the fund.

The record is one of constantly improving investment performance. In 1948, 21 out of 26 plans had earnings of less than 3 per cent, with 18 experiencing yields of less than 2.75 per cent. Eight plans had yields of less than 2.50 per cent, one going as low as 1.69 per cent. One year later, 19 out of 28 plans recorded earnings of less than 3 per cent, with 16 showing a yield of less than 2.75 per cent. During 1950, 18 plans out of 30 earned less than 3 per cent and 10 plans less than 2.75 per cent. By 1951, only 14 plans failed to earn 3 per cent, and only 8 failed to earn 2.75 per cent. In 1952, all plans except 7 earned more than 3 per cent, 6 of the 7, however, earning less than 2.75 per cent. Finally, in 1953, only five trusts earned less than 3 per cent, assuming that the fund reflected in line 4 was still earning less than 3 per cent.

Analyzed in another manner, the 1948 earnings of only five trusteed plans equaled the composite rate of interest credited to group annuity contracts in that year, but the earnings in those five cases were greatly in excess of the insurance companies' rate. In subsequent years, the number of trusteed plans whose earnings equaled or exceeded the composite rate credited to group annuity contracts in those years rose to 9, 11, 16, 18 and 20 in that order.

If a generalization may be ventured from this sample, it might

TABLE 13

INVESTMENT EARNINGS OF THIRTY TRUSTEED
PENSION PLANS 1948-1953

Line	Size of Fund	1948	1949	1950	1951	1952	1953
1		4.97%	4.09%	4.65%	4.30%	4.17%	4.40%
2	Over	2.49	2.57	2.70	3.09	3.28	3.33
3	$50,000,000	2.60	2.71	2.80	2.67	2.69	2.98
4		1.69	2.26	2.39	2.48	2.79	—
5		9.60	8.63	10.44	8.90	7.79	6.55
6	$25,000,000	8.25	5.66	8.55	7.07	6.08	—
7	to	4.01	4.99	6.73	9.37	4.63	4.49
8	$50,000,000	2.08	1.98	2.52	2.12	2.18	2.89
9	$10,000,000	2.59	2.64	2.08	2.94	3.09	3.35
10	to	2.63	2.77	2.73	2.90	3.03	3.22
11	$25,000,000	2.98	2.99	2.99	3.01	3.00	3.00
12		2.87	4.16	4.89	5.72	4.56	4.64
13		—	—	2.78	4.13	3.77	3.68
14		2.56	2.60	3.01	3.02	3.06	3.64
15		—	3.53	3.33	3.11	3.28	3.61
16		2.51	2.73	2.81	3.34	3.47	3.59
17		2.81	3.16	3.60	3.05	3.53	3.52
18		2.74	2.67	3.47	3.18	3.13	3.44
19		2.40	2.62	3.55	2.30	4.10	3.37
20	$ 1,000,000	—	—	2.78	3.50	3.19	3.28
21	to	2.74	3.12	2.90	2.96	3.77	3.23
22	$10,000,000	2.55	2.69	2.80	2.76	3.17	3.17
23		3.09	3.52	4.03	3.80	3.37	3.16
24		2.55	2.71	2.78	2.70	2.74	3.11
25		2.64	2.81	3.14	3.55	3.51	3.07
26		—	2.69	2.73	2.85	3.12	3.07
27		2.25	2.23	2.18	2.37	2.53	3.05
28		2.04	2.24	2.46	2.28	3.04	3.03
29		1.88	2.38	2.42	2.10	2.57	2.60
30		2.21	2.62	2.57	2.51	2.51	2.56

Source: Adapted from an exhibit prepared by a well-known firm of pension consultants.

be concluded that through 1950, the insurance companies had a far more impressive record than that of the trust companies. There were wide variations among the various trusts, reflecting basic differences in investment policy, and a few plans showed returns greatly in excess of the composite rate earned by the seven leading group annuity companies. By 1951, a definite trend toward common stock investments was under way, and the results are unmistakably apparent in the earnings exhibit. Those trusts which do not engage in any equity investment show a yield below the standards of the insurance companies, while those that do pursue a common stock investment policy record a yield substantially better than that of the insurance companies, the margin of superiority depending upon the extent of equity investment and the emphasis placed on capital gains. Unusually high yields generally reflect a special situation such as investment in the common or preferred stock of the employer.

EXPENSES

A third factor that has a bearing on the cost of a pension plan is that of expenses. In neither insured nor trusteed plans can expenses be regarded as a major element of cost, with the exception of individual insurance and annuity contracts. Interestingly, greater differences in the expense element exist among the various types of insured plans than between trusteed plans and their closest insurance counterpart—the group annuity contracts.

Expense Element in Insured Plans.—The expenses incurred in connection with insured pension plans may be broadly classified as (1) acquisition costs, (2) administrative costs, and (3) taxes.

The most significant item among the acquisition costs is the commissions paid to the field forces for the development and servicing of the business. In this area arise the principal differences in the expense element of the various plans. In the case of an individual contract plan, the commission is the same as that payable on a contract which is not part of a pension trust, unless a special contract is used for pension purposes, in which case the commission would probably be lower. The commission normally varies with the type of contract and the size of the premium. A typical first-year commission payable on a retirement income contract issued at age 45, the average age of issue in many pension trusts, might be 25 per cent of the first year gross premium, with the percentage being smaller at ages above 45 and larger at ages below 45. A renewal commission of 5 per cent of the gross premium for the next nine years would constitute a typical pattern of renewal commissions.

The commissions on group permanent contracts are normally much smaller than those payable on individual contracts. The scale used by one of the leading companies in the group permanent field for the basic group permanent contract—retirement endowment at 60 or 65—is as follows:

Portion of Annual Premiums	Commissions as Percentage of Adjusted Gross Premiums		
	1st year	Next 9 years	Next 10 years
First $ 5,000	20%	4.5%	2.25%
Next $ 20,000	16	3.75	1.875
Next $ 50,000	12	3.0	1.5
Next $ 75,000	9	2.5	1.25
Next $100,000	6	2.0	1.0

The commission paid on that portion of the annual premium in excess of $250,000 is adjusted to fit individual circumstances. The foregoing scale appears to be representative of those used by other important group permanent companies.

The smallest commissions are payable under group annuity contracts. Once more it seems preferable to present typical scales rather than to attempt a generalization. One large company, extremely active in the group annuity field, provides commissions according to the following scale:

Portion of Annual Premiums	Commissions as Percentage of Gross Premiums	
	1st year	2nd to 10th year
First $ 20,000	7.0%	1.5%
Next $ 30,000	3.0	1.5
Next $450,000	1.0	0.6
Over $500,000	0.4	0.3

Another company, equally active in the group annuity field, pays according to the following scale:

Portion of Annual Premiums	Commissions as Percentage of Gross Premiums	
	1st year	2nd to 10th year
First $100,000	3.0%	1.0%
Next $400,000	1.0	0.5
Over $500,000	0.4	0.2

The principal difference between the two scales lies in the treatment of small cases, although there is a difference, small but relatively significant, in the renewal commissions at all levels.

Other acquisition costs include commissions or comparable payments to field supervisors, salaries of home office representatives who assist in the installation of the plans, fees for medical examinations, where required, expense of constructing initial records, and the cost of issuing the necessary contracts and certificates. Premium taxes on first year premiums might well be considered an acquisition expense but, in view of their importance, have been separately classified.

The administrative expenses of an insured pension plan are basically those attributable to the record-keeping and actuarial functions. In this category are expenses connected with premium accounting, reserve valuation, dividend calculation, benefit payments, and similar functions. In this area, also, the per unit expenses of group permanent and group annuity contracts are much lower than those of individual insurance and annuity contracts because of bulk handling. This is particularly true of noncontributory deposit administration and immediate participation guarantee contracts under which no accounts are established by the insurance company for individual employees until the benefits vest or until the employees retire. Investment expenses are normally charged against investment income and are not treated as administrative expenses. Each pension plan must bear its pro rata share of the insurance company's overhead, which falls in the category of administrative expense.

Life insurance companies are subject to the usual types of taxes, such as Federal and state income taxes, Social Security taxes, transfer taxes, and the like, but, in addition, they are subject to a special tax on premiums levied by the various states. While most states levy a tax on ordinary insurance premiums, at least those of companies domiciled in other states, only seventeen states tax annuity premiums on any basis. These taxes on annuity premiums range from ½ per cent in South Dakota to 3 per cent in Idaho, the most common being 2 per cent. Neither New York nor Pennsylvania taxes annuity premiums. In the aggregate, less than 1 per cent of group annuity premiums has been absorbed by state premium taxes, but such taxes have consistently accounted for a third or more of all group annuity expenses.

In order to meet these expenses, and for other purposes, the insurance companies add a special charge, called loading, to their net premiums to arrive at the gross premium paid by the policyholder. The loading, however, does not necessarily, and in fact usually does not, measure the additional cost to the policyholder attributable to expenses, since a portion of the loading may be returned in the form of dividends or may be used to accumulate a contingency reserve which would otherwise have had to come out of the net premium or from surplus. It is more accurate to state that, in the normal case, the loading represents the maximum potential expense that may be incurred under the contract. It is conceivable that under certain old policies, expenses may currently exceed the loading element, the deficiency being offset by mortality savings and excess interest, but under normal circumstances expenses can be assumed to be considerably less than the loading.

With this explanation, it may be pointed out that the loading on a retirement annuity or retirement income contract, one of which is likely to be used with an individual policy pension trust, while varying among companies and possibly with age of issue, might be in the neighborhood of 20 per cent of the net premium. The loading on group permanent contracts, like commissions, is lower than that of individual contracts, typically amounting to 12 or 13 per cent of the gross premium. The loading on group annuity contracts, 5 to 8 per cent of the gross premium, is the lowest of all. Even so, the loading under the group annuity contract is grossly redundant, except for small cases. The greater portion of the loading is not used to meet current expenses but is allocated to the accumulation of a contingency fund or returned to the employer in the form of dividends.

The actual expenses incurred by an insurance company under group annuity contracts are reported separately in the annual statements filed with the state insurance departments. The twelve-year record of such expenses for the seven leading group annuity companies is presented in Table 14.

TABLE 14

GROUP ANNUITY EXPENSES AS A PERCENTAGE OF PREMIUMS
WEIGHTED AVERAGE FOR SEVEN LEADING COMPANIES FOR PERIOD
1942-1953

Year	Total Expenses	Commissions	Taxes*	All Other
1942	2.83%	.53%	.94%	1.36%
1943	2.78	.50	.95	1.33
1944	2.50	.49	.88	1.13
1945	2.54	.48	.72	1.34
1946	2.69	.42	.83	1.44
1947	2.69	.43	.80	1.46
1948	2.61	.38	.80	1.43
1949	2.87	.40	1.02	1.45
1950	2.40	.32	.84	1.24
1951	2.56	.33	.90	1.33
1952	2.57	.32	.98	1.27
1953	2.57	.31	.75	1.51

* Does not include Federal income taxes.
Source: Kenneth Black, Jr., op. cit., p. 172.

In the table, group annuity expenses are broken down into commissions, taxes, and "all other," and expressed as a percentage of premiums. It will be noted that, in the aggregate, commissions constitute an insignificant cost of doing business. In 1953, they amounted to only .31 of 1 per cent of the premiums collected by the companies. The percentage has declined as renewal commissions exert an ever-stronger influence, and the trend may be expected to continue as renewal commissions expire on the older plans. Taxes have been a far more significant item, in later years being about 2½ times as large as commissions. At no time during the twelve-year period did total expenses exceed 2.87 per cent of premiums and in the latest year they amounted to only 2.57 per cent.

The foregoing expense ratios reflect the composite expense rates of seven companies for all types of group annuity contracts, including the deposit administration and immediate participation guarantee forms, and for all cases, irrespective of size or duration. Yet the expense rate varies significantly with the size of the case and, to a lesser extent, with the species of group annuity contract. The influence of size and duration can be observed in Table 15.

TABLE 15

ESTIMATED EXPENSES OF DEFERRED GROUP ANNUITY
CONTRACT BY SIZE AND DURATION OF PLAN[a]

Annual Premiums or Purchase Payments	Number of Eligible Lives			
	100	500	1000	2500
	First Ten Years of Contract			
$ 25,000	7.22%	—%[c]	—%[c]	—%[c]
50,000	5.07	7.21	—[c]	—[c]
100,000	3.66	4.74	5.98	—[c]
250,000	2.56	2.99	3.49	4.99
500,000	2.20	2.41	2.66	3.41
1,000,000	—[b]	1.90	2.03	2.40
	Sixth Through Fifteenth Years			
$ 25,000	4.90	—[c]	—[c]	—[c]
50,000	3.17	5.12	—[c]	—[c]
100,000	2.21	3.19	4.32	—[c]
250,000	1.64	2.03	2.48	3.84
500,000	1.45	1.64	1.87	2.55
1,000,000	—[b]	1.40	1.51	1.85
	Eleventh Through Twentieth Years			
$ 25,000	4.34	—[c]	—[c]	—[c]
50,000	2.63	4.58	—[c]	—[c]
100,000	1.84	2.81	3.94	—[c]
250,000	1.36	1.75	2.20	3.56
500,000	1.20	1.40	1.62	2.30
1,000,000	—[b]	1.22	1.33	1.67

a Based on the expense studies of one of the largest group annuity companies; expenses expressed as a percentage of the premium or purchase payments during each of the periods indicated. Investment expenses not included.

b Combinations not found in practice.

c Combinations not acceptable to the company because of the small average premium per life.

Table 15 shows for certain combinations of active lives and annual premiums the expenses which will be incurred during three different periods of a deferred group annuity contract, according to the expense analysis of one of the oldest and largest group annuity companies. The expenses are expressed as a percentage of the total premium payments under the contract during each of the three periods studied. Only prospective *actual* expenses are reflected, no allowance being made for amounts set aside to meet expenses that will arise beyond the twenty-year period, which amounts would become a part of the reserve for future expenses.

For any given number of lives the expense ratio declines as the premium volume increases, while for any given premium volume the expense rate increases with the number of lives, a reflection of the expense of record maintenance. Furthermore, for any specific combination of lives and premiums the expense ratio declines with each successive period. The latter phenomenon is primarily traceable to the fact that renewal commissions for any given set of premiums expire at the end of ten years and thereafter only premium taxes and administrative expenses are reflected in the expense estimates. The expenses of the first period are strongly influenced by first-year commissions and other acquisition expenses, while the second period reflects no first-year commissions and renewal commissions for only five years. No commissions nor acquisition expenses are reflected in the data for the third period.

During the first ten years the expenses range from a high of 7.22 per cent in a case of 100 lives and an annual premium of $25,000, to a low of 1.90 per cent in a case of 500 lives and an annual premium of $1,000,000—an unusual combination. With respect to cases below 100 lives, the expense rate goes above the high of 7.22 per cent shown in the table, rising to 11 per cent for plans covering only ten lives, when account is taken of the special administrative charge levied in such cases. According to the projections, the expense ratio during the second ten years may go as low as 1.20 per cent with the 100 lives and $500,000 premium combination, or to 1.67 per cent in the much more plausible combination of 2500 lives and $1,000,000 of premiums.

Comparable prospective expense ratios for deposit administration contracts issued by the same company are given in Table 16. This table reflects the savings in administrative expense attributable to unallocated funding, since commissions and premium taxes—the other major elements of expense—are identical to those incurred under the deferred group annuity contract. For all combinations the expense ratios under the deposit administration contract are lower

TABLE 16

ESTIMATED EXPENSES OF DEPOSIT ADMINISTRATION
CONTRACT BY SIZE AND DURATION OF PLAN[a]

Annual Premiums of Purchase Payments	Number of Eligible Lives				
	100	500	1000	2500	10,000
First Ten Years of Contract					
$ 25,000	6.22%	—%[c]	—%[c]	—%[c]	—%[c]
50,000	4.55	5.40	—[c]	—[c]	—[c]
100,000	3.37	3.79	4.17	—[c]	—[c]
500,000	2.08	2.17	4.24	2.46	—[c]
1,000,000	—[b]	1.75	1.79	1.89	2.42
2,000,000	—[b]	—[b]	1.56	1.61	1.87
Sixth Through Fifteenth Years					
$ 25,000	3.98	—[c]	—[c]	—[c]	—[c]
50,000	2.70	3.52	—[c]	—[c]	—[c]
100,000	1.94	2.36	2.72	—[c]	—[c]
500,000	1.34	1.42	1.50	1.71	—[c]
1,000,000	—[b]	1.25	1.29	1.40	1.90
2,000,000	—[b]	1.17	1.19	1.24	1.49
Eleventh Through Twentieth Years					
$ 25,000	3.43	—[c]	—[c]	—[c]	—[c]
50,000	2.15	2.98	—[c]	—[c]	—[c]
100,000	1.57	1.98	2.35	—[c]	—[c]
500,000	1.09	1.18	1.25	1.46	2.48
1,000,000	—[b]	1.08	1.11	1.22	1.73
2,000,000	—[b]	1.03	1.05	1.10	1.35

a Based on the expense studies of the same company whose findings were reported in Table 15.
b Combinations not found in practice.
c Combinations not acceptable to the company because of the small average premium per life.

than their counterparts under the deferred group annuity contract.

It is well to remember that these cost projections are based on current expense levels and are therefore subject to modification if the expense components undergo a change in the future.

In addition to the foregoing expenses which are incurred by the insurance company and passed on to the employer, the latter incurs some administrative expenses within his own organization and, occasionally under deposit administration and IPG contracts, fees to actuarial consultants.

Expense Element in Trusteed Plans.—The expenses incurred under trusteed plans are of three types: (1) actuarial fees, (2) trustee fees, and (3) employer administrative costs.

Trust companies do not provide actuarial facilities as a part of their pension service. The employer, therefore, must retain his own actuarial consultant and compensate him independently of any fees paid to the trustee. Charges will be incurred for two types of service: (1) those incident to the establishment of the plan and (2) those related to the year-to-year operations of the plan. These charges will vary with the nature and magnitude of the services provided, as well as among actuarial firms, but it is possible to indicate the general range of fees. The fee for establishment of the plan, including the so-called development fee, will generally fall within a range of $5,000-$15,000, while the annual fee for valuation, preparation of Treasury reports, and other normal actuarial services will usually run around 50 per cent of the installation charge or within a range of $2,500 to $7,500. For extremely small cases, the fees will fall below those indicated, while for the exceptionally large cases the fees will run considerably higher than those indicated above.

The principal charge levied by the trustee is the fee for investment services. This charge is levied annually and is based on the size of the fund. There is no standard scale of charges, but competition has produced fees that are roughly comparable. A representative fee among the banks in the New York area is ¼ per cent of the first $1,000,000 in the pension fund, 1/10 per cent of the next $4,000,000, and 1/20 per cent of the excess over $5,000,000. Banks in other areas tend to charge somewhat higher rates. A typical scale of charges among Midwestern banks, for example, is ½ per cent of the first $50,000, ¼ per cent of the next $1,950,000, 6/40 per cent of the next $2,000,000, 1/10 per cent of the next $2,000,000, and 3/40 per cent of the next $2,000,000, and 1/20 per cent of the excess over $8,000,-000. Some banks specify a limit beyond which the charge will be subject to negotiation. Smaller banks tend to charge a higher fee than larger banks. Since the investment fee is based on total accumulations under the plan, it tends to constitute an increasing percentage of annual contributions.

If the trustee prepares and mails the checks to retired employees, an additional charge is made. The charge is usually a specified amount per check, subject to a minimum annual charge. The New York banks tend to charge ten cents per check, with a minimum annual charge of $250, while a typical scale in the Midwest is seventy-five cents per check on the first 100 checks, twenty-five cents per check on the next 1,900 checks, and fifteen cents per check on the excess above 2,000 checks. Any special administrative services performed by the trust company, such as the preparation of booklets or other explanatory material, are subject to additional charges.

The employer also incurs certain administrative expenses within his own organization. He must maintain the basic personnel records from which he can certify to the trustee the benefits to be paid to each employee, as well as the time when the payments are to be made. For purposes of employee relations or for other reasons, the employer may handle the check-writing function. He may also have to make decisions with respect to actuarial assumptions, investment policies, and other broad matters affecting the plan. The investment function in particular may make heavy demands on the executive staff, since a pension committee of the employer is frequently given the responsibility of approving all investments made by the trustee.

To a large extent, the administrative functions of the employer are the same whether the plan be insured or trusteed. While the relative magnitude of employer administrative expenses under insured and trusteed plans is a subject of considerable controversy and wide disagreement, the broader responsibility of the employer under a trusteed plan should logically entail greater demands on the executive staff than under an insured plan. Any differences, however, should be relatively insignificant in the total cost picture.

Comparison of Expenses Under Insured and Trusteed Plans.— Precise quantitative comparisons of expenses of insured and trusteed pension plans are difficult, if not impossible, to develop because of differences in the nature, incidence, and accounting treatment of the expenses involved. It seems preferable, therefore, to restrict the analysis to a statement of principles.

In the interest of clarity and consistency, investment expenses should be treated as deductions from gross investment earnings rather than as expenses per se. This procedure is dictated by the basic differences in insurance and trust company investment practices which may be reflected in both gross yield and investment expenses. A prime example is the insurance company emphasis on real estate mortgages which combine a relatively high gross yield with relatively heavy acquisition and servicing costs.

A valid expense analysis, therefore, involves a balancing of (1) acquisition expenses (primarily commissions), (2) premium taxes, (3) insurance company administrative expenses, and (4) employer administrative and legal expenses incurred under insured plans against (1) fees of actuarial consultants and (2) employer administrative and legal expenses incurred under trusteed plans.

Employer administrative and legal fees might well offset each other under the two types of plan, but it is more likely that they will be higher under the trusteed plan. The offsetting items to the fees of actuarial consultants are insurance company acquisition and administrative expenses. In general, the latter will exceed the former, the margin being wide in the case of individual contract plans and narrowing down to less than one percentage point in the case of some group annuity contracts. In fact, over a period of twenty or thirty years the expenses of a deposit administration contract, exclusive of premium taxes and investment expenses, might conceivably run as low as the fees of the actuarial consultant for the same period. This would not be true, of course, if the employer retains a consulting actuary in connection with his deposit administration plan, which is occasionally the case. On the other hand, the trust company also incurs acquisition expenses which, it must be assumed, will be passed on to the employer in one form or another. At the present time such expenses appear to be inconsequential.

The premium tax levied on insured plans has no counterpart among trusteed plans and is a penalty the employer pays for electing an insured plan. All insured plans, however, do not pay such tax, since only seventeen states levy a tax on group annuity premiums. Some companies pro rate the taxes paid on group annuity premiums over all group annuity policyholders, irrespective of the location of the employees, while others assess the tax of a particular state against only those policyholders having covered employees in that state. Therefore, if an employer has no employees in a state which taxes group annuity premiums and is insured by a company which does not pro rate such taxes, he would avoid the tax. On the other hand, an employer insured by a company which does not pro rate would, in most of the seventeen states, pay a tax of 2 per cent of contributions.

It is essential in comparing expenses of insured and trusteed plans to keep in mind that the expenses of insured plans are prefunded. The loading contained in an insurance premium is designed to take care of all expenses incurred at any time in connection with the benefit purchased by the premium. Therefore, if an insured plan should be terminated at any point, the accumulated reserves would be adequate to absorb any expenses incurred in the future, as well as to provide all benefits purchased to that point. In other words, the loading represents the maximum potential expenses under the plan.

Expenses under a trusteed plan, on the other hand, are financed on a pay-as-you-go basis. The benefits may be funded in advance, but the expenses are almost always handled on a current basis. If a trusteed plan should terminate, the employer would continue to incur expenses for whatever period the trust would have to be administered. To compare the loading under an insured plan with the reported expenses of a trusteed plan is to compare the total potential expenses, past and future, of the former with only the past expenses of the latter. Such a comparison is improper and misleading.

TURNOVER

The effect of turnover on the cost of a pension plan has been discussed in a previous chapter. It was pointed out that the rate of turnover is a major determinant of cost, although its influence may be modified to some extent by the vesting provisions of the plan, as well as by the eligibility requirements. In a typical plan only a small percentage of the employees who qualify for coverage will ever qualify for benefits. This is true whether the plan be of the insured or trusteed variety. Moreover, there is no reason to believe that the rate of turnover will be influenced to any measurable degree by the type of financing adopted. Nevertheless, the funding medium does determine the time when the turnover factor exerts its influence, as well as the manner in which the influence is exerted.

Under plans which use allocated funding, no allowance is made in the premiums for anticipated turnover, credit being given as the turnover occurs. Under unallocated funding media, turnover is often discounted in advance, adjustments being made only for variations of actual from projected experience. The practical significance of this difference in procedure is that a larger initial outlay is required under those plans which do not discount for turnover. Only if the lowest initial outlay is a matter of paramount concern should turnover be a factor in the choice of funding medium.

As a matter of practice, turnover undoubtedly wields a stronger influence among trusteed plans than among insured plans. This is due to the fact that trusteed plans usually contain less liberal vesting provisions and less stringent requirements for coverage than insured plans. The turnover factor, therefore, has a larger area in which to operate. This is clearly a function of the plan provisions, however, and not of the funding medium.

DEFERRED RETIREMENT

Contributions to pension plans are calculated on the assumption that the employees will retire at a specified age, or according to a schedule of retirement ages. It may happen, however, that some employees will not retire at the scheduled time but will continue to work beyond such date. Under some plans, such an employee would receive his retirement benefits as if he had retired, with no reduction in salary, while under others he would not be entitled to benefits as long as he worked but upon retirement would receive the actuarial equivalent of the benefit to which he was entitled at normal retirement age. In neither case would the employer profit by the delayed retirement. Under many plans, however, retirement benefits are deferred until actual retirement, with no actuarial adjustment, and the employer is credited with the benefits which would have gone to the employee had he retired at the scheduled age. When this latter procedure is followed, the employer's cost is obviously reduced.

As is true of turnover, the number of employees who defer their retirement beyond normal retirement is unaffected by the financing vehicle utilized. However, the same type of plan which discounts for turnover may also take credit in advance for anticipated postponements of retirement. This likewise reduces the initial outlay of the employer.

EMPLOYEE CONTRIBUTIONS

It is obvious that, with a given scale of benefits, the cost of a pension plan to the employer can be reduced through employee participation in the financing. It is necessary to make the reservation concerning the scale of benefits since in some cases employee contributions are reflected in higher benefits for the employees rather than in a reduction of the employer's outlay.

Even with the same scale of retirement benefits, however, the employer's outlay is not reduced dollar for dollar by employee contributions. In the typical insured plan, employer contributions are used to purchase annuities which provide no refund in the event that the employee should die before retirement. If employees are required to participate in the financing, justice dictates that their contributions should be returned to their estates, with or without interest, in the event of death before retirement. The result is that, on the average, the employer's cost is reduced about seventy cents by each dollar contributed by the employees, the remaining 30 per cent of employee contributions being used to defray the cost of employee death benefits.[17]

All funding media do not lend themselves equally well to employee participation in financing. Some insurance companies will not administer employee contributions under deposit administration and immediate participation guarantee contracts. If contributions are to be made by employees, such companies would apply them to the purchase of regular deferred annuities. Employee contributions may be made under trusteed plans, but if common stock investments are contemplated, a separate trust may be established for employee money which would be invested in fixed-income securities, or if a single trust is used employee contributions may be earmarked for fixed-income securities.

SUMMARY OF COST FACTORS

It is apparent from the foregoing that only two elements of cost—investment earnings and expenses—are affected in the long run by the choice of funding medium. The other factors—mortality, turnover, age of retirement, and employee contributions—exert an influence on ultimate costs which is unaffected by the funding medium. The incidence or timing of the costs, however, which may be an important consideration in itself, will vary with the funding medium.

17. William W. Fellers, "Pension Costs and Cost Experience," *Pensions and Profit-Sharing* (Washington, D. C.: Bureau of National Affairs, 1953), p. 157.

With respect to investment earnings, it would appear from past performance that life insurance companies will earn a somewhat higher net rate of return than a trust fund invested exclusively in government bonds and high-grade corporate bonds and a much higher rate than one invested wholly in government bonds. If a substantial portion of the trust fund is invested in a diversified list of common stocks, however, the trust fund is likely to show a higher yield, on the basis of current common stock performance, than that of a typical life insurance company, the margin of superiority depending upon the proportion of the fund invested in equities. Most pension fund trustees consider 35 per cent to be the upper limit for common stock holdings, but in recent years this has been more than adequate to yield a return on the total fund in excess of that earned by life insurance companies with their fixed-income investments. Whether or not this situation will prevail throughout the indefinite future is in the realm of conjecture.

With respect to expenses, a fair conclusion might be that under most circumstances a trusteed plan should reflect lower expenses, any differences being attributable—but not necessarily equal to—commissions and premium taxes paid by insurance companies. Under any type of funding medium, with the exception of individual contract plans, expenses tend to be a relatively minor item of cost.

SECURITY OF BENEFITS

The cost of a pension plan is a matter which concerns the employer primarily, the employees secondarily, if at all. The security of benefits, on the other hand, is a matter with which both the employer and the employees are vitally concerned. The employees are concerned for the obvious reason that the benefits promised under the plan will, in the usual case, represent the difference between financial security and financial insecurity in old age. The employer's concern is rooted not only in humanitarian impulses but in the desire to realize the business objectives underlying the establishment of the plan.

The security behind pension promises can be measured in terms of three factors: (1) a third-party guarantee, (2) a segregated pension fund, and (3) the general financial resources and good faith of the employer. These factors are not mutually exclusive, but the classification serves to emphasize some significant points that are pertinent to the discussion.

THIRD-PARTY GUARANTEE

For all practical purposes, only one type of third-party guarantee is available for the safeguarding of pension benefits and that is the guarantee of a life insurance company. With the exception of the immediate participation guarantee contract, every dollar that is paid to an insurance company under a pension plan carries with it the company's unconditional guarantee that a benefit of a specified amount will be paid pursuant to the terms of the plan. For the purpose of exposition, the insurance company's guarantee may be analyzed from the standpoint of mortality, interest, expenses, and the other factors that enter into the cost of a pension plan, but the paramount consideration from the point of view of the employer and employees is the *composite* guarantee—the company's promise to pay a specified benefit for each dollar contributed. The company may lose under one of its basic assumptions and gain under another, but its commitment remains fixed. The nature and significance of the guarantee should not be obscured by the fact that the *rate schedules* for future contributions may not be guaranteed or may be guaranteed only for a limited period. That is a matter which relates to prospective cost, not security. Whether the rate schedule is guaranteed for the lifetime of the contract or only for a limited period, a dollar, once paid over to the insurance company, immediately becomes entitled to a rate guarantee that will remain with it until it is converted into a retirement benefit. Thus, the security of benefits already purchased is precisely the same, whether they are to be paid under an individual insurance or annuity contract, a group permanent contract, a deferred group annuity, or a deposit administration group annuity. It should be recalled, however, that under deposit administration plans, only employee contributions, if any, are applied to the purchase of benefits for active employees, so that only retired employees enjoy the type of security available under conventional insurance contracts. No benefits are ever purchased under an immediate participation guarantee contract, and the only guarantee provided by the insurance company is the limited rate guarantee offered by a few companies. In effect, however, retired employees enjoy the same security of benefits available under other types of insured plans through an insurance company requirement that a fund of minimum size be maintained. That, however, becomes a function of adequacy of the pension fund, which is the next source of security to be considered.

The arrangement under which a trust company administers the funds of an uninsured plan does not give rise to a third-party guarantee, since the obligation of the trust company is limited to the investment and disbursement of funds turned over to it by the employer.

SEGREGATED PENSION FUND

The significance of a third-party guarantee diminishes as a segregated fund, irrevocably committed to the payment of pension benefits, approaches and is maintained at the level conservatively estimated to be sufficient to liquidate the accrued liability of the plan, including that arising out of credited past service. In the same vein, the guarantee provided under insured plans is effective only as to benefits already purchased, or monies paid in, under the plan. Under any type of plan, therefore, the level of funding, or the extent to which funds have been accumulated, is of crucial importance.

The level of funding under any type of pension plan is a function of two variables: (1) the conservatism of the cost projections, and (2) the rate at which the sums estimated to be required—whatever the basis of the estimates—are accumulated. Under the allocated funding types of insured plan, the insurance company dictates both the conservatism of the cost projections and the rate of accumulation. The cost projections are reflected in the premiums and the rate of funding in the requirement that all benefits—those relating to both past and current service—be purchased in full before the employee retires.

The employee who reaches retirement while the plan is still in operation is assured, therefore, that he will receive all the benefits to which he is entitled. If the plan should terminate before a particular employee reaches retirement, he is assured that all benefits for service after the plan was established have been purchased in full. The same cannot be said of past service benefits. Benefits for past service would not have been purchased in full under an individual contract or group permanent plan, the unpurchased portion depending upon the number of years the contract had to run. The status of such benefits under a deferred group annuity would depend upon the funding policy pursued by the employer. The benefits could have been purchased in full, in part, or to no extent. However, under any of these three types of contracts, whatever portion of past service benefits has been purchased up to the point of termination is definitely credited to the individual employees and, of course, guaranteed.

In connection with deposit administration and immediate participation guarantee group annuities, only the retired employees are assured of receiving all the benefits to which they are entitled under the plan. The position of the active employees depends upon the status of the unallocated fund. The rate at which the active life fund is accumulated is determined, within Treasury regulations, by the employer and his actuarial consultant. Treasury regulations require, as a minimum, that contributions equal to current service costs and interest on the initial past service liability be made, but the employer is accorded considerable leeway in formulating his current service costs. For example, the employer may discount his contributions for death, interest, turnover, and delayed retirement, using any reasonable assumptions. Whether the fund would be adequate, as of any given time, to purchase benefits for all service, past and current, would depend upon the employer's funding policy and the skill and conservatism with which cost projections were made. There is no assurance that the fund would be adequate even to purchase all current service benefits in full. In any case, the rights of a particular employee are subject to the formula for allocation prescribed by the plan, and many plans assign priority to certain classes of employees or classes of benefits. Some employees may receive their benefits in full, while others receive nothing.

Under a trusteed pension plan, all employees, active and retired, must look to the solvency of the trust fund for the security of their benefits, since no outside agency is lending its guarantee to the promise of the employer. The funding policy of the trusteed plan, therefore, is particularly significant.

The trusteed plan is subject to the same Treasury regulations on funding as are applicable to insured plans, but in each case these regulations are aimed primarily at the prevention of *overfunding* rather than *underfunding*. Treasury approval of a pension plan carries with it no assurance that the employer's funding policy is adequate to provide the benefits promised under the plan. Contributions under a trusteed plan must be adequate to cover the normal cost of the plan plus interest on the initial accrued liability, but, as in the case of deposit administration and immediate participation guarantee contracts, the employer has wide discretion in estimating his costs. Liberal assumptions are frequently made with respect to such cost-reducing factors as mortality, interest, turnover, and delayed retirement.

Wide variations exist among trusteed plans as to the rate of funding. Some are funding at the maximum rate permitted under Treasury regulations, while others are funding at the minimum rate. Still others—perhaps the majority—are pursuing a middle course of meeting the normal cost and amortizing the accrued liability over a period of 20 or 30 years.

Inasmuch as the retired employees are usually given a prior lien on the assets of a terminated plan, they are virtually assured of receiving their benefits under a plan which has been funded beyond the minimum level. Even under minimum funding conditions, the accumulated fund should be adequate after a number of years to provide benefits in full to the retired group of employees. As under any unallocated funding medium, however, active employees have no assurance of receiving the benefits for which they have qualified.

It is sometimes said in regard to the security of benefits that a trusteed plan is not permitted to accumulate a contingency reserve. The basis for such a statement is the fact that *in any one tax year* gains from experience more favorable than the assumptions must be credited against the employer's contributions for the following year. Yet it is possible for the plan to accumulate the equivalent of a contingency reserve by methods which are entirely acceptable to the Treasury. The most obvious method is through the use of assumptions less favorable than the experience is likely to be, particularly with respect to interest earnings and turnover. Some plans assume no turnover. While the gains in any particular year, as stated above, must be recognized and credited against the employer's contribution for the following year, the liabilities of all future years are presumably overstated, resulting in the creation of excess reserves. The same result can be achieved through conservative valuation of assets, particularly common stocks.

It should be observed, however, that excess reserves in the form of conservative assumptions are held by life insurance companies, *in addition* to contingency reserves.

GENERAL FINANCIAL RESOURCES

In one sense, the financial resources of the employer are the primary source of security in any pension plan, since, if the employer retains the will and ability to meet the obligations of the plan into the indefinite future, he could dispense with the other two safeguards. The employer does just that under a disbursement or pay-as-you-go plan, and, as a consequence, the employees are totally dependent upon the future resources of the employer. Even in the case of a fully funded plan, the employees must rely on the financial ability of the employer for benefits arising out of service to be performed in the future. However, with respect to benefits which have accrued as a result of past service, using the term in its broadest sense, the financial resources of the employer are important, in the case of insured plans, only if all benefits have not been purchased, and, in the case of trusteed plans, only if the accumulated fund, plus future interest earnings, should prove inadequate to provide the benefits promised under the plan.

As long as a plan is a going concern, it is generally assumed that the employer, with the support of employee contributions, will eventually make the contributions to provide all benefits in full. If the plan should terminate, the primary source of reliance would be the accumulated fund, supplemented in the case of insured plans, by the insurance company's guarantee. Should the fund prove inadequate, supplemental contributions by the employer would then become a matter of paramount consideration.

A realistic appraisal of the situation leads to the conclusion that the prospects of supplementary employer contributions are not too bright. Until a plan has been in effect for ten years without a substantive amendment, it can be terminated without retroactive tax penalties only for reasons of "business necessity," the most common of which is inability to meet the financial obligations of the plan. If the employer can prove to the Treasury that he lacks the financial resources to continue the plan, it seems unlikely that he would voluntarily assume the obligation of making good a deficiency in the fund. If a plan remains in operation for more than ten years, it would become such an integral phase of the employer's personnel policy that one must assume that it would be terminated only for the most compelling financial reasons. In some cases, of course, an employer may terminate a plan in order to avoid the creation of additional liabilities, with the full intention of meeting those which have been created in the past.

A question may well be raised at this point as to the legal obligation of the employer to make up any deficit in the pension fund. The answer seems clear in the case of a voluntary unilateral plan in which the employer customarily reserves the right to terminate the plan at any time, and specifically limits his legal obligation to the funds already contributed. With respect to this type of plan, an eminent legal authority has stated: ". . . Under . . . a funded unilateral company plan the employees qualifying for pensions may obtain vested rights to pension benefits, [but] they can look only to the trustee or to the insurance company, to whom the pension fund has been entrusted, for the payment of their pension benefits. If that fund should prove inadequate, the employees normally have no legal recourse against the company itself to compel additional contributions or to require the company to assume direct liability for the payment of the pensions."[18]

The answer is not so clear with respect to negotiated bilateral plans. The employer's obligation depends upon the terms of the particular collective bargaining agreement. Under one general type of agreement, the employer assumes a legal obligation to provide lifetime benefits in the appropriate amount to all employees who retire during the term of the labor contract.[19] The obligation under this type of agreement is to *pay pensions* rather than to make a definite *contribution to a pension fund*. However, if insufficient funds are contributed during the term of the labor contract to provide lifetime benefits to all employees who retire during that period, the employer presumably could be compelled to make the necessary additional contributions. The employer owes no liability to those employees who do not qualify for benefits—and actually retire—

18. Arthur H. Dean, "Accounting for the Cost of Pensions—A Lien on Production," *Harvard Business Review*, Vol. XXVIII, No. 4, July, 1950, p. 33.
19. *Ibid.*, pp. 34-35.

during the term of the contract and need not make any contributions on their behalf.

Under another common type of bilateral pension agreement, the employer's obligation is couched in terms of funding requirements. Some of the agreements require terminal funding, while others specify that the employer shall make contributions sufficient to keep the plan "actuarially sound." It is not clear whether compliance with such funding requirements will relieve the employer of any further liability under the contract.

To the present, the employer's liability under bilateral pension agreements is purely a matter of conjecture, since the issue has not come before the courts.

FLEXIBILITY

Another factor that must be considered in evaluating the relative merits of the various media of financing is that of flexibility. The advocates of trusteed plans tend to emphasize the importance of flexibility, while the proponents of insured plans are inclined to play down its significance. In an effort to cast some light on the issue, this section points out the areas in which the need for flexibility may exist and then indicates the extent to which the required flexibility can be provided under each of the available funding media. The topic can be discussed under the two general headings of benefit structure and funding procedure.

BENEFIT STRUCTURE

The broad problem in this area is that of adapting the funding medium to the specifications of the plan. If the benefit provisions of the plan follow the normal or conventional pattern, the benefits can be provided satisfactorily under any of the available financing forms. Certain types of provisions may be incorporated into a plan, however, which will require a degree of flexibility not available under all forms of financing.

For example, a plan which provides that OASI benefits are to be deducted, in full or in part, from the benefits that would otherwise be payable requires a more flexible funding medium than one whose benefits are independent of OASI. The same is true when the benefit formula of a plan is subject to periodic change, as is the case under negotiated bilateral plans. A provision which permits early retirement with full benefits would create complications for some types of insured plans. Finally, the payment of disability benefits other than those available under conventional early retirement provisions would not be feasible under some insurance contracts.

With respect to the adaptability of the various funding media, it can be said that the trusteed approach lends itself to any of the specifications outlined above plus any others that might be desired. By the very nature of the arrangement, a trusteed plan is capable of providing any type of benefit which the employer is willing to provide. This is one of the strong appeals of the trusteed method. In general, however, the flexibility of the trusteed plan is matched by the deposit administration and immediate participation guarantee contracts, although a more involved procedure might be entailed in some instances. Theoretically, the deferred group annuity can be adapted to any set of specifications, but, as a general practice, it is confined to plans which provide a unit of benefit for each year of service with no complicated adjustments. It is not unusual, however, to find the deferred group annuity used with final pay plans. Disability benefits could be provided only on a pay-as-you-go basis or through the facilities of a separate fund. Individual and group permanent contracts are wholly unsuited to plans which contain unusual benefit specifications, although disability benefits are available under the group permanent contracts of some companies.

Funding Procedure

In one sense, the entire question of flexibility is concerned with the funding process, since any set of benefits can be provided so long as a means can be found of predicting and accumulating the sums of money that will be required. The unusual types of benefit specifications mentioned in the preceding section are troublesome only because they create a problem of estimating how much money will be needed to provide the benefits. The funding medium must permit the necessary degree of flexibility in projecting the costs and accumulating the funds. Yet flexibility with respect to the two functions of projection and accumulation may be desirable in connection with any set of benefit specifications, whether simple or complex.

Flexibility with respect to cost projections is primarily a question of whether advance recognition is to be given to the factors of turnover, disability, delayed retirement, and salary changes or whether recognition will be accorded only as the experience develops. Latitude also exists with respect to the basic assumptions relating to mortality, interest, and expenses. Costs may be estimated with a reasonable margin of safety or they may be calculated with no allowance for possible adverse experience.

The employer and his actuarial consultant have complete latitude, within the limits of Treasury regulations, in estimating the costs that will be incurred under a trusteed plan. As has been indicated previously, credit is commonly taken for anticipated turnover and delayed retirement. Moreover, the consulting actuary is likely to assume a higher rate of investment earnings than that assumed by a life insurance company. There is a possibility that he will assume a higher rate of mortality among both active and retired employees than would an insurance company actuary. Finally, no allowance will generally be made for future expenses, the assumption being that these will be handled on a pay-as-you-go basis.

This method of estimating costs always produces a figure lower than the costs projected by an insurance company, sometimes 20 to 25 per cent lower. It must be remembered, however, that such cost projections are estimates in every sense of the word and may be quite different from the costs that finally emerge. Every factor that can affect the original estimate and the ultimate true cost is subject to fluctuation as events develop in the future. While it must be assumed that the cost estimates are prepared in good faith and in accordance with the best judgment of the consulting actuary, it must be said, in all fairness, that the actuary assumes no financial responsibility in connection with his estimates.

Complete latitude also exists under deposit administration and immediate participation guarantee contracts with respect to benefits accruing to active employees. The cost estimates may be prepared by an independent actuary or by the insurance company, but in either case it is customary to discount for turnover and delayed retirement. A less conservative set of assumptions relating to mortality, interest earnings, and expenses may also be used. The whole effect is to reduce the initial outlay and possibly reduce to some extent the security underlying the accrued benefits of the active employees.

The employer has no latitude with respect to benefits payable to retired employees under the deposit administration and immediate participation guarantee contracts or in connection with any benefits payable under the other types of insured plans. The costs are calculated according to the insurance company assumptions, and no account of turnover, disability, and delayed retirement is taken until the events occur. The situation is quite different here since the insurance company guarantees its estimate of costs and places its entire resources behind its guarantee. Under such circumstances, it is to be expected that the cost estimate would be higher than one prepared by an independent actuary but the true cost, in either case, will depend upon actual experience. Advocates of trusteed plans view this inflexibility of insured plans as a major disadvantage, while insurance company representatives regard it as one of the strongest assurances that the employees will receive the benefits which they have earned.

Once the cost estimates for a particular set of benefits have been developed, flexibility may exist as to the *rate* at which the sums estimated to be needed are accumulated. Sufficient flexibility to permit an employer to take optimum advantage of tax deductions and to adjust his contributions to his earnings experience is regarded as a desirable objective so long as it does not impair the "will to fund" and, hence, the solvency of the plan.

The minimum rate of funding is dictated by the Treasury requirement that contributions equal current costs plus interest on the initial past service liability. Beyond this point, however, considerable flexibility may be permitted under many forms of financing.

As might be surmised, the employer, under a trusteed plan, can set his own pace in funding. He may "freeze" his past service liability and never fund it. If, however, he is amortizing the past service liability, he may decide to forego his past service contribution in some year or years. In fact, after the initial past service liability has been partially amortized, he may skip all contributions, including those for current service, for a year or several years.

Apart from the insurance company requirement that sufficient funds be on hand at all times to provide benefits in full to those employees who have retired, the employer enjoys the same latitude

in funding under the deposit administration and immediate participation guarantee contracts that he does under the trusteed approach.
The same disadvantages attend the too liberal exercise of the privilege of foregoing contributions.

Under a deferred group annuity, the employer is usually required
to meet all current service costs, even though a portion of the past
service liability has been liquidated. Considerable flexibility can be
achieved, however, in the rate at which the past service liability is
liquidated. Many companies will permit an employer to amortize the
past service liability over a period of twenty or thirty years. Furthermore, if a portion of the past service liability has been funded, subsequent contributions for that purpose can be omitted in particular
years. Under some contracts, contributions for both current and past
service may be temporarily suspended, with or without the insurance company's consent, so long as the benefits to be paid under
the contract are not affected at any time and the unfunded past
service does not exceed the initial past service liability.

No flexibility exists relative to individual and group permanent
contracts other than that obtainable under normal reinstatement
privileges and—in the case of individual contracts—a possible automatic premium loan feature. The special "stop and go" provision
found in some group permanent contracts is, of course, a source of
flexibility but is administratively complicated.

A final and broader aspect of flexibility relates to the facility with
which a change in funding agencies can be accomplished. Such a
step normally has serious implications, and it should be taken only
after a careful and dispassionate consideration of all pertinent factors, including the impact on the employee group. The employees
may question the change in funding agency if it appears that the
employer is merely attempting to reduce his pension outlays, without passing along any part of the anticipated savings to the employees in the form of more liberal benefits.

Under a trusteed plan the employer normally reserves the right
to change trustees at any time, subject, of course, to a reasonable
notice, or to terminate the trust and transfer the plan to an insurance
company. It should be noted that the latter transfer involves only a
termination of the *trust* and not of the *plan*. Adequate precautions
must be taken in such a maneuver to avoid the possibility that the
tax authorities will rule that a termination of the plan has occurred.

If the employer exercises his right to change funding agencies, the assets comprising the trust property can be transferred intact to the new trustee, if the trust is to be continued, or, if the trust is to be terminated in favor of an insured plan, such of the assets as are legally and financially acceptable to the insurance company could presumably be credited against the premium obligations of the plan, the remainder of the fund, if any, being converted into cash and applied as premiums. No specific charge is levied for termination, since the trustee is compensated on a current basis for its services.

As a matter of practice, many insurance companies will accept only cash. In any event, a transfer of trust assets would be of little advantage to the employer, since the insurance company would hardly accept the assets at any value greater than current market value.

Funds cannot be transferred with such facility under insured plans. Under no circumstances will the insurance company relinquish responsibility for payment of benefits to those employees who have already retired. Under some group annuity contracts, particularly those of the deposit administration and IPG types, funds accumulated for employees not yet retired can be transferred to another agency at the request of either the insurance company or the employer. Even though such contracts contain no reference to the right of transfer, it is usually understood that, should the occasion arise, a transfer of funds could be arranged on a negotiated basis.

In the event of a transfer of funds under a group annuity contract, the insurance company assesses a liquidation charge. The charge may be contractual or it may be adjusted to individual circumstances, but in either case it would not normally exceed 5 per cent of the fund. The liquidation charge is intended to cover not only the expenses incident to the transfer itself, which should be relatively insignificant unless investment losses are sustained, but also all expenses, including commissions and premium taxes, incurred on amounts paid into the fund. In addition, restrictions are normally imposed on the rate at which the money can be withdrawn, a ten-year period of liquidation frequently being stipulated. This right may not be invoked, however.

A contractual right of transfer exists under individual insurance and annuity contracts in the form of cash surrender and loan values.

When an employer wishes to transfer an individual contract plan to another agency he can either surrender the policies for cash or exercise the loan privilege, the liquidation charge being determined by the manner in which the nonforfeiture values are calculated. The loan privilege would normally be exercised only where the plan contained a restriction on cash surrenders. A change in funding medium that is to be effective only as to future benefits can be accomplished by a transfer of the individual contracts, with the transferee continuing premium payments on the original basis.

SERVICE

A final factor to be considered is that of service. While this factor does not lend itself to precise delineation and rigorous analysis, broadly speaking it can be said to embrace those functions associated with the installation of the plan, periodic valuations, disbursement of pension monies, and routine record keeping.

An evaluation of this factor must concern itself with the quantity and quality of the services provided by agencies other than the employer. In the case of insured plans, the services are normally provided by the insurance company, although some services may be performed by independent actuaries, particularly during the exploratory or developmental stage of the plan. In the case of trusteed plans, the services are provided by the trustee and the consulting actuary.

Generalizations as to the range and calibre of services provided by the various funding media are of doubtful value because of the extreme variations in practices among even the same type of funding agencies. It appears, however, that less variation exists among insurance companies than among the agencies servicing trusteed plans. For example, the range and quality of actuarial services provided by a particular firm of consulting actuaries might greatly surpass those furnished by an insurance company under typical circumstances, while the services of another might not approach the minimum standard of a life insurance company. Nevertheless, any differences that might exist in this area are not attributable to the funding mechanism, as such, but to the choice of consulting actuary.

In connection with the disbursement function, however, the insurance companies appear to enjoy a definite advantage. This is attributable to their superior facilities for keeping track of persons who have retired and those who have left the service of the employer with deferred benefits. Trust companies operate in a limited geographical area and must rely heavily on their correspondent banks in playing the role of paymaster to a constantly increasing group of pensioners scattered throughout the country. Their difficulties are compounded when benefits are vested and many years elapse between the termination of the employee's service and the commencement of his retirement income.

Life insurance companies, on the other hand, tend to operate over a wide area and those engaged in pension underwriting have representatives in every community of any consequence. They are in a position to render personalized service to their body of pensioners, wherever they might be located. Their far-flung agency system is of especial significance in connection with a plan which provides vested benefits.

CONCLUSION

It must be apparent at this juncture that no funding medium is inherently superior to all others. Each has its peculiar advantages and disadvantages. A particular funding medium might be ideal for one set of circumstances and completely unsuitable for another. Plan specifications, particularly the benefit formula, will have a strong influence on the employer's choice of medium. So will cost considerations, especially the anticipated return on invested funds. In the final analysis, however, the decision is likely to hinge on the relative importance which the employer attaches to the related factors of flexibility and responsibility.

Varying degrees of flexibility can be obtained among the available funding media, but one of the inexorable facts of pension life is that control is always accompanied by responsibility. As the degree of employer control over the financing and administration of a pension plan increases, so does his responsibility for the functioning of the plan. Under the individual contract pension trust, for example, the employer has very little flexibility but, by the same token, his responsibilities are virtually limited to the payment of premiums. He enjoys freedom from investment worries and uncertainty over the magnitude of the financial obligations he has assumed. Under other types of insured plans the employer gains more flexibility but assumes more direct responsibility for the success of the plan, the ultimate in both flexibility and responsibility being represented by the IPG group annuity. Finally, under a self-administered trusteed plan the employer has almost complete control over the provisions, financing, and administration of the plan, the only limitations being found in the governing tax laws and the terms of a labor-management agreement, if any; in exchange for this control, however, the employer inherits full responsibility for the operation of the plan.

Increasing numbers of employers are placing flexibility and control ahead of freedom from responsibility. This is especially true of the larger employers who feel that they can afford to assume all risks inherent in a pension undertaking. The desire to control the investment of the pension fund and particularly to take advantage of common stock investments, is frequently the decisive factor. Small and medium-sized firms tend to prefer the lower order of responsibility identified with insured plans, especially those of the allocated funding type, notwithstanding the accompanying restrictions on the employer's freedom of action. Underlying the choice in each case should be an appreciation of the employees' interest and an acceptance of the premise that having established a pension plan an employer is morally obligated to provide the benefits which it promises. Only on the basis of such a philosophy can the private pension movement become a significant force in mankind's perennial quest for old-age security.

Appendices

Appendix A

PART I

COST CALCULATIONS FOR SINGLE PREMIUM FUNDING
1937 STANDARD ANNUITY MORTALITY TABLE 3% INTEREST

| | Total Prospective Benefits Upon Which Costs Are Based | | | | |
| Age Bracket | Current Service (1% of Col. 4)* | Past Service (1% of Col. 4 x Col. 6)* | Single Premium Cost Factors | Normal Cost (Col. 7 x Col. 9) | Accrued Liability (Col. 8 x Col. 9) |
(1)	(7)	(8)	(9)	(10)	(11)
15–19	$ 600	$ 600	1.896	$ 1,138	$ 1,138
20–24	2,530	5,060	2.212	5,596	11,193
25–29	4,640	18,560	2.585	11,994	47,978
30–34	4,550	27,300	3.027	13,773	82,637
35–39	4,510	40,590	3.560	16,056	144,500
40–44	4,600	59,800	4.215	19,389	252,057
45–49	4,590	78,030	5.040	23,134	393,271
50–54	4,480	94,080	6.112	27,382	575,017
55–59	4,340	112,840	7.570	32,854	854,199
60–64	3,900	120,900	9.665	37,694	1,168,499
65 and over	....	124,740	10.914	.....	1,361,412
Totals	$38,740	$682,500		$189,010	$4,891,901

* See Table 7, p. 147.

PART II
COST CALCULATIONS FOR LEVEL ANNUAL PREMIUM AND AGGREGATE FUNDING

Age Bracket	Prospective Benefits upon Which Costs Are Based [1% of Col. 4 x (Col. 6 + Yrs. to 65)]*	Level Premium Cost Factor for Attained Age	Initial Annual Cost on Attained Age Level Premium Method (Col. 12 x Col. 13)	Level Premium Cost Factor for Entry Age†	Normal Cost on Entry Age Normal Method (Col. 12 x Col. 15)
(1)	(12)	(13)	(14)	(15)	(16)
15–19	$ 29,400	.077	$ 2,264	.074	$ 2,176
20–24	113,850	.095	10,816	.087	9,905
25–29	194,880	.120	23,386	.100	19,488
30–34	177,450	.153	27,150	.114	20,229
35–39	166,870	.200	33,374	.125	20,859
40–44	165,600	.272	45,043	.132	21,859
45–49	160,650	.389	62,493	.138	22,170
50–54	152,320	.606	92,306	.145	22,086
55–59	147,560	1.116	164,677	.145	21,396
60–64	132,600	3.398	450,575	.145	19,227
65 and over	124,740	10.914	1,361,412	. . .	. . . . .
Totals	$1,565,920		$2,273,496		$179,395

PART II—continued
COST CALCULATIONS FOR LEVEL ANNUAL PREMIUM AND AGGREGATE FUNDING

Age Bracket	Present Value Factors	Present Value of Prospective Benefits (Col. 12 x Col. 17)	Temporary Annuity Factors	Present Value of Future Normal Costs (Col. 16 x Col. 19)	Present Value of Future Earnings (Col. 4 x Col. 19)*
(1)	(17)	(18)	(19)	(20)	(21)
15–19	1.896	$ 55,742	24.589	$ 53,506	$ 1,475,340
20–24	2.212	251,836	23.204	229,836	5,870,612
25–29	2.585	503,765	21.613	421,194	10,028,432
30–34	3.027	537,141	19.806	400,656	9,011,730
35–39	3.560	594,057	17.775	370,769	8,016,525
40–44	4.215	698,004	15.503	338,880	7,131,380
45–49	5.040	809,676	12.958	287,279	5,947,722
50–54	6.112	930,980	10.087	222,781	4,518,976
55–59	7.570	1,117,029	6.786	145,193	2,945,124
60–64	9.665	1,281,579	2.844	54,682	1,109,160
65 and over	10.914	1,361,412	. . . . .	. . . . . .	. . . .
Totals		$8,141,221		$2,524,776	$56,055,001

* See Table 7, p. 147.
† Based on assumed entry ages: Col. (2)–Col. (6), Table 7, p. 147.

Appendix B

PART I

COST CALCULATIONS FOR SINGLE PREMIUM FUNDING
GA-1951 MORTALITY TABLE, 2½% INTEREST

| Age Bracket | Total Prospective Benefits Upon Which Costs Are Based | | Single Premium Cost Factors | Normal Cost (Col. 7 x Col. 9) | Accrued Liability (Col. 8 x Col. 9) |
| | Current Service (1% of Col. 4)* | Past Service (1% of Col. 4 x Col. 6)* | | | |
(1)	(7)	(8)	(9)	(10)	(11)
15–19	$ 600	$ 600	2.757	$ 1,654	$ 1,654
20–24	2,530	5,060	3.129	7,916	15,833
25–29	4,640	18,560	3.554	16,491	65,962
30–34	4,550	27,300	4.040	18,382	110,292
35–39	4,510	40,590	4.602	20,755	186,795
40–44	4,600	59,800	5.258	24,187	314,428
45–49	4,590	78,030	6.051	27,774	472,160
50–54	4,480	94,080	7.062	31,638	664,393
55–59	4,340	112,840	8.403	36,469	948,195
60–64	3,900	120,900	10.258	40,006	1,240,192
65 and over	....	124,740	11.272	.....	1,406,069
Totals	$38,740	$682,500		$225,272	$5,425,973

* See Table 7, p. 147.

PART II

COST CALCULATIONS FOR LEVEL ANNUAL PREMIUM AND AGGREGATE FUNDING

Age Bracket	Prospective Benefits upon Which Costs Are Based [1% of Col. 4 x (Col. 6 + Yrs. to 65)]*	Level Premium Cost Factor for Attained Age	Initial Annual Cost on Attained Age Level Premium Method (Col. 12 x Col. 13)	Level Premium Cost Factor for Entry Age†	Normal Cost on Entry Age Normal Method (Col. 12 x Col. 15)
(1)	(12)	(13)	(14)	(15)	(16)
15–19	$ 29,400	.100	$ 2,940	.097	$ 2,852
20–24	113,850	.121	13,776	.112	12,751
25–29	194,880	.149	29,037	.126	24,555
30–34	177,450	.186	33,006	.143	25,375
35–39	166,870	.238	39,715	.155	25,865
40–44	165,600	.315	52,164	.162	26,827
45–49	160,650	.440	70,686	.170	27,311
50–54	152,320	.669	101,902	.177	26,961
55–59	147,560	1.203	177,515	.177	26,118
60–64	132,600	3.573	473,780	.177	23,470
65 and over	124,740	11.272	1,406,069	. . .	. . . . .
Totals	$1,565,920		$2,400,590		$222,085

PART II—continued

COST CALCULATIONS FOR LEVEL ANNUAL PREMIUM AND AGGREGATE FUNDING

Age Bracket	Present Value Factors	Present Value of Prospective Benefits (Col. 12 x Col. 17)	Temporary Annuity Factors	Present Value of Future Normal Costs (Col. 16 x Col. 19)	Present Value of Future Earnings (Col. 4 x Col. 19)*
(1)	(17)	(18)	(19)	(20)	(21)
15–19	2.757	$ 81,056	27.469	$ 78,342	$ 1,648,140
20–24	3.129	356,237	25.776	328,670	6,521,328
25–29	3.554	692,604	23.872	586,177	11,076,608
30–34	4.040	716,898	21.736	551,551	9,889,880
35–39	4.602	767,936	19.346	500,384	8,725,046
40–44	5.258	870,725	16.682	447,528	7,673,720
45–49	6.051	972,093	13.750	375,526	6,311,250
50–54	7.062	1,075,684	10.549	284,412	4,725,952
55–59	8.403	1,239,947	6.987	182,486	3,032,358
60–64	10.258	1,360,211	2.871	67,382	1,119,690
65 and over	11.272	1,406,069	. . . . .	. . . . . .	. . . .
Totals		$9,539,460		$3,402,458	$60,723,972

* See Table 7, p. 147.
† Based on assumed entry ages: Col. (2)–Col. (6), Table 7, p. 147.

Appendix C

Part I

Cost Calculations for Single Premium Funding
1937 Standard Annuity Mortality Table 2½% Interest
Moderate Turnover

| Age Bracket | Total Prospective Benefits Upon Which Costs Are Based | | Single Premium Cost Factors | Normal Cost (Col. 7 x Col. 9) | Accrued Liability (Col. 8 x Col. 9) |
	Current Service (1% of Col. 4)*	Past Service (1% of Col. 4 x Col. 6)*			
(1)	(7)	(8)	(9)	(10)	(11)
15–19	$ 600	$ 600	.192	$ 115	$ 115
20–24	2,530	5,060	.535	1,354	2,707
25–29	4,640	18,560	.879	4,079	16,314
30–34	4,550	27,300	1.339	6,092	36,555
35–39	4,510	40,590	1.926	8,686	78,176
40–44	4,600	59,800	2.665	12,259	159,367
45–49	4,590	78,030	3.629	16,657	283,171
50–54	4,480	94,080	4.909	21,992	461,839
55–59	4,340	112,840	6.597	28,631	744,405
60–64	3,900	120,900	9.388	36,613	1,135,009
65 and over	....	124,740	11.360	.....	1,417,046
Totals	$38,740	$682,500		$136,478	$4,334,704

* See Table 7, p. 147.

PART II

COST CALCULATIONS FOR LEVEL ANNUAL PREMIUM AND
AGGREGATE FUNDING

Age Bracket	Prospective Benefits upon Which Costs Are Based [1% of Col. 4 x (Col. 6 + Yrs. to 65)]*	Level Premium Cost Factor for Attained Age	Initial Annual Cost on Attained Age Level Premium Method (Col. 12 x Col. 13)	Level Premium Cost Factor for Entry Age†	Normal Cost on Entry Age Normal Method (Col. 12 x Col. 15)
(1)	(12)	(13)	(14)	(15)	(16)
15–19	$ 29,400	.026	$ 764	.021	$ 617
20–24	113,850	.044	5,009	.037	4,212
25–29	194,880	.066	12,862	.048	9,354
30–34	177,450	.097	17,213	.061	10,824
35–39	166,870	.142	23,696	.072	12,015
40–44	165,600	.210	34,776	.077	12,751
45–49	160,650	.323	51,890	.084	13,495
50–54	152,320	.535	81,491	.090	13,709
55–59	147,560	1.040	153,462	.090	13,280
60–64	132,600	3.388	449,249	.090	11,934
65 and over	124,740	11.360	1,417,046	. . .	. . . . .
Totals	$1,565,920		$2,247,458		$102,191

PART II—*continued*

COST CALCULATIONS FOR LEVEL ANNUAL PREMIUM AND
AGGREGATE FUNDING

Age Bracket	Present Value Factors	Present Value of Prospective Benefits (Col. 12 x Col. 17)	Temporary Annuity Factors	Present Value of Future Normal Costs (Col. 16 x Col. 19)	Present Value of Future Earnings (Col. 4 x Col. 19)*
(1)	(17)	(18)	(19)	(20)	(21)
15–19	.192	$ 5,645	7.509	$ 4,633	$ 450,540
20–24	.535	60,910	12.181	51,306	3,081,793
25–29	.879	171,300	13.261	124,043	6,153,104
30–34	1.339	237,606	13.760	148,938	6,260,800
35–39	1.926	321,392	13.561	162,935	6,116,011
40–44	2.665	441,324	12.680	161,683	5,832,800
45–49	3.629	582,999	11.229	151,535	5,154,111
50–54	4.909	747,739	9.179	125,835	4,112,192
55–59	6.597	973,453	6.342	84,222	2,752,428
60–64	9.388	1,244,849	2.771	33,069	1,080,690
65 and over	11.360	1,417,046	. . . . .	. . . . . .	. . . .
Totals		$6,204,263		$1,048,199	$40,994,469

* See Table 7, p. 147.
† Based on assumed entry ages: Col. (2)–Col. (6), Table 7, p. 147.

Appendix D

IMPACT OF MORTALITY IMPROVEMENT

The trend toward lower rates of mortality has been described in the text of this volume. This trend has created problems for insurance companies and others engaged in the underwriting of annuities. This Appendix describes the efforts of insurance companies to anticipate the financial effects of continued improvement in annuitant mortality.

The traditional or conventional method of coping with the improvement in annuitant mortality has been the use of a much lower guaranteed rate of interest than is likely to be earned plus, in many cases, a setback in the 1937 Standard Annuity Table. While the use of an extremely conservative rate of interest has provided an effective, and convenient, margin of safety in the past, there is evidence that this device will prove incapable of absorbing the cost of decreasing death rates in the future.[1] Moreover, the use of an unrealistic rate of interest as a margin for mortality improvement is confusing to laymen and may be misunderstood by an employer exploring the cost of a proposed plan. There is a growing feeling that each element entering into the cost structure should rest on reasonable assumptions and be capable of justification to a layman. The efficacy of the setback procedure also appears to be limited inasmuch as the obsolescence of the 1937 Standard Annuity Table varies by age and sex. The device may produce adequate premiums in the aggregate, but it is almost certain to bring about an even greater distortion of equities by age and sex than that inherent in the unmodified form of the Table.

In an effort to provide a more satisfactory basis for the writing of annuities, Wilmer A. Jenkins of the Teachers' Insurance and Annuity Association, and Edward A. Lew, of the Metropolitan Life Insurance Company, undertook to develop a new annuity table. Their objective was to develop a table that would not only accurately reflect current mortality among annuitants but would also make an allowance, on a realistic and equitable basis, for future improvement in mortality. Out of this project emerged an annuity table which has been widely acclaimed as a milestone in the study of annuitant mortality. The development of the table which is now known as the Annuity Table for 1949 is described in the first volume of the *Transactions of the Society of Actuaries*.[2]

1. See Ray M. Peterson, "Group Annuity Mortality," *Transactions of the Society of Actuaries,* Vol. IV, 1952, p. 273.
2. Pp. 369-466.

At the younger ages (55 and below for males, and 50 and below for females) the Table reflects the experience of active lives under group annuity contracts, while at the older ages the experience under individual immediate nonrefund annuities is reflected.[3] The individual annuity experience for the period 1941-46 was utilized, with the experience for calendar years 1939, 1940, 1946, and 1947, centering around 1943, being used for the group annuity contracts. The experience under both sets of contracts was adjusted to bring it up to 1949.

To provide a margin for future improvement in mortality, two sets of projection factors were prepared. One set, known as "projection scale A," assumes that annuitant mortality will continue to decline indefinitely into the future at the same annual rates of decrease that have prevailed in recent decades. The other set, "projection scale B," assumes that the future will produce smaller rates of decrease in mortality at the younger ages, where past reductions have already engendered very low mortality rates, and somewhat higher rates of decrease than those of the past at ages over sixty, which ages should benefit most greatly from current intensive efforts to reduce the toll from cardiovascular-renal diseases and cancer. Projection scale A might be regarded as retrospective in its outlook, while projection scale B is prospective in nature. Both projection scales assume that future mortality rates among annuitants will vary with the year of exposure, or the year passed through, rather than with the year of issue of the annuity or the year of birth.

As has been pointed out, the Annuity Table for 1949 is based on the experience of individual annuitants at those ages represented in the critical period of benefit disbursements. Yet the Jenkins and Lew investigation revealed that the experience of group annuity retired lives possesses demonstrably different characteristics from individual annuity experience. To provide a table that would reflect the special characteristics of group annuities, Ray M. Peterson of the Equitable Life Assurance Society undertook an investigation of group annuitant mortality, the results of which appear in the 1952 *Transactions of the Society of Actuaries*.[4] The table which grew out of this study has been designated the Group Annuity Table for 1951.

This Table was basically derived from the mortality experience of group annuitants—the first published table to be derived in that manner. At ages below 56, the rates are those of the Annuity Table for 1949 adjusted for one year's decrease according to the Jenkins and Lew projection scale B. At ages over 65, the rates are based on the intercompany group annuity retired lives experience for the years 1946-50, with an allowance for three years' decrease in mortality according to projection scale B. Mortality rates for the gap between ages 56 and 65 were derived by extrapolation.

3. The volume of experience under individual immediate nonrefund annuities at the younger ages was too meager to be reliable.
4. Vol. IV, pp. 246-307.

The use of projection factors was designed to adjust the mortality rates to the 1951 level. At that point the basic table was considered to be representative of the *average* actual experience of all occupational groups for the year 1951. On the theory that certain groups of employees, which cannot be identified on an *a priori* basis, will experience lighter mortality than the average, it was deemed necessary to introduce an arbitrary margin of safety. This was accomplished by reducing the mortality rates for males at all ages by 10 per cent and those for females by 12½ per cent. This type of adjustment provides a margin that increases with age which was thought desirable in view of the relative unreliability of the data at the oldest ages.

Peterson then prepared a set of projection factors through which the Table can be kept up-to-date. He designated his set of factors as "projection scale C," in deference to scales A and B prepared by Jenkins and Lew. Projection scale C is 1⅓ times projection scale B, subject to a maximum annual rate of 1.25 per cent. Peterson argues that since current death rates for group annuitants are higher than those of individual annuitants, future progress in medical care, sanitation, and nutrition should exert a slightly stronger influence on group annuitant mortality. In other words, there is more room for improvement. The same reasoning would seem to dictate a higher scale of factors for males than for females, but the desire to avoid undue complexity motivated Peterson to use the same scale for both sexes.

There is divided opinion among actuaries as to the advisability of introducing into annuity premiums and reserves a specific margin for future improvement in mortality.[5] The objections to the use of projection factors are technical in nature and revolve around the administrative complications that would be introduced. The necessity of making provision against future mortality improvement has not been questioned; the issue is the manner in which it should be accomplished. Neither has Peterson's projection scale C been questioned, other than that the rates of decrease at the younger ages may be too small. It would seem advisable, therefore, to take a look at the financial implications of continued improvement in annuitant mortality, as well as that which has occurred in recent years.

With respect to mortality after 65, the 1937 Standard Annuity Table, the most widely used table for pension calculations, shows a life expectancy of 14.40 years for males age 65. In other words, a male upon reaching 65 can expect to live, on the average, another 14.40 years. The Ga-1951 Table with Projection, on the other hand, estimates that a male now age 65 will live 14.86 years longer on the average. This is not a striking difference, of course, but the use of projection factors assumes an ever-lengthening life expectancy. Thus, the Ga-1951 Table with Projection forecasts a life expectancy at age 65 of 15.51 years for a male

5. See, for example, "Discussions on Group Annuity Mortality," *Transactions of the Society of Actuaries*, Vol. IV, 1952, pp. 707-55.

now (1953) age 55. Furthermore, a life expectancy of 16.15 years at age 65 is predicted for a male now 45, with the expectancy rising to 16.75 years for a male now 35. In other words, a two-year extension in the life expectancy of males age 65 is envisioned over the next thirty years. This represents an increase of 16 per cent.

Somewhat smaller increases in life expectancy are predicted for females. The life expectancy of a female age 65 is 17.55 years according to the 1937 Standard Annuity Table. The Ga-1951 Table with Projection, on the other hand, shows a life expectancy of 17.74 years for females now age 65 and projects a life expectancy of 18.30 years in 1963, 18.84 years in 1973, and 19.35 years in 1983.

What does a longer life expectancy mean in terms of dollars? The payment of $1,000 per year for the lifetime of a male employee age 65 requires the accumulation of a sum of $11,555, if the cost of the benefits is calculated on the basis of the 1937 Standard Annuity Table and 2½ per cent interest, with no loading. If the cost is calculated on the more conservative basis of the 1937 Standard Annuity Table with a one year setback and 2¼ per cent interest, the sum required is $12,206. The sum required to provide a life income of $1,000 per year to a male employee reaching 65 in 1953 is $11,920 according to the Ga-1951 Table with Projection and 2½ per cent interest, or somewhat less than the sum required on the most conservative basis of valuation in general use today. Nevertheless, the cost will increase with the passage of time and by 1963, according to the Ga-1951 Table with Projection, it will require a principal sum of $12,376 to provide a life income of $1,000 to a male employee age 65. A male employee reaching 65 in 1973 will represent a commitment of $12,810 for each $1,000 of annual income, whereas the comparable obligation by 1983 will amount to $13,224.

This is only part of the picture. Not only will it cost more in the future to provide an income of a specified amount to an employee who attains the age of 65, but a larger percentage of employees will live to reach 65. According to the 1937 Standard Annuity Table, five males out of every seven alive at age 35 will survive to 65. The Ga-1951 Table with Projection, however, estimates that six out of every seven males alive at age 35 will survive to 65, or 16 per cent more than under the other assumption. The chances of survival from age 45 to 65 are 11 per cent better under the Ga-1951 Table with Projection than under the 1937 Standard Annuity Table. Interestingly enough, the Ga-1951 Table with Projection gives a man age 35 today a slightly better chance of reaching 65 than a man age 45 today!

The picture for the future, then, is one of more employees living to 65 to receive a more expensive benefit. The increased longevity after 65 is the more significant factor and will affect all pension plans in substantially the same manner, the principal mitigating circumstance being the deferment of retirement to an age beyond 65. The impact of the lower rate of mortality before retirement, however, is more difficult to assess, being dependent upon the vesting provisions of the plan, the death benefits, if any, and the rate of withdrawal. When full or liberal vesting is provided, the improved chances of survival should add significantly to the cost of the plan. If there are no vested rights, or if vesting is provided for only after an extended period of service, the turnover factor will overshadow mortality as a determinant of the plan's cost. A normal rate of turnover would tend to minimize the effect of the greater chance of survival. If the plan provides death benefits other than return of the employee's contributions, if any, the savings in death benefits would be a significant offset against the higher retirement costs.

Selected Bibliography

Ackerman, Laurence J., "Arbitration—A Facet of Pension Planning and Pension Administration," *The Journal of the American Society of Chartered Life Underwriters*, Vol. VI, No. 3, 1952, pp. 244-255.

——, and McKain, Walter C., Jr., "Retirement Programs for Industrial Workers," *Harvard Business Review*, Vol. XXX, No. 4, July-August, 1952, pp. 97-108.

Baker, Helen, *Retirement Procedures Under Compulsory and Flexible Retirement Policies* (Princeton, N. J.: Princeton University—Industrial Relations Section), 1952, 65 pp.

Bevan, J. A., *et al.*, "Discussion of Pension Trusts," *Transactions of the Society of Actuaries*, Vol. V, 1953, pp. 63-67.

Black, Kenneth, Jr., *Group Annuities* (Philadelphia: University of Pennsylvania Press), 1955, 280 pp.

——, "Group Annuities Under the Immediate Participation Guarantee Contract," *The Journal of the American Society of Chartered Life Underwriters*, Vol. VIII, No. 2, 1954, pp. 135-145.

Blagden, H. E., "Actuarial Note: A New Mortality Basis for Group Annuities," *Transactions of the Society of Actuaries*, Vol. II, No. 4, 1950, pp. 322-327. Also Discussion, pp. 328-330 by R. M. Peterson and H. R. Bassford.

Blanchard, Fessenden S., *Where to Retire and How* (New York: Dodd, Mead and Company), 1952, 299 pp.

Boyce, Carroll W., *How to Plan Pensions: A Guidebook for Business and Industry* (New York: McGraw-Hill Book Company), 1950, 479 pp.

Bronson, Dorrance C., "Pensions—1949," *Transactions of the Society of Actuaries*, Vol. I, 1949, pp. 219-255. Also Discussion, pp. 256-294.

——, *et al.*, "Discussion of Pensions," *Transactions of the Society of Actuaries*, Vol. II, 1950, pp. 476-484.

Buck, George B., Jr., *et al.*, *Pensions and Profit Sharing* (Washington: Bureau of National Affairs, Inc.), 1953, 272 pp.

Carlson, Julia, *Employee-Benefit Plans in the Electric and Gas Utility Industries* (Washington: Federal Security Agency—Division of Research and Statistics), Bureau Memorandum No. 73, 1952, 150 pp.

Chancellor of the Exchequer, *Report of the Committee on the Taxation Treatment of Provisions for Retirement* (London: Her Majesty's Stationery Office), 1954, 159 pp.

Cochran, Howe P., *Scientific Employee Benefit Planning* (Boston: Little, Brown and Company), 1954, 354 pp.

Collective Bargaining Handbook for Workers Security Programs (Detroit: UAW-CIO Social Security Department), 1949, 60 pp.

Couper, Walter J., and Vaughan, Roger, *Pension Planning* (New York: Industrial Relations Counselors, Inc.), 1954, 245 pp.

Crabbe, R. J. W., and Poyser, C. A., *Pension and Widows' and Orphans' Funds* (Cambridge: Cambridge University Press), 1953, 240 pp.

224 Selected Bibliography

Daoust, Joseph H., "Area Pension Plans," *Labor Law Journal*, January, 1954, pp. 47-58.

Dean, Arthur H., "Accounting for the Cost of Pensions—A Lien on Production" (in two parts) *Harvard Business Review*, Vol. XXVIII, No. 4, July, 1950, pp. 25-40; No. 5, September, 1950, pp. 102-122.

Dearing, Charles L., *Industrial Pensions* (Washington: Brookings Institution), 1954, 310 pp.

Duncan, Robert M., "A Retirement System Granting Unit Annuities and Investing in Equities," *Transactions of the Society of Actuaries*, Vol. IV, 1952, pp. 317-343.

Eisner, S. L., *et al.*, "Discussion of Group Retirement Plans," *Transactions of the Society of Actuaries*, Vol. III, 1951, p. 119.

Employee Benefit Plan Review, Monthly (Chicago: Charles D. Spencer and Associates).

Employee Welfare and Benefit Programs, Research Technical Report 7, Industrial Relations Center, University of Minnesota, November, 1950, 49 pp.

Enriching the Years (Albany: New York State Joint Legislative Committee on Problems of the Aging), 1953, 199 pp.

Equitable Society Pension Forums for Group Annuity Clients, Proceedings of the (New York: Equitable Life Assurance Society of the United States), 1953, 57 pp.

Federal Reserve Bank of New York, "Private Pension Plans," *Monthly Review of Credit and Business Conditions*, December, 1953, pp. 185-188.

Friedson, Abe, and Zisman, Joseph, *Nineteen Employee-Benefit Plans in the Airframe Industry* (Washington: Federal Security Agency—Division of Research and Statistics), January, 1951, 63 pp.

Fuerth, D. S., "Legal Aspects of the Group Annuity Business," *Insurance Law Journal*, October, 1950, pp. 714-721.

Goldstein, Meyer M., "Current Problems on Pension Plans," *The Journal of the American Society of Chartered Life Underwriters*, Vol. VI, No. 3, pp. 234-243.

Greenough, William C., *New Approach to Retirement Income* (New York: Teachers Insurance and Annuity Association of America), 1951, 55 pp.

Guertin, A. N., *et al.*, "Discussion of Annuitant Mortality Trends," *Transactions of the Society of Actuaries*, Vol. IV, 1952, pp. 345-353.

———, *et al.*, "Discussion of Employee Welfare Plans," *Transactions of the Society of Actuaries*, Vol. I, 1949, pp. 568-574.

Hall, Harold R., *Some Observations on Executive Retirement* (Boston: Harvard University Graduate School of Business), 1953, 298 pp.

———, "Executives' Financial Preparation for Retirement," *Harvard Business Review*, Vol. XXXI, No. 1, January-February, 1953, pp. 83-96.

Hanover Pension Bulletin (New York: Hanover Bank) Monthly.

Henderson, C. R., "A Better Pension Program," *Harvard Business Review*, Vol. XXX, No. 1, January-February, 1952, pp. 62-74.

Hennington, H. H., *et al.*, "Discussion of Retirement Plans," *Transactions of the Society of Actuaries*, Vol. IV, 1952, pp. 160-165.

Hohaus, R. A., "Reinsurance of Retirement Plans," *Transactions of the Actuarial Society of America*, Vol. XXVI, 1925, pp. 480-506.

———, "Group Annuities," *Record of the American Institute of Actuaries*, Vol. XVIII, Part I, No. 37, 1929, pp. 51-72.

———, "Further Remarks on Group Annuities," *Record of the American Institute of Actuaries,* Vol. XXIII, Part II, No. 48, 1934, pp. 328-359.

Holzman, Robert S., *Guide to Pension and Profit Sharing Plans* (Mount Vernon, N. Y.: Farnsworth Publishing Company), 1953, 64 pp.

Houseman, Raymond F., "Some Practical Aspects of The Calculation of Employer Contributions Under Group Annuities of the Deposit Administration Type," *Transactions of the Society of Actuaries,* Vol. IV, 1952, pp. 231-245.

Ilse, Louise Walters, *Group Insurance and Employee Retirement Plans* (New York: Prentice-Hall), 1953, 438 pp.

Improving Social Security (Washington: United States Chamber of Commerce), 1953, 128 pp.

Jenkins, W. A., and Lew, E. A., "A New Mortality Basis for Annuities," *Transactions of the Society of Actuaries,* Vol. I, 1949, pp. 369-466.

Johnson, George E., "The Variable Annuity," *The Journal of the American Society of Chartered Life Underwriters,* Vol. VII, No. 1, 1952, pp. 67-73.

Journal of Commerce, The (New York), Annual editions on employee benefit plans.

Justin, Jules J., "Pension Plans—Check List for Administrators," *Harvard Business Review,* Vol. XXVIII, No. 6, November, 1950, pp. 114-122.

Kimball, Ingalls, "Industrial Pensions," *Annals of The American Academy of Political and Social Science,* Vol. 161, 1932, pp. 33-39.

Latimer, Murray Webb, *Industrial Pension Systems in the United States and Canada* (New York: Industrial Relations Counselors, Inc.), 1932, 2 vols.

Mathiasen, Geneva, ed., *Criteria for Retirement; A Report of a National Conference on Retirement of Older Workers* (New York: Putnam's Sons), 1953, 233 pp.

McGill, Dan M., "Insurance and Pension Costs As a Barrier to the Employment of Older Workers," *Proceedings* of the Second Conference on *The Problem of Making a Living While Growing Old,* sponsored jointly by Temple University Bureau of Economic and Business Research and Pennsylvania Department of Labor and Industry, 1953, pp. 136-148.

Montgomery, Doris, "Pensions—In the American Manner," *Journal of the American Society of Chartered Life Underwriters,* Vol. V, No. 1, pp. 16-27.

Murphy, R. D., "Mortality Among Annuitants," *Journal of the American Society of Chartered Life Underwriters,* Vol. II, No. 4, pp. 354-362.

———, "Significant Annuity Developments," *Life Insurance Trends at Mid-Century* (David McCahan, Editor), Philadelphia: University of Pennsylvania Press, 1950, pp. 84-99.

Myers, J. W., "Governmental and Voluntary Programs for Security," *Harvard Business Review,* Vol. XXVIII, No. 2, March, 1950, pp. 29-44.

Myers, R. J., *et al.*, "Forums on Old Age Benefits," Discussion, *Transactions of the Society of Actuaries,* Vol. II, 1950, pp. 108-132.

Negotiated Pension Plans (Washington: Bureau of National Affairs, Inc.), 1949, 248 pp.

O'Neill, Hugh, *Modern Pension Plans,* Principles and Practices (New York: Prentice-Hall), 1947, 382 pp.

Owen, A. S., "Pension Schemes and Funds—The Problem of Transfers of Employment," *Journal of the Insurance Institute of London,* Vol. XLI, Session 1952-1953, pp. 7-24.

Pension Plans and Common Stock (New York: Morgan Stanley and Company), 1950, 52 pp.

Pension Plans Under Collective Bargaining; A Reference Guide for Trade Unions (Washington: American Federation of Labor), 1952, 105 pp.

Permanent and Total Disability Benefit Provisions in Industrial Retirement Plans (Washington: United States Department of Health, Education, and Welfare—Social Security Administration), June, 1950, 44 pp.

Peterson, Ray M., "Group Annuity Mortality," *Transactions of the Society of Actuaries,* Vol. IV, 1952, pp. 246-307.

———, "Certainties and Uncertainties in Pension Planning," *The Journal of the American Society of Chartered Life Underwriters,* Vol. VIII, No. 1, 1953, pp. 5-28.

"Portable Pensions," *The Economist,* Vol. CLXVI, No. 5715, March 7, 1953, pp. 651-653.

Prentice-Hall Pensions and Profit-Sharing Service (New York: Prentice-Hall).

Preparing Employees for Retirement (New York: American Management Association), (Personnel Series, No. 142), 1951, 27 pp.

Rae, William M., "The Ultimate Inflexibility of a Self-Insured Pension Plan," *The Journal of the American Society of Chartered Life Underwriters,* Vol. IX, No. 1, 1954, pp. 86-90.

Recent Pension Plans: Collectively Bargained Programs Established in New York State Between July 1951 and January 1953 (Albany: New York Department of Labor—Division of Research and Statistics), Publication No. B-68, June, 1953, 60 pp.

Robbins, Rainard B., *Impact of Taxes on Industrial Pension Plans* (New York: Industrial Relations Counselors, Inc.), 1949, 82 pp.

———, *Pension Planning in the United States* (New York: Teachers Insurance and Annuity Association of America), 1952, 197 pp. (Edited by W. C. Greenough)

———, "The Effect of Social Security Legislation on Private Pension Plans," *Journal of the American Association of University Teachers of Insurance,* Vol. V, No. 1, 1938, pp. 47-56.

Rowe, Evan K., and Paine, Thomas H., "Pension Plans Under Collective Bargaining," *Monthly Labor Review* (Part I—Extent and Nature of Vested Rights in Pension Plans and Their Relationship to the Problems of Labor Mobility), March, 1953, pp. 237-248; (Part II—Compulsory Retirement), May, 1953, pp. 484-489; (Part III—Types and Amount of Benefits), July, 1953, pp. 714-722.

Sedgwick, R. Minturn, "A New Pension Plan," *Harvard Business Review,* Vol. XXXI, No. 1, January-February, 1953, pp. 70-82.

Sibson, Robert E., *Survey of Pension Planning* (Chicago: Commerce Clearing House), 1953, 184 pp.

Simons, Gustave, "Payroll Flexibility Through Employee Trusts," *Harvard Business Review,* Vol. XXVI, No. 4, July, 1948, pp. 441-453.

"Social Contribution by the Aging," *The Annals of the American Academy of Political and Social Science,* entire issue, January, 1952, Vol. CCLXXIX.

Social Security Bulletin (Washington: United States Department of Health, Education, and Welfare—Social Security Administration), Monthly.

Solenberger, Willard E., "Pension Programming from a Labor Viewpoint," *The Journal of the American Society of Chartered Life Underwriters,* Vol. VIII, No. 2, 1954, pp. 125-134.

Strong, Jay V., *Employee Benefit Plans in Operation* (Washington: Bureau of National Affairs), 1951, 348 pp.

Study of Industrial Retirement Plans (New York: Bankers Trust Company), 1953, 145 pp.

Survey Report of Private Employee Benefits in Distribution Covering Retail, Wholesale, Service, Combination Businesses (Washington: United States Chamber of Commerce), 1954, 31 pp.

TPF&C Pension Tax Manual (Philadelphia: Towers, Perrin, Forster and Crosby), 4th Edition, 1949, and Supplement.

Trowbridge, Charles L., "Fundamentals of Pension Funding," *Transactions of the Society of Actuaries,* Vol. IV, 1952, pp. 17-43. Discussion by Cecil J. Nesbitt, *et al.,* pp. 657-683.

Turner, Arthur N., *Employment and Retirement in an Aging Population—A Bibliography* (Boston: Harvard University Graduate School of Business Administration), 1951, 50 pp.

Van Eenam, Weltha, and Penman, Martha E., *Analysis of 346 Group Annuities Underwritten in 1946-50* (Washington: Federal Security Agency), 1952, 56 pp.

Warters, D. N., "Group Insurance on Level Premium Plans," *Transactions of the Actuarial Society of America,* Vol. XLVIII, 1947, pp. 95-115. Also Discussion, pp. 296-300 by W. R. Williamson and J. H. Smith.

"What is Actuarial Soundness in a Pension Plan," Proceedings of Panel Meeting, *Journal of the American Association of University Teachers of Insurance,* Vol. XX, No. 1, March, 1953, pp. 35-69.

Zisman, Joseph, *Fifty Employee-Benefit Plans in the Basic Steel Industry* (Washington: Federal Security Agency—Bureau of Research and Statistics), Bureau Memorandum No. 65, November, 1947, 103 pp.

———, and Carlson, Julia, *Seventy-three Employee-Benefit Plans in the Petroleum Refining Industry* (Washington: Federal Security Agency), Bureau Memorandum No. 70, April, 1951, 264 pp.

INDEX

Accrued liability
  Aggregate cost method, 145, 151-157
  Attained age level premium funding, 143, 149, 150, 152-157
  Attained age normal, 145
  Definition, 126
  Entry age normal, 143, 144, 145, 149-157
  Freezing, 130, 144, 145, 204
  Single premium funding, 142, 148, 149, 152-157
"Active life fund"
  (See Deposit Administration plan)
Actuarial consultant
  Combination plan, 125
  Deposit Administration plan, 187, 190, 197, 203, 204, 207
  Fees, 187, 188, 190
  IPG, 112, 197, 203, 204, 207
  Responsibility for cost estimates, 203
  Self-administered Trusteed plan, 116, 117, 120, 203, 204, 207
A F of L, 26, 27
Age requirements
  As to coverage, 33, 34, 138
  As to disability benefits, 62
  As to early retirement, 50
  As to normal retirement, 48, 49
  As to vesting, 59, 60
Age set-backs
  Group permanent optional retirement, 79, 80, 81
  To offset mortality improvement, 92, 162
  To reflect differences in male and female mortality, 162, 165
Aged
  Economic status, 4
  Number of, 1
  Participation in labor force, 2, 3
  Responsibility for, 5
American Annuitants Table, 92

American Men (5), Table, 81
Annuity forms
  (See Benefits, retirement)
Annuity Table, 1949, 81
Annuity table, static, 93
Arbitrary Rule
  (See Coverage of pension plans)
Automatic retirement age, 48, 49, 52
Auxiliary fund
  Combination plan, 121-125
  Group Permanent plan, 78, 79, 81, 82, 84

Bankers Trust Company, 32, 33, 36, 59, 60, 65, 67
Bell System, 38
Benefit of survivorship, 143, 149
Benefits, death
  Combination plan, 121, 122
  Deferred Group Annuity plan, 61, 90, 91
  Deposit Administration plan, 104
  General, 61, 62
  Group Permanent plan, 77, 78, 80, 121
  Individual Contract plan, 71, 72, 73
  Self-administered Trusteed plan, 61, 114, 115
Benefits, disability
  Deferred Group Annuity plan, 91, 202
  Deposit Administration plan, 105, 202, 204
  General, 50-52, 62, 63, 114, 202, 204
  Group Permanent plan, 80, 81, 202
  Individual Contract plan, 73, 74
  IPG plan, 114, 202, 204
  Self-administered Trusteed plan, 63, 115, 116, 202, 204
Benefits, retirement
  Annuity forms
    Cash refund, 46, 54
    Instalment refund, 46, 54

Combination plan—*Continued*
Use with group permanent, 78, 79, 81, 82, 84
Valuation factors, 123, 124
Vesting, 122
Combined Annuity Table, 91
Commingling of assets, Self-administered Trusteed plan, 114
Commissioner of Internal Revenue, 22, 30-32, 134, 136
Common stock investments, 171, 172, 175, 176, 180, 194, 198, 209
Common trust fund, 170, 175
Compensation
Effect on benefits, 34, 37, 38, 40, 42, 103, 140
Impact on funding, 140, 142, 143, 145
Complete funding, 141
Conditional vesting, 58, 59
Contingency reserves, 93, 94, 99, 109-112, 138, 169, 183, 198, 199
Continuous service, 38, 39
"Conventional" plan, 32, 33, 48, 59
Coverage of pension plans
Arbitrary Rule, 30
Bases of exclusion
Age, 33, 34
Amount of pay, 32
Length of service, 32, 33
Type of employment, 31
Discretionary Rule, 30
Number of employees, 28, 84
Prohibition against discrimination, 21, 22, 30, 31
Credibility, 83, 99
CSO Mortality Table, 81, 122
Current service cost
(See Funding-Normal Cost)

Dean, Arthur H., 200
Dearing, Charles L., 16
Deferred Group Annuity plan
Allocation of past service contributions, 88, 89
Benefits
Death, 61, 90, 91
Disability, 91, 202
Guarantees, 195-197
Retirement, 86, 89
Withdrawal, 89, 90

Deferred Group Annuity plan—*Continued*
Change of funding medium, 206
Contingency reserves, 93, 94, 99, 138
Coverage, 84
Deferred retirement credit, 98
Dividends, 98-100, 138
Employee certificate, 85
Employee contributions, 86, 90
Employer withdrawal credit, 95-98
Expenses, 93, 96, 138, 180-186, 190, 206
Experience account, 98-100, 169
Flexibility, 88, 196, 202-205
Funding, 87-89, 142, 159, 196, 197, 204, 205
Good health requirement, 97, 98
Investment earnings, 175-178
Loading, 87, 93, 96, 138, 183, 191
Master contract, 85
Modification of the contract, 100
Mortality, 168, 169
Normal annuity form, 91
OASI offset, 42, 43, 142
Optional annuity forms, 91
Past service liability, 87-89
Premiums
Minimum annual, 85
Rate factors, 87, 92, 93
Rate guarantees, 94, 95, 168, 169
Reinstatement, 101
Servicing of pensioners, 207, 208
Special administrative charge, 85
Statutory requirements, 84, 85
Termination, 100, 101, 196, 197
Turnover, 87, 191
Underwriting requirements, 85
Vesting, 86, 89, 90, 91, 101
Deferred retirement
Effect on benefits, 52, 53, 192
Effect on pension plan cost, 192, 197, 198, 203, 204
Deferred Wage Concept, 15, 16, 65, 66
Definite benefit formulas
(See Benefits, retirement)
"Definitely determinable" benefits, 22, 74, 75
"Deposit account"
(See Deposit Administration plan)

Equitable Life Assurance Society of
the United States, The, 167
"Erroneous actuarial computation,"
64, 65, 135
Expenses
Actuarial fees, 187, 188, 190
Administrative, 180, 182-190
Check-writing fees, 188, 189
Commissions, 180-186, 190, 206
Comparison between insured and
trusteed plans, 189-191, 194,
206
Deferred Group Annuity plan, 93,
96, 138, 180-186, 190, 206
Deposit Administration plan, 106,
109, 110, 138, 182, 184, 186,
187, 190, 206
Employer administrative, 187, 189,
190
Funding of, 138, 183, 191
Group Permanent plan, 138, 181-
183
Individual Contract plan, 138, 180,
190
Investment, 185, 188, 189, 190
IPG, 111, 112, 138, 182, 184, 187,
206
Legal fees, 190
Loading, 183, 191
Prorating of premium taxes, 190
Self-administered Trusteed plan,
121, 138, 188-191, 194, 203
Taxes, 180, 182-185, 190, 206
Trustee fees, 188-190
Experience account, 98-100, 107, 111,
112, 169

Federal OASI
Average monthly wage, 8, 9
Benefits, 6, 8, 9, 44
Coverage, 5-7
Currently insured status, 9
"Drop out" provision, 7, 9
Earnings limitation, 7, 8
Financing, 10, 11
Fully insured status, 7
Impact on private pensions, 27, 32,
42, 49, 68, 103, 108, 114, 142,
202
Integration of private pensions with
Excess plan, 44-47

Federal OASI—*Continued*
Integration of private pensions—
Continued
General, 32, 40-42, 51, 52
Offset plan, 42, 43
Stepped-up benefits plan, 47, 48
Integration with other Federal
plans, 11
New start, 7
Old-age insurance benefit, 8
Primary insurance amount, 8
Social Security adjustment option,
52, 55, 56
Federal Reserve system, 4
Federal Security Agency, 36, 39, 42,
52, 59, 66, 67
Fellers, William W., 193
Five Per Cent Rule
(See Funding)
Flexibility
As to benefits, 103, 109, 114, 201,
202
As to contributions, 88, 106, 112,
125, 133, 142
As to coverage, 103, 109
As to investments, 171, 172
Combination plan, 125
Deferred Group Annuity plan, 88,
196, 202-205
Deposit Administration plan, 102,
103, 106, 109, 197, 202-205
Group Permanent plan, 202-205
Individual Contract plan, 205-208
IPG plan, 109, 110, 112, 197, 202-
205, 209
Self-administered Trusteed plan,
114, 197, 198, 202-205, 209
Funding
"Accrual rate," 145
Accrued liability, 126, 142, 144,
145, 148-157, 196, 204, 205
Advance funding
Arguments against, 131, 133
Arguments for, 131-133
Definition, 130
Methods of, 148, 149, 152-157
Aggregate, 134, 145, 151-157
Attained age level premium,
87, 142, 143-145
Attained age normal, 145
Entry age normal, 145

The composition, makeup and plastic plates for this book were produced by Ruttle, Shaw & Wetherill, Inc., Philadelphia. The text type is Linotype Caledonia, leaded 2 points. The title page was set in Monotype Graphic Light #101. Graphic Light was used for Chapter Titles. The book was printed letterpress by Allen, Lane & Scott, Inc., Philadelphia, on Warren's #1854, basis 60, supplied by Schuylkill Paper Co., Philadelphia. It was bound by National Publishing Co., Philadelphia, in Holliston Record Buckram English Finish. Design by Guenther K. Wehrhan.